Entrepreneurship and the Growth of Firms

Per Davidsson

Professor of Entrepreneurship, Brisbane Graduate School of Business, Queensland University of Technology, Australia

Frédéric Delmar

Professor, Strategy and Organization, EM Lyon, France

Johan Wiklund

Professor of Entrepreneurship, Jönköping International Business School, Sweden

Edward Elgar
Cheltenham, UK • Northampton, MA, USA

Published by
Edward Elgar Publishing Limited
Glensanda House
Montpellier Parade
Cheltenham
Glos GL50 1UA
UK

Edward Elgar Publishing, Inc.
136 West Street
Suite 202
Northampton
Massachusetts 01060
USA

A catalogue record for this book
is available from the British Library

Library of Congress Cataloguing in Publication Data

Davidsson, Per.
    Entrepreneurship and the growth of firms / Per Davidsson, Frédéric Delmar,
    Johan Wiklund.
        p. cm
    Includes bibliographical references and index.
        1. Entrepreneurship 2. Entrepreneurship—Research. 3 Business enterprises.
    I. Delmar, Frédéric. II. Wiklund, Johan. III. Title.

HB615.D32 2006
338′.04—dc22
                                                                              2006008420

ISBN: 978 1 84542 575 3

Typeset by Cambrian Typesetters, Camberley, Surrey
Printed and bound by CPI Group (UK) Ltd, Croydon, CR0 4YY

Contents

Figures

vii

Tables

Acknowledgements

The publishers with to thank the following who have kindly given permission for the use of copyright material:

Ashgate Publishing Ltd for: Delmar, F. (1997), 'Measuring growth: methodological considerations and empirical results', in R. Donckels and A. Miettinen (eds), *Entrepreneurship and SME Research: On its Way to the Next Millennium*, pp. 190–216.

Babson College for: Delmar, F. and P. Davidsson (1999), 'Firm size expectations of nascent entrepreneurs', in P.D. Reynolds, W.D. Bygrave, S. Manigart, C. Mason, G.D. Meyer, H.J. Sapienza and K.G. Shaver (eds), *Frontiers of Entrepreneurship Research 1999*, vol 19, pp 99–104.

Blackwell Publishing Ltd for: Davidsson, P., F. Delmar and J. Wiklund (2000), 'Entrepreneurship as growth; growth as entrepreneurship', in M.A. Hitt, R.D. Ireland, S.M. Camp and D.L. Sexton (eds), *Strategic Entrepreneurship: Creating a New Mindset* (pp. 328–42); Davidsson, P. and J. Wiklund (2000), 'Conceptual and empirical challenges in the study of firm growth', in D. Sexton and H. Landström (eds), *The Blackwell Handbook of Entrepreneurship* (pp. 26–44); Wiklund, J. (1999), 'The sustainability of the entrepreneurial orientation–performance relationship', *Entrepreneurship Theory and Practice*, **24**(1), 37–48; and Wiklund, J., P. Davidsson and F. Delmar (2003), 'What do they think and feel about growth? An expectancy – value approach to small business managers' attitudes towards growth', *Entrepreneurship Theory and Practice*, **27**(3), 247–69.

Elsevier Ltd for: Delmar, F., P. Davidsson and W. Gartner (2003), 'Arriving at the high-growth firm', *Journal of Business Venturing*, **18**(2), 189–216.

Every effort has been made to trace all the copyright holders but if any have been inadvertently overlooked the publishers will be pleased to make the necessary arrangements at the first opportunity.

1. Introduction

Per Davidsson, Frédéric Delmar, Johan Wiklund

We – the three authors-editors of this volume – all started our respective research careers with a doctoral dissertation where the phenomenon of small firm growth had a central place. We have since returned to this topic in several other texts; together, alone and in collaboration with other colleagues. In this volume we have collected many of our most important works on firm growth. It is our hope that the bringing together of the knowledge we have developed in this area over the last two decades will provide readers with a comprehensive understanding of firm growth and assist other researchers in reaching further and deeper into this phenomenon.

Below we will first review our respective dissertation studies. While the main contents of these are not included in this volume the main results are relevant for the completeness of the picture we paint. It may also be useful for the reader to better understand the backgrounds of the authors and editors. We will then briefly comment on each of the eight works that are included in full. Alongside these presentations we will insert in suitable places some insights we have gained from other projects and papers that are for various reasons not included in this volume.

PRELUDE: THE DISSERTATION STUDIES

It all started with Per Davidsson's (1989a) dissertation study 'Continued Entrepreneurship and Small Firm Growth' – a title which introduces the connection between entrepreneurship and growth that reappears in the title of the current volume and which is scrutinized in one of the included chapters. A striking feature of this work is its – by today's standards – breadth and scope. An indication of this is its main question: 'Why do some firms continue to develop and expand, whereas others remain small and behave conservatively?' (p. 3). Moreover, it draws upon psychology and sociology as well as several strands of research in economics and management. In terms of approach it includes examples of pure exploration (Chapter 8) as well as deductive hypothesis testing based on theory (Chapter 7) or prior empirical work (Chapter 6), but its main approach (Chapter 1–5) is best described as abductive – a wrestling back and forth between theoretical ideas and empirical observations (cf. Alvesson and Sköldberg, 2000). Data collection for the work included case studies based on semi-structured qualitative interviewing supplemented by possibly the first entrepreneurship/small business application of conjoint methodology in the pilot study (Davidsson, 1986), and a main study supplementing data from a combined phone and mail survey with secondary data from statistical records. The presented data analyses include parametric and non-parametric univariate and bivariate methods as well as regression analysis, cluster analysis, discriminant analysis and a particular structural equations modeling (SEM) technique called partial least squares analysis (PLS) – which also appears in Delmar's and Wiklund's theses (cf. Hulland, 1999; Wold and Jöreskog, 1982).

   This breadth reflects European research culture in general (at least at the time) and the cross-disciplinary research area in which it was created (Economic Psychology). To a considerable extent, however, it also reflects the status of the entrepreneurship/small business field of research (then often regarded as one and the same). Research in this area was at that time decidedly phenomenon-driven rather than theory-driven, so if one asked a broad question like 'What contributes to the growth and non-growth of small firms?' one would have to include a broad range of aspects and factors, otherwise the study would appear to be obviously lacking. Further, there was actually very little to build on in terms of theory and previous studies narrowly focusing on the growth of small firms and it was immensely more difficult to locate what actually existed before the occurrence of the internet and electronic databases of scholarly publications, so broad search along multiple routes was needed in order to find enough material to build a theoretical framework.

   Existing research was typically on a rather low level of abstraction and with vague notions of the causal mechanisms involved – effectively long laundry lists of factors suggested or demonstrated to be somehow associated with small firm growth. This is also where the main contribution of this dissertation work lies (cf. Davidsson, 1991). A theoretical model is suggested which portrays all the specifics as aspects of three over-arching antecedents of firm growth: ability, need and opportunity. Further, it is argued that managerial action is governed by perceptions of these three factors, whereas outcomes are also influenced directly by objective ability, need and opportunity, whether correctly perceived or not. This introduces a level of abstraction that was uncommon in this literature at the time. In the empirical analysis it was demonstrated that PLS allowed the simultaneous analysis of up to 72 manifest variables, all regarded as aspects of either growth or the three over-arching, explanatory factors. The empirical results supported the importance of all three but pointed out need as the relatively most important dimension. On an operational level this means that owner-managers who were higher in need for achievement (Murray, 1938) and lower in economic satisfaction had markedly higher growth motivation, and that firms that were older and larger had lower rates of actual growth (the argument being that firms that are larger, or which have existed longer at a given size, are less likely to strictly need to grow in order to survive or to yield a sufficient income to the owner-manager).

Frédéric Delmar's dissertation builds largely on the results from Davidsson's dissertation and uses the same methodological approach and type of analysis (PLS). If Davidsson was eclectic, blending several approaches in the study of small firm growth, Delmar decided to focus attention on the psychology of the entrepreneur. At that time, there was a debate about the value of psychological research in entrepreneurship (Gartner, 1988; Shaver and Scott, 1991). The questioning of the value of such research originated mostly in the lack of use of state-of-the-art psychological theory in entrepreneurship research. In order to overcome such limitations, Delmar developed a model of entrepreneurial behavior and firm growth based on a current social psychological approach. The model emphasized the role of intrinsic vs. extrinsic motivation; the interaction between ability and motivation; the role of task characteristics; and the need to distinguish between entrepreneurial performance and business performance. The results of Delmar's analyses confirmed the results of Davidsson's study. Entrepreneurial behavior or managerial action was influenced by perceived ability, need, and opportunity also in this study.

The distinction between entrepreneurial behavior and firm performance is an important development of Davidsson's original model. It is important because it emphasizes the evolution of a firm as a complex phenomenon that takes place in a dynamic environment only partly under the control of the entrepreneur. Based on available information, entrepreneurs might make correct or incorrect decisions but regardless, external circumstances could lead to unanticipated outcomes potentially reversing what was anticipated.

Furthermore, the complexity also leads to the number of choices of how to reach a particular firm-level outcome. The results from Delmar's dissertation showed that many of these decisions are made based on personal values and interests (intrinsic motivation) of the entrepreneur. The more intrinsically motivated the entrepreneur is by the prospects of growth, the more likely he or she is to engage in a growth process and succeed. On the other hand, if the growth process is chosen for extrinsic reasons, the entrepreneur is less likely to succeed in the endeavor.

Task characteristics and perceived ability were important determinants of achieved growth as well as growth motivation. Those entrepreneurs that had already experienced growth and employed staff that was open to changes were more likely to engage in and achieve further growth. Hence, there was a strong interaction among previous performance, attribution of ability and firm performance.

Johan Wiklund's dissertation entitled 'Small firm growth and performance: entrepreneurship and beyond' was completed in 1998. It received the 1998 NFIB best dissertation award, which is awarded by the Entrepreneurship Division of the Academy of Management. As the title indicates, the dissertation builds on the preceding works by Davidsson and Delmar. The focus on the study lies on the actual activities and strategies that small firms utilize in order to achieve growth. The argument is made that regardless of the motivations and access to resources of the individual small business manager, he or she must be able to devise the appropriate strategies in order to take advantage of growth opportunities. This focus clearly sets this dissertation apart from those of Davidsson and Delmar who put the individual on center stage.

In reviewing the literature it became clear that most empirical studies using growth as the dependent variable relied on cross-sectional data. This is far from ideal as growth represents a process of change. In cross-sectional studies, the strategies and management practices used by the small business could thus represent effects of the growth taking place up to the point of data collection rather than causes of that growth process. In order to avoid such problems, the thesis used a longitudinal design collecting information on the independent variables at one point of time and the resulting growth outcomes later. It also took into account that small businesses may grow by setting up subsidiaries and by mergers and acquisitions and not only by organically expanding one organizational unit. The results supported that in particular those small businesses that pursued aggressive growth strategies tended to rely on a combination of internal growth and external growth mechanisms, which at the time was a novel finding. The finding spurred further investigation into how mergers, acquisitions and strategic alliances could be used by small firms to fuel growth (Wiklund and Shepherd, 2005a).

Specifically, the study used the entrepreneurial orientation (EO) construct developed by Miller (1983) and Covin and Slevin (1986; 1989) to tap into the strategic activities of the small firms. EO refers to a firm's strategic orientation, capturing specific entrepreneurial aspects of decision-making styles, methods, and practices. As such, it reflects how a firm operates rather than what it does and is a relevant conceptualization of entrepreneurship in existing firms.

In part, the focus of the thesis reflects that conceptual development had taken place since Davidsson's dissertation was published nine years earlier. Several valuable theoretical contributions had been made. However, the literature on small firm growth far from represented one coherent field and a major contribution of the thesis was its amalgamation of previous research into one coherent research model. The model suggests that the motivations of the entrepreneur, the resources that the small business can access and the environmental conditions all affect growth. However, these effects are indirect, mediated by the strategies that the small business pursues, in this case its entrepreneurial orientation. To a large extent, the empirical results supported the model. The strategic choices made by small business managers affect its growth to a substantial degree, even when a broad range of other factors are taken into account, thereby challenging ecological and institutional theories emphasizing inertia and path dependence. Indirect positive effect of environmental dynamism on growth mediated by EO suggests that in dynamic environments, where market demand is constantly shifting, opportunities become abundant and growth is highest for firms having an orientation for pursuing new opportunities because they have a good fit between their strategic orientation and the environment. These ideas were developed further in an article testing how configurations of EO, environmental dynamism and the access to resources affect small business performance (Wiklund and Shepherd, 2005b).

THE WORKS INCLUDED IN THIS BOOK

Part I: The Conceptual and Empirical Complexity of the Firm Growth Phenomenon

What we have learnt more than anything else through our dissertations and other research is that firm growth is a complex phenomenon. It is not unidimensional. It is hard to predict and assess. Further, it can manifest itself in various ways, and consequently it can have differential effects on several different levels. This is important for researchers to realize because otherwise they will rush out and conduct ill-conceived studies employing poor or misplaced operationalizations applied to too heterogeneous samples of firms – and run the risk of learning nothing or drawing erroneous conclusions. It is equally important for managers and policy-makers to understand the multi-faceted nature of firm growth. For managers, different forms of growth may be easier or harder to achieve. These will also pose different challenges as regards internal turmoil in the organization, and have different effects on results in the shorter and longer terms. For policy-makers the challenges include telling the difference between sound consolidation and unsound concentration of industries as firms grow larger; the static efficiency of large scale vs. the dynamic effectiveness of diversity; and genuine job creation as distinct from mere movement of jobs through acquisition-based firm growth.

In the entrepreneurship literature it is often taken for granted that growth is entrepreneurial and that growth is good. In our work we have found reason to question the uncritical acceptance of both of those notions. In

'Entrepreneurship as Growth; Growth as Entrepreneurship' – the first chapter in Part 1 – we take a deeper look at the connection between entrepreneurship and growth, a theme we had all had reason to contemplate in our respective dissertation works. The original context for this manuscript was a by-invitation research meeting on the interface between entrepreneurship and strategy held at the Kauffman Foundation facilities in Kansas City in 2001, which later led to the publication of a book edited by the conference organizers (Hitt, Ireland, Camp and Sexton, 2002). In that context, we wanted to explore growth as an obvious area of potentially fruitful collaboration and cross-fertilization between entrepreneurship and strategy research as well as examine for what aspects of firm growth entrepreneurship researchers were likely apt to make unique contributions.

We find that old or implicit notions of entrepreneurship defined as 'owner-management of independent firms' naturally include growth as an aspect of entrepreneurship. Contemporary definitions are more exacting: either 'entrepreneurship' is reserved for an emergent stage and growth is regarded as a different (and later) phenomenon, or only such growth that is based on the introduction of new offerings in the market is indicative of entrepreneurship. As young and small firms tend to grow organically whereas old and large ones primarily grow through acquisition (cf. below) the assumption that growth reflects entrepreneurship is reasonable for the former type of firms but questionable for the latter. We further argue that the growth of particular business activities, such as the launching of a new product, represents a phenomenon that has greater relevance for entrepreneurship researchers than has the growth of the firm as a business organization. This marks a difference compared with strategic management, where firm performance is the dependent variable of choice.

The second selection for Part I – 'Conceptual and Empirical Challenges in the Study of Firm Growth' – has a similar origin and first publication outlet. This chapter was prepared for a by-invitation conference organized by Donald Sexton in Fort Lauderdale in 1999, for the last in his series of 'State of the Art of Entrepreneurship Research' books (Sexton and Landström, 2000; Sexton and Kasarda, 1992; Sexton and Smilor, 1986, 1997; cf. Kent, Sexton and Vesper, 1982). It reflects issues arising in connection with empirical studies we were involved in at the time, such as Wiklund's thesis work as well as Davidsson–Delmar's project on high-growth firms (the three chapters in Part III of this book are from these two projects). Our discussions of the need for theoretical input and longitudinal design emanate mainly from the experiences from Davidsson's thesis project and the groundwork for Wiklund's dissertation project. So do our discussions of the need to be careful not to equate one entrepreneur with one firm. This mix-up of levels of analysis has been a very common mistake or shortcoming in entrepreneurship research. We have recently had reason to revisit the issue in more general terms than just discussing growth (Davidsson, 2004 forthcoming) and it has also been highlighted by other authors (Sarasvathy, 2004; Scott and Rosa, 1996). If the fundamental interest is on the individual level and the study uses psychological theory as a starting point, then the study needs to consider all the businesses the individual is involved in and not just one that happens to be included due to firm-based rather than individual-based sampling. If the interest is genuinely at the firm level, then in many cases the founder represents but a fraction of the human capital available to the firm.

This chapter on conceptual and empirical challenges also discusses the fundamental elusiveness of the growing firm, with empirical illustration from the high-growth firm study. In short, the problem is that growth implies change. At the same time the researcher does not want the firm to change so much that at the end of the observation period it can no longer meaningfully be regarded 'the same' firm, because if the firm does not in some meaningful manner remain the same there is no way we can assess how much 'it' has grown! In addition, this chapter provides an elaborate discussion of the challenges and importance of matching theories, knowledge interests, firm conceptualizations and operationalizations of growth so that they fit logically together. While this discussion may not offer complete and satisfactory solutions for all researchers' design dilemmas we think it provides illuminating food for thought for any researcher about to conduct a study of firm growth. We are aware of no corresponding discussion elsewhere in the literature.

The next chapter – 'Measuring growth: methodological considerations and empirical results' – discusses the choice of specific operationalizations of growth at much greater depth. It actually preceded the previous two chapters in time as it first appeared in *Entrepreneurship and SME Research: On its Way to the Next Millennium* (Donckels and Miettinen, 1997). The origin of the chapter is the observation Delmar made when writing his dissertation and trying to understand what was already known on firm growth and what results had been replicated in different studies. Instead of finding a homogenous field centered on common concepts he found a plethora of different and unrelated results. A source to this lack of theory and empirical development was the heterogeneity of different growth measures – researchers use a wide variety of concepts to measure growth. These differences in measurement affect the relationship among the independent variables and the dependent variable, and hence theory development. In order to examine the previous statement, 55 growth studies were reviewed, and data from a sample of small businesses were used to examine the effects of different growth measures.

As different measures were used, a direct comparison among studies is made difficult, if not impossible. It was found that most studies were based on samples from manufacturing industries. Furthermore, the results indicated little knowledge of the effects of the choice time period, and the effect of the choice of indicator. It was also found that growth measured in absolute or relative changes yielded totally different results. Other authors later found similar results among large stock listed companies (Weinzimmer, Nystrom and Freeman, 1998). A major contribution of the included text is that it highlights the need to treat the operationalization of growth very carefully. A failure to do so will hamper the development of growth research.

While at the time of this writing the manuscripts selected for Part I are four to eight years old, we feel that they still hold up as sources of essentially sound advice for researchers interested in studying firm growth and – at least to some extent – for practitioners contemplating the consequences of different modes of firm growth. However, we have also learnt more since these works were published. As a result we would today more emphasize that if the true interest is in firm performance rather than growth specifically. it is not really defensible to use growth as the sole performance indicator. Growth is not necessarily an indicator of sound, sustainable development in the best interest of the firm's various stakeholders. On the contrary, in recent work we have concluded that trying to 'grow profitable' from a starting point of below-average profitability may be a very risky prospect more likely to lead to poor performance along both dimensions than to the ideal state of profitable growth (Davidsson, Steffens and Fitzsimmons, 2005). Therefore, if the interest is really in performance rather than growth specifically the study should at least include other performance measures alongside growth (Dahlqvist, Davidsson and Wiklund, 2000; Wiklund, 1998).

When growth is the true interest and under emphasized issue in the above readings is that researchers should be wary not to make unwarranted linear assumptions. Non-growth or shrinkage may in part be a different phenomenon than just 'less growth'. Hence, one should not necessarily expect variables to have the same relative effect on size changes along the entire spectrum (Cooper, Gimeno-Gascon and Woo, 1994; Dahlqvist et al., 2000; Penrose, 1959). Further, we would today be less inclined to suggest that sales growth is the best indicator overall. From a technical standpoint we have learnt from ongoing research that employment growth is actually the indicator that has the highest correlation with other alternative growth measures (sales growth, equity growth, income growth, and assets growth) and is most robust to different operationalizations (Wiklund and Shepherd, 2005a). Other on-going work has revealed that it is possible to find theoretical explanations for when sales and employment growth are more and less highly correlated. More specifically, hypotheses derived from transaction cost economics can help explain why sales growth is sometimes not accompanied by corresponding employment growth, at least in resource-constrained environments (Chandler, McKelvie and Davidsson, 2005). Overall, we would today even more emphasize the importance of letting theoretical considerations govern the choice of growth indicator (Wiklund and Shepherd, 2005a). Other researchers have demonstrated that theory-driven research on growth within relatively homogenous samples of firms is a sound way to go for firm growth research (Baum and Locke, 2004). With more homogenous samples it may also be possible to use industry-specific growth indicators that may be the best choice for the particular industry although they cannot be employed when a more heterogeneous sample is studied. We would also suggest that it is sounder practice to test several growth indicators separately rather than using just one indicator or an index combining several indicators to a growth index that is assumed to be uni-dimensional. If several measures are used separately the researcher will likely arrive at a more complete understanding of the phenomenon than when just one measure is selected.

Part II: Growth Aspirations and Motivation

Davidsson's dissertation study (Davidsson, 1989a, 1991) used both growth motivation and actual growth as dependent variables. However, as the study was cross-sectional in design he could not strictly prove that the two were causally related. It was only through the similarity of influence of arguably time-invariant independent variables in two separate analyses using outcome variables that he could make a case for the manager's growth motivation having its own, important role to play with respect to achieving actual growth apart from objective characteristics of the firm and its environment. In more recent work we have directly investigated the relationship between the manager's growth motivation and the actual, subsequent growth of the firm. Building on the theory of planned behavior (Ajzen, 1991), Wiklund and Shepherd (2003) showed that the access to growth opportunities in the environment and the access to resources needed for devising growth strategies moderate the relationship between growth motivation and growth. Delmar and Wiklund (2003) used cross-lagged regression analysis to tease out the causality between growth motivation and growth, demonstrating that while effects run both ways the effect of motivation on growth is stronger than the reverse. These supportive results make the studies included in Part II more relevant as we now know that growth aspiration/motivation is not just an unsatisfactory and unproven proxy for 'the real thing' but actually has independent predictive power with respect to subsequent growth.

The chapter 'Firm size expectations of nascent entrepreneurs' was one of the first papers based on the Swedish counterpart to the Panel Study of Entrepreneurial Dynamics (Gartner, Shaver, Carter and Reynolds, 2004). It was presented at the Babson Conference in 1999 and included in the proceedings *Frontiers of Entrepreneurship Research* (Reynolds et al., 1999). Before we actually had any longitudinal data from the project we used growth aspirations as a dependent variable, as did some of our international colleagues who were in the same situation. Thus, we were here interested in examining the factors affecting the future firm size expectations of nascent entrepreneurs. The proposed model was based on four different components that were tested together as well as separately in order to assess their unique and combined effect on size expectations. The four components are: initial human capital; personal/business goals; environmental and business context; and activities to organize the new firm. The dependent variable reflects the growth trajectories that new firms can take.

The results show that growth aspirations are modest. While it was difficult to predict intended start size we had some success at predicting expected early growth. Moreover, the results show that nascent entrepreneurs expecting high growth also expected a larger start size. Their goal was more often to make the future business their main income source. Other studies on growth ambitions of nascent entrepreneurs reach similar conclusions. First, nascent entrepreneurs are relatively modest in their aspirations. For example, Human and Matthews (2004) show that aspirations are typically low for US-based nascent entrepreneurs as well. The median expected revenue after five years is a mere US$100 000, and on a dichotomous attitudinal item 78 per cent say they prefer to keep the firm at a manageable size rather than growing it as large as possible. Despite the low aspirations other research indicates they are still over-optimistic about what they will be able to achieve (Schoett and Bager, 2004). In summary, the analyses of nascent entrepreneurs' growth aspirations have helped create a realistic image of the modesty of the typical new venture start-up.

Data from another of our projects, The 1994 Start-up Cohort, has confirmed that it is not just early growth aspirations that are modest. Young firms in Sweden show very modest actual growth on average (Dahlqvist and Davidsson, 2000; Dahlqvist et al., 2000). In 'What do they think and feel about growth? An expectancy-value approach to small business managers' attitudes toward growth' – the second selection for Part II – we delve deeper into the reasons behind this. This chapter has a long history. The core set of questions on expected consequences of growth was included in Davidsson's dissertation study and the topic of the first journal article emanating from it (Davidsson, 1989b). However, it was only mentioned as a side issue in the dissertation itself. The question package was included but remained a side issue in Delmar's and Wiklund's respective thesis studies as well. In 1997 Wiklund took the initiative to perform a joint analysis of the three data sets in what was to become an award-winning Babson paper that year (Wiklund, Davidsson,

Delmar and Aronsson, 1997). It then took a full six years – due more to our own preoccupation with other commitments than an overly lengthy review process – before the version included here appeared in the journal *Entrepreneurship Theory and Practice*.

Building on expectancy-value theory, the article shows that small business managers' attitudes towards growth can be reasonably well explained by the consequences that they expect from growth. Given that three large data sets were merged for the study, we were able to split the sample in multiple ways and conduct fine-grained analyses. A consistent finding across the multiple analyses is that expectations concerning the effect of growth on employee well-being come out as the most important determinant of growth attitude. It suggests that the 'soft qualities' of the small business are of great concern to small business managers. Had this result appeared in a single study, skeptics could have regarded it a peculiarity of little consequence. When replicated in three studies and multiple sub-sample analyses, the suggestion that this non-financial concern may be more important than financial ones (for example, the personal income variable included in the study) in determining overall growth attitude has to be taken seriously. In sum, the concern for the atmosphere of the work place and the well-being of the staff (including the business owner) appears to provide a relevant explanation to the lack of growth aspirations found in our own and others studies noted in the above.

The chapter also points to the value of replication, which is common in many scientific fields but largely missing in entrepreneurship. The same measures were used in three samples including somewhat different firms and different phases of the business cycle. Other than the consistent strong effects of employee well-being, each of the samples only produces three or four results that were statistically significant at the conventional 5 per cent level. However, while not statistically significant across all studies, all effects were positive, and the likelihood of finding positive effects this large or larger in three separate studies of this size is actually extremely small. The fact is that all the results of the combined studies support the theory.

We have advocated replication in studies of growth also elsewhere. The Dahlqvist et al. (2000) article deliberately tests if results obtained by a single study replicate in a different context. Some do, suggesting great generality for these particular findings, while others don't, warranting additional testing. However, we have also noted that – at least among new firms – growth results are likely not to replicate because researchers operationalize growth in very many different ways and identical growth measures across studies are very rare. The problem with this is that the correlation between different growth measures is low suggesting limited concurrent validity (Wiklund and Shepherd, 2005a). We therefore recommend that researchers replicate growth research utilizing identical growth measures.

Part III: Patterns and Determinants of Actual Growth

It is probably fair to suggest that the majority of firm growth studies are geared toward explaining variance in growth rates across firms and to attribute relative strength of explanatory power to the independent variables included in the analyses. Although our respective dissertation projects have such an exercise as their main objective it is not the focus we have chosen for the selection of manuscripts for this section on actual growth. As regards 'factors influencing growth' across all kinds of firms and contexts we would hold that the research community has probably come as far as it can come: a wide range of known factors on the individual, firm and environment levels have some influence, and no single factor has a dominant influence (see for example, Storey, 1994). In order to reach further we would suggest researchers turn to theory-driven analysis of the influence of specific sub-sets of factors in specific contexts (Baum and Locke, 2004).

Nonetheless, our first selection for Part III – 'The sustainability of the entrepreneurial orientation performance relationship' is about performance prediction. However, this manuscript, which originates from the continued data collection from the sample studied for Wiklund's dissertation and first appeared in *Entrepreneurship Theory and Practice* in 1999, is not about the total and relative influence of a laundry list of common sense based growth predictors. Instead, it is narrowly focused on the role of an important and recurring concept in entrepreneurship studies: entrepreneurial orientation. Even more importantly, it is one of few examples of studies addressing a huge but largely ignored issue in management studies: over what time span should the independent variables reasonably be assumed to exert their influence on business outcomes? On the one hand it is reasonable to assume that it takes some time for entrepreneurial initiatives to pay off suggesting studying performance outcomes over long periods of time. For example, the income streams from new product launches are not immediate. On the other hand, over longer periods of time, the business may go through changes so that the level of the independent variables change, or factors not included in the model may intervene and disturb the relationships between independent and dependent variables. The empirical results showed that EO had positive implications for the performance in the subsequent year as well as in the following year, but that the results were stronger in the latter case. This suggests that the performance implications of EO on performance are long term rather than short term. This supports the underlying logic of the EO construct as a strategic variable and not simply a quick fix.

The study used 'performance' and not 'growth' as the dependent variable. Yet it is included in this volume on growth. The reason is that the performance construct was measured by a range of indicators relating to multiple dimensions of growth as well as multiple indicators of financial performance, including objective as well as self-perceived measures. There has been a debate in the literature about the most suitable indicators of small business performance and the decision was made to take a broad view on these issues, as recommended by some authors (Birley and Westhead, 1990). Interestingly, there was a high correlation among the different indicators and they could be summed to an index with favorable measurement properties (Cronbach's Alpha above 0.70). This suggests that small businesses that expand their operations also perform better financially. Although this is not the major finding of the article, it is important because it supports the observation that small businesses grow primarily on the basis of retained earnings and not by extending debt or outside equity. In doing so it opposes the idea that growth would be a trade-off for financial performance. This is not necessarily at odds with Davidsson et al.'s (2005) finding that firms that grow from a starting point of low profitability rarely become more profitable as a result of their expansion.

The second entry in Part III – 'High-growth firms and their contribution to employment: the case of Sweden 1987–96 – has been on a long and winding journey. It has previously appeared as a conference paper and a report to the OECD in the late 1990s before being translated and published in a scholarly journal in French (Davidsson and Delmar, 2002). It was then committed to a book project, which the editors in the end were never able to pull off, which is why – in effect – it appears as an original publication in the English language in the present volume. As its title indicates this is essentially a piece of descriptive policy research. As such, it can serve as a warning example to young researchers: without theoretical interpretation it does not matter how good the data are and how interesting the results might seem to a researcher or practitioner in that country at that time; it is simply not very interesting to others a few years later what percentage of job creation was attributable to certain industries, regions and firm size classes.

However, despite its somewhat atheoretical character this paper has – largely due to its unique data – some features that make it deserve being included here. Most importantly, the study is probably the only one so far of this scope that distinguishes between organic and acquisition-based growth. This made it possible for us to detect rather dramatic differences by firm age and size class regarding *how* rapidly growing firms achieve their growth. In short, young and small firms grow organically while older and larger ones achieve expansion more or less exclusively through acquisition of other units already in existence. This implies these categories of firm fulfill different roles in the economy and clearly demonstrates that firm growth does not necessarily translate to employment growth in the economic system of which the firms form part. Another unique feature of the study is that it follows the firms' development through an entire business cycle. It turns out that the high-growth firms, as a group, appear much less affected by the swings in the economy than the majority of 'other' firms. A deeper analysis (not reported in the paper) shows that the high-growth firms are able to maintain their growth in the downturn by increasing their emphasis on acquisitions as the room for organic growth diminishes with the general recession. In the battle between 'population ecology' (Hannan and Freeman, 1977) and 'strategic choice' (Child, 1972) this suggests that at least a significant minority of firms is able to shape its own destiny, supporting the conclusions from Wiklund's dissertation study.

The final chapter – 'Arriving at the high growth firm' – first appeared as a Babson paper under a different title and was later published in *Journal of Business Venturing* in its present form (and adding Bill Gartner as co-author). It utilizes the same data set as the previous paper but analyses it in a different way. With its focus on different patterns and measures of growth it neatly connects back to the challenges and measurement issues discussed in Part I. We here observe the heterogeneity of how firms actually grow. Using cluster analysis techniques we find seven distinct growth patterns that firms might use. These growth patterns differ in pace, in content, and regularity, and are dependent on the age, size and the industry affiliation of the firm concerned. For example we found that firms that were able to grow substantially both in terms of employees and in sales were mostly found among small- and medium-sized firms in knowledge-intensive industries, whereas firms that chose expansion by acquisition often were older, part of a company group and located in traditional industries such as paper and pulp; steel and manufacturing.

These results indicate that the question of '*how* do firms grow' is as relevant a question as '*why* do firms grow'? Because we show that growth patterns are to some degree ordered, there might be a potential for gaining a deeper understanding of how firm growth occurs. Apparently, firms differ in why they start to grow and how they grow. The consequences of growth do also differ on a number of levels of analyses. A firm that grows by acquisition is faced with different problems than a firm that grows organically. In the first case, the special problems related to merging two different cultures arise, but the firm may be able to rapidly achieve a new strategic posture. In the second case, integration of new employees can be done under different circumstances, but it might be hard to rapidly find sufficient resources to meet the demand of growth.

Moreover, with a focus on the process of firm growth, we might also address one of our initial observations in this introductory chapter: growth implies change, and it is important to understand the origin of these changes; how and what has changed, and what has persisted in the growing firm. A growing firm might change location, legal structure, company structure and products. Still, as researchers we often regard the firm as the same unique entity, which may be an unjustifiable conclusion.

CONCLUSION

While the selection of papers for this volume gives a fair overview of our personal research efforts regarding firm growth it cannot, of course, do justice to what the research community as a whole has had to say about firm growth. However, it is our hope that this collection of chapters will serve as an interesting overview of insights into this phenomenon as well as a source of inspiration to conduct new studies that reach further. A conventional approach in this concluding section would be to spell out detailed advice for future research. However, we feel that the works selected for the volume already include enough of that sort. Instead, we hope that readers find inspiration from connections across these works and their prior knowledge to come up with new research questions and approaches beyond what we are able to conceive of. That would be an instance of Schumpeterian 'entrepreneurship' in the form of 'new combinations' (Schumpeter, 1934) leading to 'growth' – in this case of collective, cumulative knowledge.

REFERENCES

Ajzen, I. (1991), 'The theory of planned behavior', *Organizational Behavior and Human Decision Processes*, **50**, 179–211.

Alvesson, M. and K. Sköldberg (2000), *Reflexive Methodology; New Vistas for Qualitative Research*, Thousand Oaks, CA: Sage.

Baum, J. R. and E. A. Locke (2004), 'The relationship of entrepreneurial traits, skill, and motivation to subsequent venture growth', *Journal of Applied Psychology*, **89**(4), 587–98.

Birley, S. and P. Westhead (1990), 'Growth and performance contrasts between "types" of small firms', *Strategic Management Journal*, **2**, 535–57.

Chandler, G. N., A. McKelvie and P. Davidsson (2005), 'A transaction cost perspective on the relationship between growth in sales and employment', paper presented at the Academy of Management meeting, Honolulu.

Child, J. (1972), 'Organizational structure, environment and performance: the role of strategic choice', *Sociology*, **6**(1–22).

Cooper, A. C., F. J. Gimeno-Gascon, and C. Y. Woo (1994), 'Initial human and financial capital as predictors of new venture performance', *Journal of Business Venturing*, **9**(5), 371–95.

Covin, J. G. and D. P. Slevin (1986), 'The development and testing of an organizational-level entrepreneurship scale', in R. Ronstadt, J. A. Hornaday, R. Peterson and K. H. Vesper (eds), *Frontiers of Entrepreneurship Research 1986*, Wellesley, MA: Babson College, pp. 628–39.

Covin, J. G. and D. P. Slevin (1989), 'Strategic management of small firms in hostile and benign environments', *Strategic Management Journal*, **10** (January), 75–87.

Dahlqvist, J. and P. Davidsson (2000), 'Business start-up reasons and firm performance', in P. D. Reynolds, E. Autio, C. Brush, W. D. Bygrave, S. Manigart, H.

Sapienza and K. Shaver (eds), *Frontiers of Entrepreneurship Research 2000*, Wellesley, MA: Babson College, pp. 46–54.

Dahlqvist, J., P. Davidsson and J. Wiklund (2000), 'Initial conditions as predictors of new venture performance: a replication and extension of the Cooper et al. study', *Enterprise and Innovation Management Studies*, 1(1), 1–17.

Davidsson, P. (1986), *Tillväxt i små företag: en pilotstudie om tillväxtvilja och tillväxtförutsättningar i små företag* [*Small Firm Growth: A Pilot Study on Growth Willingness and Opportunity for Growth in Small Firms*] (Studies in Economic Psychology No. 120, Stockholm: Stockholm School of Economics.

Davidsson, P. (1989a), 'Continued Entrepreneurship and Small Firm Growth', doctoral dissertation, Stockholm; Stockholm School of Economics.

Davidsson, P. (1989b), 'Entrepreneurship – and after? A study of growth willingness in small firms', *Journal of Business Venturing*, 4(3), 211–26.

Davidsson, P. (1991), 'Continued entrepreneurship: ability, need, and opportunity as determinants of small firm growth', *Journal of Business Venturing*, 6(6), 405–29.

Davidsson, P. (2004), 'Researching Entrepreneurship', New York: Springer.

Davidsson, P. (forthcoming), 'Method challenges and opportunities in the psychological study of entrepreneurship', in J. R. Baum, M. Frese and R. A. Baron (eds), *The Psychology of Entrepreneurship*, Mahway, NJ: Erlbaum, Chapter 13.

Davidsson, P. and F. Delmar (2002), 'Les entreprises à forte croissance et leur contribution à l'emploi: le cas de la Suède 1987–1996', *Revue Internationale PME*, 14(3–4), 164–87.

Davidsson, P., P. Steffens and J. Fitzsimmons (2005), 'Growing profitable or growing from profits. Putting the horse in front of the cart?', Academy of Management Best Paper Proceedings.

Delmar, F. (1996), 'Entrepreneurial behavior and business performance', doctoral dissertation, Stockholm: Stockholm School of Economics.

Delmar, F. and P. Davidsson (1999), 'Firm size expectations of nascent entrepreneurs', in P. D. Reynolds, W. D. Bygrave, S. Manigart, C. Mason, G. D. Meyer, H. J. Sapienza and K. G. Shaver (eds), *Frontiers of Entrepreneurship Research 1999*, vol 19, Wellesley, MA: Babson College, pp. 90–104.

Delmar, F. and J. Wiklund (2003), 'The effect of the entrepreneur's growth motivation on subsequent growth: a longitudinal study', paper presented at the Academy of Management Meeting, Seattle.

Donckels, R. and A. Miettinen (eds) (1997), *Entrepreneurship and SME Research: On its Way to the Next Millennium*, Aldershot, UK: Ashgate.

Gartner, W. B. (1988), ' "Who is an entrepreneur?" is the wrong question', *American Small Business Journal*, 12(4), 11–31.

Gartner, W. B., K. G. Shaver, N. M. Carter and P. D. Reynolds (2004), *Handbook of Entrepreneurial Dynamics: The Process of Business Creation*, Thousand Oaks, CA: Sage.

Hannan, M. T. and J. H. Freeman (1977), 'The population ecology of organizations', *American Journal of Sociology*, 82(5), 929–64.

Hitt, M., D. Ireland, M. S. Camp, D. L. Sexton (eds) (2002), *Strategic Entrepreneurship: Creating a New Mindset*, Oxford, UK: Blackwell.

Hulland, J. (1999), 'Use of partial least squares (PLS) in strategic management research: a review of four recent studies', *Strategic Management Journal*, 20, 195–204.

Human, S. L. and C. H. Matthews (2004), 'Future expectations for the new business', in W. B. Gartner, K. G. Shaver, N. M. Carter and P. D. Reynolds (eds), *Handbook of Entrepreneurial Dynamics: The Process of Business Creation*, Thousand Oaks: Sage, pp. 386-400.

Jöreskog, K. G. and H. Wold (1982), 'The ML and PLS techniques for modeling with latent variables', in H. Wold (ed.), *Systems Under Indirect Observation*, vol 2, Amsterdam: North-Holland, pp. 263-70.

Kent, C. A., D. L. Sexton and K. H. Vesper (1982), *Encyclopedia of Entrepreneurship*, Englewood Cliffs, NJ: Prentice Hall.

Miller, D. (1983), 'The correlates of entrepreneurship in three types of firms', *Management Science*, **29**, 770-91.

Murray, H. A. (1938), *Explorations in Personality*, New York: Oxford University Press.

Penrose, E. (1959), *The Theory of the Growth of the Firm*, Oxford: Oxford University Press.

Reynolds, P. D., W. D. Bygrave, S. Manigart, C. Mason, G. D. Meyer, H. J. Sapienza et al. (eds) (1999), *Frontiers of Entrepreneurship Research 1999*, vol 19, Wellesley, MA: Babson College.

Sarasvathy, S. (2004), 'The questions we ask and the questions we care about: reformulating some problems in entrepreneurship research', *Journal of Business Venturing*, **19**(5), 707-20.

Schoett, T. and T. Bager (2004), 'Growth expectations by entrepreneurs in nascent firms, baby businesses and mature firms', in T. Bager and M. Hancock (eds), *The Growth of Danish Firms. Part 2 of the Global Entrepreneurship Monitor, Denmark 2003*, Copenhagen: Boersens, pp. 219-230.

Schumpeter, J. A. (1934), *The Theory of Economic Development*, Cambridge, MA: Harvard University Press.

Scott, M. and P. Rosa (1996), 'Opinion: has firm level analysis reached its limits? Time for a rethink', *International Small Business Journal*, **14**(4), 81-9.

Shaver, K. G. and L. R. Scott (1991), 'Person, process, choice: the psychology of new venture creation', *Entrepreneurship Theory and Practice* (Winter), 23-45.

Sexton, D. and K. Kasarda (1992), *The State of the Art in Entrepreneurship*, Boston, MA: PWS Publishing.

Sexton, D. and R. W. Smilor (1986), *The Art and Science of Entrepreneurship*, Cambridge, MA: Ballinger.

Sexton, D. L. and R. W. Smilor (1997), *Entrepreneurship 2000*, Chicago, IL: Upstart Publishing.

Sexton, D. L. and H. Landström (2000), *The Blackwell Handbook of Entrepreneurship*, Oxford, UK: Blackwell.

Storey, D. J. (1994), *Understanding the Small Business Sector*, London: Routledge.

Weinzimmer, L. G., P. C. Nystrom and S. J. Freeman (1998), 'Measuring organizational growth: issues, consequences and guidelines', *Journal of Management*, **24**(2), 235-62.

Wiklund, J. (1998), 'Small firm growth and perofrmance: entrepreneurship and beyond', doctoral dissertation, Jönköping International Business School, Jönköping.

Wiklund, J., P. Davidsson, F. Delmar and A. Aronsson (1997), 'Expected consequences of growth and their effect on growth willingness in different samples of small firms', in P. D. Reynolds, W. D. Bygrave, N. M. Carter, P. Davidsson, W. B. Gartner, C. M. Maston and P. P. McDougall (eds), *Frontiers of Entrpreneurship Research 1997*, Wellesley, MA: Babson College, pp. 1-16.

Wiklund, J. and D. Shepherd (2003), 'Aspiring for, and achieving growth: the moderating role of resources and opportunities', *Journal of Management Studies*, **40**(8), 1911–41.

Wiklund, J. and D. Shepherd (2005a), 'Knowledge accumulation in growth studies: the consequences of methodological choices', paper presented at the ERIM expert workshop Perspectives on the Longitudinal Analysis of New Firm Growth, 18–19 May, Erasmus University, Rotterdam, The Netherlands.

Wiklund, J. and D. Shepherd (2005b), 'Entrepreneurial orientation and small business performance: a configurational approach', *Journal of Business Venturing*, **20**(1), 71–91.

PART I

The Conceptual and Empirical Complexity of
the Firm Growth Phenomenon

2. Entrepreneurship as growth; growth as entrepreneurship*[1]

Per Davidsson, Frédéric Delmar, Johan Wiklund

INTRODUCTION

An increasing number of scholars identify themselves as 'entrepreneurship researchers' (and educators), and would refer to the field of research they are affiliated with as 'entrepreneurship research'. Many of these researchers would also have a second home in some other application area such as small business, family business, or innovation; in a business sub-discipline like marketing, finance, or strategic management; or in a discipline such as psychology, sociology or economics. Apart from occasionally making it into mainstream journals, the North American members of this community of scholars would regard *Journal of Business Venturing* and *Entrepreneurship Theory and Practice* as primary outlets for their research as well as important reading for their professional development (Romano and Ratnatunga 1997). Further, they are likely regulars at the Babson College/Kauffman Foundation Entrepreneurship Research Conference and/or members of the Entrepreneurship Division of the Academy of Management. In other parts of the world other journals, conferences and associations could be added, but the North American ones would not be entirely disregarded.

Entrepreneurship – the concept as well as the phenomenon – certainly attracts at least occasional interest also from researchers who do not fit the above description. However, it is the (admittedly heterogeneous) community of researchers described above, and their research, that we have in mind when we in the following refer to 'entrepreneurship researchers' and 'entrepreneurship research'.

Within this rapidly expanding field, business growth has become a major theme. Gartner (1990) showed that 'growth' was one out of eight themes that professional users commonly associated with the entrepreneurship concept. Livesay (1995) chose *Entrepreneurship and the Growth of Firms* as the title for his two-volume collection of essential readings in the field. In 1997, growth was chosen as the theme for the Babson/Kauffman Conference. It may further be noted that 26 studies in Delmar's (1997) methodological review of research on firm growth were published in either *Journal of Business Venturing* or *Entrepreneurship Theory and Practice*. Thirteen of the studies had some variant of the word 'entrepreneur' in the title. In his partly overlapping review of 53 studies on growth, Wiklund (1998) included 20 that were published in these two journals, and another 12 appeared in other publications that were clearly identifiable as outlets for entrepreneurship research, such as *Entrepreneurship and Regional Development* or *Frontiers of Entrepreneurship Research*. Again, 13 of the studies had some variant of the word 'entrepreneur' in the title.

This shows that many researchers evidently associate 'growth' with 'entrepreneurship' and vice versa. However, entrepreneurship researchers are not alone in showing an interest in business growth. Rather, growth is a major theme both in economics and management studies (Acs and Audretsch 1990, Evans 1987, Greiner 1972, Kazanjian and Drazin 1989, Penrose 1959). For the young and formative field of entrepreneurship research this gives reason to seriously reflect upon a couple of issues. First, there is the risk that the entrepreneurship researchers re-invent worse versions of wheels that are already in operation in other fields, thus failing to make a meaningful contribution. Second, there is the risk that they over-extend their own field, thus creating obstacles rather than contributions to a clear and thorough understanding of entrepreneurial processes. To avoid these risks, entrepreneurship researchers have reasons to ask themselves:

- Are there particular aspects of business growth that fall naturally within the domain of entrepreneurship?
- If so, is interest in these issues unique to entrepreneurship research (suggesting potential for unique contribution) or do other fields of research share them (suggesting potential for fruitful collaboration)?

The purpose of this chapter is to attempt to answer these questions. We will approach this task by first asking 'Is entrepreneurship growth?' Starting from a number of contemporary and influential definitions of entrepreneurship we discuss the possible inclusion or exclusion of growth implied by these definitions. We then turn to the converse question: 'Is growth entrepreneurship?' We will argue that specific types or stages of firm growth do satisfy theoretical criteria to qualify as 'entrepreneurship'. Having identified the aspects of business growth that fall naturally within the domain of entrepreneurship we broaden our discussion, exploring the potential for making a unique contribution. We argue that entrepreneurship research should deal not only with the growth of the 'firm' or the 'organization', but also with the growth of specific economic activities regardless of their organizational affiliations. In the concluding section we recapitulate and further discuss our main points.

As a background, we should mention that all three authors wrote their doctoral dissertations on entrepreneurship and small firm growth (Davidsson 1989, Delmar 1996, Wiklund 1998). In addition, all three authors have subsequently been personally involved in conceptual and methodological work on the topic of growth, as well as in several longitudinal empirical studies, ranging from growth aspirations during the pre start-up phase of independent new ventures to acquisition-based expansion of large corporations (for example, Davidsson and Delmar 1997, 1998, Davidsson and Wiklund 2000, Delmar 1997, Delmar and Davidsson 1998, 1999, Wiklund and Davidsson 1999, Wiklund, Davidsson, Delmar and Aronsson 1997). This chapter is best regarded as the result of a process of wrestling between theory and data that has been going on with greater or lesser intensity for well over a decade. Our early conceptual views affected which questions the studies were designed to address. Various results of the studies in turn affected our conceptual views. Although the present chapter is conceptual, we will draw upon and occasionally make reference to our earlier empirical work as well.

IS ENTREPRENEURSHIP GROWTH?

Having set the stage we can now turn to our first main question: 'Is entrepreneurship growth?' We have mentioned already that Gartner (1990) showed that growth was one out of eight themes that professional users commonly associated with the entrepreneurship concept. However, his study also made clear that not all would agree on that issue. This suggests that a discussion of whether or not entrepreneurship entails growth has to start with the definition of entrepreneurship.

This, of course, is no small part of the problem we are addressing. Through history, the words 'entrepreneur', 'entrepreneurial' and 'entrepreneurship' have been associated with many different specific economic (and other) roles and phenomena (cf. Hebert and Link 1982, Kirzner 1983). Contemporary academic usage of the terms is somewhat more restricted, but this does not mean that researchers are anywhere near a consensus as to what is the legitimate use of the concept 'entrepreneur' and its derivatives.

If we selectively pick one definition, the problem we are addressing could be made simple enough. For example, Cole (1949 [1995]) defined entrepreneurship as a purposeful activity to initiate, maintain and grow ('aggrandize') a profit-oriented business. Here, growth is part of the very definition. Cole (1949, p. 88) included mere 'maintenance' of a business while stressing 'freedom of decision'. Still today, much research that is presented under the entrepreneurship label deals with any management issues in small, owner-managed businesses, thereby implicitly adopting a view of entrepreneurship similar to

Cole's. Recent conceptual discussion of entrepreneurship, however, has favored a view where issues related to small firms or family-owned businesses do not automatically qualify as dealing with entrepreneurship. At the same time, these views may include processes in organizations that are not owner-managed in the concept of entrepreneurship.

In Table 2.1 we have compiled the modern conceptualizations that, arguably, have attracted the most interest and following. As a detailed examination will reveal, a common characteristic of these conceptualizations is that they make no mention of firm size. Neither do they restrict the entrepreneurship domain to owner-managed firms.

In other respects the definitions differ. Gartner's view – which he is careful to present as a suggestion for re-direction rather than a formal 'definition' – is that entrepreneurship is the creation of new organizations. This choice of focus has two origins. One was a perceived lack of treatment of organizational emergence in organization theory. Somehow organizations were assumed to exist; theories started with existing organizations (cf. Katz and Gartner 1988). The other was a frustration with the preoccupation that early entrepreneurship research had with personal characteristics of entrepreneurs. For these reasons, Gartner (1988) suggested that entrepreneurship research ought to be the behavioral study of organizational emergence. Conceptually, this does not leave room for including growth in the concept of entrepreneurship. Growth is a different organizational phenomenon, requiring other theoretical explanations (Gartner 2001, Gartner and Brush 1999).

The other definitions are broader and/or less precise. Low and Macmillan (1988) share with Gartner (1988) the view that entrepreneurship research should be more process-oriented. Their suggested definition of the field is 'creation of new enterprise'. In their wish to include aspects of what most researchers associated with the term 'entrepreneurship' at the same time as they try to give the field at least some firm direction, Low and Macmillan remain somewhat vague about exactly what is to be included under their definition. However, they consistently use 'new venture' and 'new enterprise' rather than 'new firm' or 'new organization' when they outline their own thoughts. They explicitly discuss pursuit of opportunities within existing firms, and say that they are interested in '*all* entrepreneurial phenomena that impact economic progress' (p. 151, original emphasis). Our understanding of this is that their suggested main focus of entrepreneurship research is the *creation of new economic activity,* regardless of what type of organization introduces it. Low and Macmillan (1988) do not explicitly address growth, but increases of the size of an existing organization resulting from its successful internal efforts to establish 'new enterprise' would, by implication, be entrepreneurship manifesting itself as growth.

Stevenson and his collaborators (see Table 2.1) start from experiences with

Table 2.1   Different views on entrepreneurship

Scholar(s)	Definition or conceptualization of entrepreneurship	Role of entrepreneurship research
Gartner (1988)	'Creation of new organizations' (p. 18)	Answer the question 'How do organizations come into existence?' (p. 26); in particular 'what individuals do' (p. 27) to make this happen
Low and MacMillan (1988)	'Creation of new enterprise' (p. 141)	'[E]xplain and facilitate the role of new enterprise in furthering economic progress' (p. 141)
Stevenson and Jarillo (1990), cf. Stevenson and Gumpert (1985), Stevenson, Roberts and Grousbeck (1985), Stevenson and Sahlman (1986)	'The process by which individuals – either on their own or inside organizations – pursue opportunities without regard to the resources they currently control' (p. 23)	Study the process of pursuit of opportunity from a behavioral perspective (implicit main focus)
Venkataraman (1997), cf. Shane and Venkataraman (2000)	'[T]he discovery and exploitation of profit-able opportunities for private wealth, and as a consequence for social wealth as well' (p. 132)	'[T]o understand how opportunities to bring into existence future goods and services are discovered, created, and exploited, by whom, and with what consequences (p. 120)

large, established organizations and the relative lack of capacity for novelty that they sometimes show. These authors share with Gartner (1988) the view that entrepreneurship research should focus on behavior, although their emphasis is on entrepreneurship within existing organizations. Their main argument is pursuit of opportunity regardless of current resources vs. getting a safe return on resources already owned or controlled. Opportunity is the central concept, and especially opportunities for new economic activities.

Stevenson and Jarillo (1990) state that '[A]n opportunity is, by definition, something beyond the current activities of the firm' (p. 23). Further, they explicitly include growth as they say that 'Entrepreneurship is the function through which growth is achieved (thus not only the act of starting new businesses)' (p. 21) and describe entrepreneurial behavior as 'the quest for growth through innovation' (p. 25).

Venkataraman's (1997) view is influenced by thoughts from economics and somewhat more macro-oriented than the previous ones. It shares with Stevenson and Jarillo (1990) the strong focus on opportunity. Importantly, opportunities to enhance the efficiency of the production of existing goods are *not* regarded as entrepreneurial. Entrepreneurship deals with opportunities for *future* goods and services (Shane and Venkataraman 2000, p. 220). Again, we would hold that new economic activity is a reasonable summary descriptive term. With respect to growth, it is important to note that Venkataraman (1997, cf. Shane and Venkataraman 2000) includes not only *discovery* in his delineation of the field, but also *exploitation*. While it may be argued that discovery (or opportunity recognition) is the fundamental and distinguishing feature of entrepreneurship relative to management (Fiet 1996, Gaglio 1997, Kirzner 1973), an inevitable counter-argument is that without action towards making creative ideas become real it would be awkward indeed to maintain that any entrepreneurship has been carried out. Schumpeter (1934, ch. 2) already made this argument quite forcefully. If exploitation is included in the definition of entrepreneurship, it must logically follow that the growth that results from a better exploitation strategy of a given opportunity (relative to a worse exploitation strategy) is entrepreneurship manifested as growth.

Based on this discussion of definitions we would argue that the contemporary discourse on the meaning of 'entrepreneurship' offers two main alternatives (cf. Sharma and Chrisman 1999). The first, most clearly articulated by Gartner (1988), holds that entrepreneurship is the creation of new organizations. This view certainly has a lot to commend it. It has a clearly defined focus, thereby avoiding the risk of over-extending the field. It addresses an ecological void that has been given only cursory treatment in economics and management studies. This has also led other scholars to adopt it (Aldrich 1999, Sharma and Chrisman 1999, Thornton 1999) although some would exchange 'creation' for 'emergence' thus de-emphasizing behavioral and strategic aspects.

The main problem with Gartner's (1988) approach is why the area of interest he delineates should be called 'entrepreneurship' rather than 'organization creation'. While pointing out an important and clearly defined arena for research, Gartner's (1988) definition in fact disregards most of the themes that users of the concept associate with entrepreneurship (Gartner 1990). There is no explicit consideration of innovation or new combinations (Schumpeter

1934, p. 66) and his approach disregards the possibility of alternative modes of exploitation for given opportunities (Shane and Venkataraman 2000, Van de Ven, Angle and Poole 1989). Therefore, if an independent inventor chooses to commercialize his/her invention through starting a new firm, this is entrepreneurship under Gartner's definition. If s/he already has a firm and uses that vehicle instead, or if an existing firm buys the invention and employs the inventor as product champion, no entrepreneurship has occurred. Conceptually, this perspective does *not* include growth.

The second view, emerging as a common theme in the other three conceptualizations offered in Table 2.1, is that entrepreneurship is the creation of new economic activity. This view includes relatively more of the connotations professional users associate with the entrepreneurship concept, and it is also more in line with a classical authority like Schumpeter (1934). The downside is that it is more vague and possibly more difficult to apply consistently in empirical work. The approach could also be criticized for not giving enough consideration to the different resource conditions facing independent start-ups and internal ventures, respectively.

Let us here define more precisely what we do and do not include in 'new economic activity'. By this concept we mean an activity that is new to the firm *and* which also changes the product or service offerings that are available on a market. The 'new to the firm' criterion requires that either an entirely new organization is created, or an existing organization starts to carry out activities that are distinctly different from what it has carried out so far. While this is a necessary criterion, it is not sufficient. The creation of a new organization for other purposes than the carrying out of new economic activity would not constitute entrepreneurship. Neither would a spin-off nor a management buy-out nor internal reorganization of an existing organization suffice as long as the organization merely continues to provide the market with the same supply as existed prior to the internal changes. It is when such changes also lead to changes in what is offered to the market that the criteria for 'new economic activity' are fulfilled. Our requirements for newness to the market are relatively mild, though. As we see it, less spectacular forms of entrepreneurship are imitative, but increase competition and therefore the incentives for all actors to improve themselves. Entrepreneurship of higher degrees is exemplified by the introduction of genuinely innovative products or services, which may shift consumption patterns and attract follower entrants, thus re-structuring industries or creating a new one.

As a minimum, then, entrepreneurship understood as the creation of new economic activity requires that a new or established firm introduces what internally is a new activity and appears at the same time as a new imitator in a market. At the high end of the spectrum, we would find the global introduction of radical innovation. According to this view, an opportunity to establish new economic activity can be pursued either within an existing organization or by establishing a new one. Both would constitute entrepreneurship. Thus, when an organization grows as a result of developing new activities the growth is a reflection of the firm's entrepreneurship. When new economic activities are added to old ones in existing organizations, this is entrepreneurship manifested as growth rather than as the creation of new organizations. Hence, under this view of entrepreneurship the question in the heading of this section can be answered affirmatively: entrepreneurship is (sometimes) growth.

We have discussed advantages and disadvantages associated with the two views. On balance, although we regard both as important areas for research, we should make it no secret that as conceptualization of entrepreneurship we prefer the latter alternative, creation of new economic activity. However, we will discuss also the 'creation of new organizations' view in the remainder of this chapter.

Admittedly, the two views we focus on do not fully capture all aspects of all contemporary definitions of entrepreneurship. A couple of exclusions should be mentioned. Although related to Schumpeter's (1934) theorizing, our definition of 'new economic activity' deviates from his description of types of economic development – often cited as his 'definition of entrepreneurship' – in that we are less willing to accept innovation regarding resource input and resource transformation (new raw materials, process innovation) as instances of entrepreneurship *per se*. We hold that it is when such internal changes affect what is offered in the market that 'new economic activity' is introduced. Kirzner (1973, 1983) would accept the discovery of any opportunity to make a profit as 'entrepreneurship'. Some such discoveries might lead neither to the creation of a new organization nor to a new economic activity as we have defined it. While narrow in other respects Kirzner's view is therefore in this regard broader than both of the views we deal with here.

In this section we have argued that the contemporary discourse presents two main views on entrepreneurship: entrepreneurship as *creation of new organizations* or as *creation of new economic activities*. 'Entrepreneurship is growth' is not a conceptually valid statement under the former view, whereas it is so under the latter view given that new economic activities add to the size of an established organization.

IS GROWTH ENTREPRENEURSHIP?

If it were accepted that entrepreneurship is (sometimes) growth, the vice versa must also be true: growth is (sometimes) entrepreneurship. When we first addressed this question we thought it was rather simple. Davidsson (1989, p. 7) expressed it as follows: '[I]s growth entrepreneurship? The answer to that question is contingent on to which extent the manager is free to choose. If economic behavior is discretionary, pursuing continued development of the firm is the more entrepreneurial choice when refraining from doing so is another feasible alternative, just like founding a firm is more entrepreneurial than not doing so.' While this still seems to us a reasonable line of argumentation we have since then in other contexts shown conceptually and empirically that the issue of business growth is very complex and multi-faceted. In fact, business growth may perhaps best be conceived of as a collective term for several rather different phenomena, requiring separate methods of inquiry as well as separate theoretical explanations (Davidsson and Wiklund 2000, Delmar 1997, Delmar and Davidsson 1998). In the present context, then, the question becomes: *what* growth can justifiably be regarded as manifestations of entrepreneurship?

As regards Gartner's (1988) organization creation view of entrepreneurship we have noted that conceptually, growth is not part of his definition. Empirical evidence suggests that the large majority of independent start-ups start very small and remain one- to three-person entities throughout their entire existence (Davidsson, Lindmark and Olofsson 1998, Delmar and Davidsson 1999). Consistent with this, Katz and Gartner (1988) separate characteristics of the person from those of the organization also for one-person businesses. However, such results suggest that restricting entrepreneurship to the study of the gestation process of 'normal' or 'average' startups only up to the point when they first start trading or first make a profit may be too restrictive. Growth up to some arbitrary level after a firm first starts as a sole trader may be necessary if it is to be meaningful to talk at all of the creation of 'organizations' as they are conceived of in organization theory, and thus fill the gap Gartner (198 8) pointed out. It may thus be advisable for research under this paradigm to include in the concept of 'emergence' or 'creation' also what other researchers might call 'early growth'. The starting point in terms of time and size would thus determine whether or not 'growth is entrepreneurship'.

For the 'entrepreneurship is new economic activity' view, the form of growth comes to the fore. Although exceptions exist (for example, Amit, Livnat and Zarowin 1989, Penrose 1959) the growth literature surprisingly rarely shows a strong interest in *how* or in *which form* firms expand. Examples of growth trajectories and their causes can be found in the literature dealing with related topics such as mergers or acquisitions (Chatterjee and Wernerfelt 1991, Hoskisson, Johnson and Moesel 1994, Markides 1995) or innovation and technological change (Tushman and Anderson 1986). A limitation of this research – for our purposes – is that the samples investigated are often composed of large firms in relatively mature industries. Furthermore, this literature is not predominantly interested in growth per se, but in how the phenomena under scrutiny change the behavior or financial performance of organizations.

Nevertheless, they do suggest different factors that might explain why firms come to grow through acquisition or by growing organically. Research on innovation and technological change focuses on the creation and diffusion of new products and services and how they affect the environmental conditions that determine the selection of firms for survival. Here, it is argued that the introduction of a new product or service leads to discontinuities, increased turbulence and uncertainty on the market. Initiators of such changes grow more rapidly than other firms (Tushman and Anderson 1986). It is implicitly clear that it is organic growth the authors have in mind, and their perspective is very close to the 'entrepreneurship as new economic activity' view.

Markides and Williamson (1996) adopt a resource-based view, and suggest that acquisition or mergers are used in order to acquire and exploit resources or assets owned by other companies, to make resources unavailable to its rivals at a competitive cost, or both. Penrose (1959) of course preceded them. In her original formulation of the resource based view, Penrose suggested that firms that exhibit organic growth have the ability to detect emerging expansion opportunities and to recombine existing resources in new ways so as to take advantage of these opportunities. In other words, Penrose argues that 'entrepreneurial resources' (or 'entrepreneurial capability') are crucial for organic growth. Acquired growth is a different process. In this case Penrose (1959) holds that the financial strength of the firm and its access to managerial slack are more important. Barney (1988) also argues that the reason organizations choose to grow through acquisitions often is excessive cash flow. Both financial and managerial slack is related to the size of the firm. This would suggest that the firm's acquisition growth is determined by the size of its resource pool rather than by its determination to develop new economic activities.

In one of our earlier studies we tested these predictions and found that firm size was indeed positively and significantly associated with acquisition growth, whereas a firm's degree of entrepreneurial strategic orientation (cf. Miller and Friesen 1982) was positively and significantly related to organic growth (Wiklund and Davidsson 1999). In another project we performed an analysis of high-growth firms broken down by firm size and age. We found very strong empirical relationships, suggesting that organic growth dominated among young and small firms whereas old and large firms grew almost exclusively through acquisition (Davidsson and Delmar 1998). This suggests that 'growth is entrepreneurship' is a reasonable generalization for young and small firms, but not for large and old ones.

We have argued already that when a firm grows as a consequence of adding new activities, we have a case of entrepreneurship manifested as growth. The short review above reinforces our view that this type of organic growth could justifiably be counted as entrepreneurship, while growth through acquisition could usually not. Returning to the definitions in Table 2.1, we find that

Venkataraman's (1997) focus on 'future goods and services' rules out growth through acquisition when the latter means moving existing production of goods and services from one organization to another. We would hold that the gist of Stevenson and Jarillo's (1990) argument also rules out acquisition growth. As suggested by Barney (1988) and Markides and Williamson (1996), acquisitions are often financial investments or serve to either protect or get synergy out of existing resources. This is in Stevenson and Jarillo's conceptualization typical 'trustee' behavior – the opposite of entrepreneurship. In our earlier discussion we found that the opportunities these authors have in mind are typically opportunities for starting new activities. This is also how we understand Low and MacMillan (1988). While their 'new enterprise' does not necessarily mean 'new to the world' it does not suffice that the activity is new only to the firm, as when existing activity is transferred from one organization to another.

From the 'entrepreneurship is new economic activity' view, then, the distinction between organic and acquired growth appears crucial for whether firm growth can be regarded as entrepreneurship or not. But what about cases where organic growth does not involve addition of new activities, but only growth in volume of an existing activity of the firm? Regarding entrepreneurship not as a dichotomous but a continuous phenomenon, Venkataraman's (1997) emphasis on discovery *and* exploitation provides some justification for regarding organic growth as a reflection of entrepreneurship even when it is 'mere' volume growth based on the original activity. The quality of the discovery – how radical a break with current practices it represents and how large a relative advantage it creates – determines its growth potential (Rogers 1995, Tushman and Anderson 1986). The quality of the exploitation determines, in turn, how much of that potential is realized. Therefore, organic growth in volume can be regarded as a (admittedly less-than-perfect) measure of the 'amount' of entrepreneurship that a particular instance of new economic activity represents.

We would be the first to admit that reality is not so simple that organic growth of firms always means they have engaged in new economic activity and that growth achieved through acquisition is never associated with genuinely new activity. In some cases, organic growth could be the result of mere volume growth of a producer of a commodity product who has just had the luck to be picked among equal alternatives by a large and growing customer. Acquisitions may in some instances reflect an aggressive strategy to rapidly buy an 'infrastructure' to be filled by the acquiring firm's own, growing activities. By and large, however, we would argue that it is reasonable to suggest that if particular firms were analyzed more closely, cases of organic growth would be much more likely to fulfill the criteria for qualifying as 'new economic activity' than would cases of acquisition growth.

In summary, we have argued in this section that when doing empirical work based on Gartner's definition of entrepreneurship it would be advisable to include what other researchers might call 'early growth' into the operationalization of 'organizational creation'. When entrepreneurship is viewed as new economic activity it is reasonable to assume that growth of firms represents entrepreneurship when the growth is achieved organically, whereas growth through acquisition does normally not represent entrepreneurship. As empirical results suggest young and small firms grow organically, whereas old and large firms grow through acquisition, there is in practice considerable overlap between the two perspectives as concerns when 'growth is entrepreneurship' appears to be a reasonable assumption.

BEYOND THE FIRM LEVEL

So far, our discussion has concerned the growth of firms or organizations. We have concluded that under the 'new economic activity' definition, organic growth of firms is a legitimate interest for entrepreneurship research. However, an interest in the growth of firms is not unique to entrepreneurship research. It would seem natural for researchers in strategic management to share to the full the interest in organic growth through the introduction of new economic activities, as one aspect of a more general interest in organizational growth (cf. Amit et al. 1989). As we have noted, it seems to be the case that also within the field of strategic management very little research has been conducted with this specific focus. Hence, this should be an area for fruitful exchange between the two sub-disciplines or interest groups.

In other respects the interests of these two lines of research differ. Although Gartner's definition focuses on the creation of a new firm (or 'organization') the other definitions in Table 2.1 are not focused on the firm level of analysis at all. This is clearly distinct from definitions of strategic management, which presuppose the existence of a firm (or organization) and an interest in its fate (Barney 1997, Schendel and Hofer 1979). The entrepreneurship definitions we favor instead point out the new economic activity as the unit of focal interest; the core interest in entrepreneurship is the emergence and growth of specific new activities.

From this perspective organic firm growth remains a proxy for entrepreneurship as long as we do not know in more detail the extent to which it represents either the introduction of new economic activity or the quality of the discovery and exploitation of opportunity for such activity. Consequently, entrepreneurship researchers should design studies where the new activity is explicitly used as the unit of analysis (cf. Davidsson and Wiklund 2000, 2001).

Ideally, the growth of such new activities should be studied at two levels.

First, it is of interest to follow the growth of the original effort, which may equal the growth of a new organization, a unit within an existing organization, or a unit which changes its organizational affiliation and/or its human champions one or more times during the course of the study. Second, we share with Venkataraman (1997), Low and MacMillan (1988) and many other entrepreneurship researchers an explicit interest in wealth creation also on the social level (see Table 2.1). From that point of view it would be of great interest to study how the new activity grows externally through imitation and – in some cases — gives rise to new populations of organizations or of practices. This interest has a large overlap with ecological or evolutionary approaches in organization theory (Aldrich 1999) as well as with research on the diffusion of innovations (Rogers 1995).

CONCLUSION

Is entrepreneurship growth? Is growth entrepreneurship? In this chapter we have given conditional affirmative answers to these questions. There is, however, one fundamental problem with associating entrepreneurship with growth that we have as yet not addressed. An organization or an activity can only grow if it is successful. If success is included in the concept of entrepreneurship, it follows that whether something constitutes 'entrepreneurship' or not can only be determined in retrospect. As a consequence, it would be difficult to study entrepreneurship in real time. As a resolution to this dilemma we suggest that entrepreneurship *as an economic phenomenon* only occurs if value is created and that entrepreneurship is ultimately measured by what effect an attempted new organization or activity has. Entrepreneurship as a scholarly domain, however, needs to study also failed attempts, and to do so in real time. Otherwise, censoring would lead to a biased view of entrepreneurship as an economic phenomenon.

We have examined two major views of entrepreneurship that were derived from definitions suggested by influential contemporary scholars: entrepreneurship as creation of new organizations and entrepreneurship as creation of new economic activity. We have argued that without any consideration of growth, entrepreneurship is reduced to a dichotomous empirical variable whose content does not fully reflect any of these definitions. Most start-ups never create much of an organization. In addition, new activities are no doubt undertaken within existing organizations, adding to their size. This suggests that entrepreneurship cannot be operationalized solely as start-up vs. non-start-up of independent new firms. Irrespective of which of the two main perspectives is chosen, some aspects of growth should be regarded as part of the entrepreneurship phenomenon.

If entrepreneurship is (sometimes) growth it follows that growth must (sometimes) be a reflection of entrepreneurship. From the 'organization creation' perspective, we have argued that empirical studies are well advised to include also what other researchers might call 'early growth' into the operationalization of emergence, and perhaps to over-sample high potential start-ups. Otherwise the research cannot fill the perceived gap between organizational non-existence and organizations as they usually appear in organization theory. From the 'new economic activity' perspective, we argued that organic firm growth is much more likely to satisfy the criteria for qualifying as entrepreneurship. Empirical research has shown that among young and small firms that expand, almost all the growth is organic. By contrast, in larger and older firms all or almost all the growth was attributable to acquisitions. Growth may thus be a reasonable indicator of entrepreneurship in the former groups, but not in the latter.

We concluded that organic growth of firms should also be a fruitful area for cross-fertilization with strategic management research. A range of research issues of mutual interest presents itself. For example, is it reasonable after a closer look to say that organic growth is entrepreneurial whereas acquisition growth is not? Under what circumstances is an organic growth strategy conducive to firm performance? Why is it that young and small firms grow organically whereas old and large firms grow through acquisitions? Is it that larger firms run out of entrepreneurial steam? If so, what structures and processes of larger organizations deter their creation of new economic activities, and what can be done to overcome these obstacles? Alternatively, is it young and small firms' lack of financial and managerial resources that force them to grow organically although acquisition growth would be more profitable or less risky? If so, what can firms do to overcome these liabilities of smallness and newness that prevent them from growing via acquisitions? These are questions that are of interest from both perspectives.

From the perspective of entrepreneurship research, however, even organic firm growth remains a proxy for the dependent variable that represents the real preference. We have argued that if entrepreneurship is defined as 'new economic activity', it follows that entrepreneurship researchers should also try to use the new economic activity itself as the unit of analysis in empirical research. Needless to say, studies using the activity itself as unit of analysis may be difficult to carry out (cf. Van de Ven, Angle et al. 1989, Van de Ven, Polley et al. 1999). Would it be possible to define 'new economic activity' in a precise enough manner to make sampling possible? How could the universe of 'new economic activities' be determined, so that representative samples could be drawn? Would the sampled units maintain a clear identity over time, so that longitudinal studies could follow units that can meaningfully be regarded 'the same' despite all the changes they go through? Are there enough theoretical concepts and established operationalizations of these available for this level of analysis? If not, could such be developed?

Clearly, tough challenges await the empirical researcher who sets out to study the growth of 'new economic activities' over time. However, several of these problems apply to the firm level of analysis as well, although researchers have learnt to habitually disregard them (Davidsson and Wiklund 2000). Moreover, we would argue that the potential for entrepreneurship research and for individual researchers to make more of a unique contribution might be much greater if these challenges are accepted.

NOTES

* Previously published as: Davidsson, P., F. Delmar and I. Wiklund (2002), 'Entrepreneurship as growth; growth as entrepreneurship', in M. A. Hitt, R. D. Ireland, S. M. Camp and D. L. Sexton (eds), *Strategic Entrepreneurship: Creating a New Integrated Mindset*, Oxford, UK: Blackwell, pp. 328–42.
1. The authors gratefully acknowledge support from the Knut and Alice Wallenberg's Foundation, the Swedish Foundation for Small Business Research (FSF), the Swedish Council for Work Life Research (RALF), and the Board for Industrial and Technical Development (NUTEK). They would also like to thank Dieter Boegenhold, Michael S. Camp, Michael Hitt, Duane Ireland, and Donald Sexton for valuable comments on earlier versions of this manuscript. The responsibility for any remaining errors and omissions is, of course, entirely the authors'.

REFERENCES

Acs, Z. J. and D. B. Audretsch (1990), 'The determinants of small-firm growth in US manufacturing', *Applied Economics*, **22**(2), 143–53.
Aldrich, H. (1999), *Organizations Evolving*, Newbury Park, CA: Sage.
Amit, R., J. Livnat and P. Zarowin (1989), 'The mode of corporate diversification: internal ventures versus acquisitions', *Managerial and Decision Economics*, **10**, 89–100.
Barney, J. B. (1988), 'Returns to bidding firms in mergers and acquisitions: reconsidering the relatedness hypothesis', *Strategic Management Journal*, **9**, 71–8.
Barney, J. B. (1997), *Gaining and Sustaining Competitive Advantage*, Reading, MA: Addison-Wesley Publishing Company.
Chatterjee, S. and W. Wernerfelt (1991), 'The link between resources and the type of diversification: theory and evidence', *Strategic Management Journal*, **12**, 33–48.
Cole, A. H. (1949), Entrepreneurship and entrepreneurial history', in *Change and the Entrepreneur*, pp. 88–107, reprinted in H. C. Livesay (ed.) 1995, *Entrepreneurship and the Growth of Firms*, vol 1, Aldershot, UK: Edward Elgar, pp. 100–22.
Davidsson, P. (1989), 'Entrepreneurship and small firm growth', dissertation prepared for the Economic Research Institute, Stockholm.
Davidsson, P. and F. Delmar (1997), 'High-growth firms: characteristics, job contribution and method observations', paper prepared for the RENT XI Conference, Mannheim, Germany (this is an early version of Chapter 8 in this volume).
Davidsson, P. and F. Delmar (1998), 'Some important observations concerning job

creation by firm size and age', in H. J. Pleitner (ed.), *Renaissance der KMU in einer globalisiertern Wirtschaft*, St. Gallen: KMU Vlg. HSa, pp. 57–67.

Davidsson, P., L. Lindmark and C. Olofsson (1998), 'The extent of overestimation of small firm job creation: an empirical examination of the "regression bias" ', *Small Business Economics*, **10**, 87–100.

Davidsson, P. and J. Wiklund (2000), 'Conceptual and empirical challenges in the study of firm growth', in D. Sexton and H. Landström (eds), *The Blackwell Handbook of Entrepreneurship*, Oxford, MA: Blackwell, pp. 26–44 (Chapter 3 in this volume).

Davidsson, P. and J. Wiklund (2001), 'Levels of analysis in entrepreneurship research: current practice and suggestions for the future', *Entrepreneurship Theory and Practice*, **25**(4, Summer): 81–99.

Delmar, F. (1996), 'Entrepreneurial behavior and business performance', dissertation prepared for The Economic Research Institute, Stockholm.

Delmar, F. (1997), 'Measuring growth: methodological considerations and empirical results', in R. Donckels and A. Miettinen (eds), *Entrepreneurship and SME Research: On its Way to the Next Millennium*, Aldershot, VA: Avebury, pp. 190–216 (Chapter 4 in the current volume).

Delmar, F. and P. Davidsson (1998), 'A taxonomy of high-growth firms', in *Frontiers of Entrepreneurship Research*, 18, Wellesley, MA: Babson College, pp. 399–43 (this is an early version of Chapter 9 in this volume).

Delmar, F. and P. Davidsson (1999), 'Firm size expectations of nascent entrepreneurs', in *Frontiers of Entrepreneurship Research*, 19, Wellesley, MA: Babson College, pp. 90–104 (Chapter 5 in this volume).

Evans, D. S. (1987), 'Test of alternative theories of firm growth', *Journal of Political Economy*, **95**, 657–74.

Fiet, J. (1996), 'The informational basis of entrepreneurial discovery', *Small Business Economics*, **8**, 419–30.

Gaglio, C. M. (1997), 'Opportunity identification: review, critique and suggested research directions', in J. Katz and J. Brockhaus (eds), *Advances in Entrepreneurship, Firm Emergence, and Growth*, Greenwich, CT: JAI Press, pp. 139–202.

Gartner, W. B. (1988), '"Who is an entrepreneur?" is the wrong question', *American Small Business Journal* (Spring), 11–31.

Gartner, W. B. (1990), 'What are we talking about when we are talking about entrepreneurship?', *Journal of Business Venturing*, **5**, 15–28.

Gartner, W. B. (2001), 'Is there an elephant in entrepreneurship research? Blind assumptions in theory development', *Entrepreneurship Theory and Practice*, **25**(4) (Summer), 27–39.

Gartner, W. B. and C. B. Brush (1999), 'Entrepreneurship as organizing: emergence, newness, and transformation', paper presented at the Academy of Management Entrepreneurship Division Doctoral Consortium, Chicago.

Greiner, L. E. (1972), 'Evolutions and revolutions as organizations growth', *Harvard Business Review*, **50**(4), 37–46.

Hebert, R. F. and A. N. Link (1982), *The Entrepreneur: Mainstream Views and Radical Critiques*, New York: Praeger.

Hoskisson, R. E., R. A. Johnson and D. D. Moesel (1994), 'Corporate divestiture intensity in restructuring firms: effects of governance, strategy, and performance', *Academy of Management Journal*, **37**(5), 1207–51.

Katz, J. and W. B. Gartner (1988), 'Properties of emerging organizations', *Academy of Management Review*, **13**(3), 429–41.

Kazanjian, R. K. and R. Drazin (1989), 'An empirical test of stage of a growth progression model', *Management Science*, **35**(12), 1489–503.

Kirzner, I. (1973), *Competition and Entrepreneurship*, Chicago, IL: University of Chicago Press.

Kirzner, I. M. (1983), 'Entrepreneurs and the entrepreneurial function: a commentary', in J. Ronen (ed), *Entrepreneurship*, Lexington, MA: Lexington Books, pp. 281–90.

Livesay, H. C. (ed) (1995), *Entrepreneurship and the Growth of Firms*, vols 1–2, Aldershot, UK: Edward Elgar.

Low, M. B. and I. C. MacMillan (1988), 'Entrepreneurship: past research and future challenges', *Journal of Management*, **14**, 139–61.

Markides, C. C. (1995), 'Diversification, restructuring and economic performance', *Strategic Management Journal*, **16**, 101–18.

Markides, C. C. and P. J. Williamson (1996), 'Corporate diversification and organizational structure: a resource-based view', *Academy of Management Journal*, **39**(2), 340–67.

Miller. D. and P. H. Friesen (1982), 'Innovation in conservative and entrepreneurial firms: two models of strategic momentum', *Strategic Management Journal*, **3**, 1–25.

Penrose, E. (1959), *The Theory of the Growth of the Firm*, Oxford, UK: Oxford University Press.

Rogers, E. M. (1995), *Diffusion of Innovations*, New York: Free Press.

Romano, C. and J. Ratnatunga (1997), 'A citation classics analysis of articles in contemporary small enterprise research', *Journal of Business Venturing*, **12**, 197–212.

Schendel, D. and C. W. Hofer (1979), 'Introduction', in D. E. Schendel and C. W. Hofer (eds), *Strategic Management: A New View of Business Policy and Planning*, Boston, MA: Little, Brown and Company.

Schumpeter, J. (1934), *The Theory of Economic Development*, Cambridge, MA: Harvard University Press.

Shane, S. A. and S. Venkataraman (2000), 'The promise of entrepreneurship as a field of research', *Academy of Management Review*, **25**(1), 217–26.

Sharma, P. and J. J. Chrisman (1999), 'Toward a reconciliation of the definitional issues in the field of corporate entrepreneurship', *Entrepreneurship Theory and Practice*, **24** (Spring), 11–27.

Stevenson, H. H. and D. E. Gumpert (1985), 'The heart of entrepreneurship', *Harvard Business Review* (March–April), 85–94.

Stevenson, H. H. and J. C. Jarillo (1990), 'A paradigm of entrepreneurship: entrepreneurial management', *Strategic Management Journal*, **11**, 17–27.

Stevenson, H. H., M. J. Roberts and H. I. Grousbeck (1985), *New Business and the Entrepreneur*, Homewood, IL: Irvin.

Stevenson, H. H. and S. Sahlman (1986), 'Importance of entrepreneurship in economic development', in R. Hisrisch (ed.), *Entrepreneurship, Intrapreneurship and Venture Capital*, Lexington, DC: Heath, pp. 3–26.

Thornton, P. H. (1999), 'The sociology of entrepreneurship', *Annual Review of Sociology*, **25**, 19–46.

Tushman, M. L. and P. Anderson (1986), 'Technological discontinuities and organizational environments', *Administrative Science Quarterly*, **31**, 439–65.

Van de Ven, A., H. L. Angle and M. S. Poole (eds) (1989), *Research on the Management of Innovation: The Minnesota Studies*, New York: Harper & Row.

Van de Ven, A. H., D. Polley, R. Garud and S. Venkataraman (1999), *The Innovation Journey*, Oxford, UK: Oxford University Press.

Venkataraman, S. (1997), 'The distinctive domain of entrepreneurship research: an editor's perspective', in J. Katz and J. Brockhaus (eds), *Advances in Entrepreneurship, Firm Emergence, and Growth*, Greenwich, CT: JAI Press, **3**, 119–38.

Wiklund, J. (1998), 'Small firm growth and performance: entrepreneurship and beyond', dissertation prepared for Jönköping International Business School, Jönköping, Sweden.

Wiklund, J. and P. Davidsson (1999), 'A resource-based view on organic and acquired growth', paper presented at the Academy of Management Pre-conference, Chicago, August.

Wiklund, J., P. Davidsson, F. Delmar and M. Aronsson (1997), 'Expected consequences of growth and their effect on growth willingness in different samples of small firms', in P. D. Reynolds, W. D. Bygrave, N. M. Carter, P. Davidsson, W. B. Gartner, C. M. Mason and P. P. McDougall (eds), *Frontiers of Entrepreneurship Research 1997*, Wellesley, MA: Babson College, pp. 1–16 (this is an early version of Chapter 6 in the current volume).

3. Conceptual and empirical challenges in the study of firm growth[1]

Per Davidsson, Johan Wiklund

INTRODUCTION

When the first author reviewed the literature on small firm growth in the mid-1980s for his dissertation work, he noted that surprisingly few studies had focused on that specific problem (Davidsson 1989a; 1989b). Today, this is no longer true. In recent years ever more comprehensive lists of studies have been compiled and reviewed. Storey (1994) compiled results from more than 25 studies. Delmar (1997) scrutinized the operationalizations of growth in 55 studies. The second author of the present chapter recently reviewed and classified close to 70 studies for his dissertation work (Wiklund, 1998), while Ardishvili, Cardozo, Harmon and Vadakath (1998) included in their classification a full 105 published and unpublished studies focusing on new and/or small firm growth.

However, rather than presenting a set of solid generalizations on the causes and effects of growth, these reviewers all tend to come up with relatively critical accounts. These criticisms concern both theoretical and methodological shortcomings. (Storey, 1994, pp. 5, 125; Cooper, 1995, p. 120; Delmar (1997, pp. 205, 212; Wiklund, 1998, pp. 6-7, 19; Ardishvili et al., 1998, p. 1).

In addition to the above evaluations of research specifically on growth, we also have the observation that longitudinal designs are generally lacking in entrepreneurship research (Cooper 1995, p. 112; Wiklund 1998, p. 7). In the latest 'state-of-the-art' volume, several authors mentioned the lack of longitudinal studies in entrepreneurship research as a major impediment (Aldrich and Baker, 1997, p. 389; Sexton, 1997, p. 407).

As a result of the shortcomings pointed out by the critics, it is still true today that knowledge about what facilitates and hinders growth is still scattered and limited. The same is true for insights into the process of firm growth. Apparently, the large number of empirical studies has not given a very high yield of generalizable knowledge. This suggests that researchers who set out to contribute meaningfully to this line of empirical research have a number of challenges to deal with. On the basis of the criticism summarized above we would suggest that some of the more important challenges are the following:

- to develop a satisfactory basic research design
- to apply a well-founded conceptualization of growth, which in turn requires a well thought-out conceptualization of 'the firm'
- to adequately match this conceptualization with the purpose of the study, the theories used, and the operationalization of growth.

In the remainder of this chapter we will elaborate our views on these challenges. In the next section we will argue that growth studies need to be longitudinal, and why this is so. We will then turn to the conceptualization of the firm and the unit of analysis in growth studies, which turns out to be a really difficult problem. After that we discuss theoretical perspectives and how these match with different conceptualizations of the firm. Finally, we turn to operationalization issues, that is the choice of growth indicators, specific ways to model growth trajectories, and the distinction between organic and acquired growth. Throughout, we also discuss how these issues relate to different purposes, that is whose knowledge interests the study aims to satisfy.

THE NEED FOR LONGITUDINAL RESEARCH ON FIRM GROWTH

Growth is a process that needs to be studied over time. To date, studies that use data from several points in time have usually been based on secondary data. Such studies may serve the purpose of testing simple theoretical propositions or estimating empirical relationships like the influence of firm age and size on growth (cf. Evans, 1987). They sometimes suffice for richer demographic profiles of growth firms, or to propose the existence of different 'types' of growth firms (Davidsson and Delmar, 1997; Delmar and Davidsson, 1998). Since they typically comprise only a minimum of variables, secondary data sets cannot, however, be used for testing or developing conceptually richer theories.

Case studies are sometimes longitudinal not only in the sense that the firm's history is investigated, but also in the sense that the firm's development is followed in real time (for example Brytting, 1991). While such studies are valuable for developing hypotheses and for suggesting interpretations of the results obtained in surveys, they will never suffice for making generalizations about relationships among variables.

Most studies on firm growth are survey based. Survey data are more or less the only alternative if we want to have data on attitudes, perceptions, strategies, and resources from a large number of cases. The problem is that with a few exceptions (for example Cooper, 1995; Wiklund, 1998) the studies are cross-sectional. This leaves the researcher with several less-than-satisfactory alternatives.

The first is to use historical growth as the dependent variable in causal analysis. This method measures a growth process that started some time ago and that ends at the time of data collection. Explanatory variables are collected at the same time and measure the present situation of the firm. In other words, explanatory variables collected today are used to predict a process of the past. This breaks with the principle that the cause must precede the effect. The researcher may justify this by assuming that the explanatory variables do not change during the period over which growth is studied. This is reasonable only when variables such as sex, age, and ethnicity are used for explaining growth. The other possible justifying assumption is that past growth predicts future growth. That is, the growth measure calculated from the past should be seen as a forecast of future growth, and the regression equation predicts this future growth. Unfortunately, there is empirical evidence that this is not a plausible assumption (for example Storey, 1994). In addition, failures are typically not included in surveys. Therefore, when past growth is used as the dependent variable, factors that increase the probability of *both* success and failure will be misinterpreted as 'success factors'. Firms' development needs to be studied in real time to avoid this error.

The second less-than-satisfactory solution is to study growth willingness rather than actual growth (cf. Davidsson, 1989b; Wiklund et al., 1997). While less problematic from a causality point of view, this introduces the question of attitude-behavior consistency (Foxall, 1984). We are left not knowing whether growth willingness is a strong predictor of subsequent growth.

The problems are essentially the same for analyses which focus on the consequences of growth rather than its antecedents. Only with longitudinal data can really satisfactory analyses for theory testing and development be undertaken. The challenge for future research is to generate funds and develop data collection procedures that make possible the building of such data sets.

WHAT IS GROWING?

A minimum requirement for knowledge development is that we know what we want to study. This implies a need for a clear conceptualization of the micro unit of the analysis. The embarrassing fact is that researchers in the field, ourselves included, have not been clear about the concept of the firm. A likely reason why this has not been much considered is that most empirical research has been cross-sectional. Theorists in their turn, have perhaps not done enough empirical research to see the conceptual problems. When growth is studied empirically and longitudinally they become apparent. Below we give some illustrations of this important point.

Consider entrepreneur X. In the late 1970s, he stumbled into becoming a part-time small business owner-manager as a result of writing some accounting software for his wife's business. Others with similar needs showed an interest, and before long X was running a high-growth firm developing and selling software for business applications. The operations continued to grow by related diversification: consulting, IT-related education programs, software development for other applications than business, and so forth. Some of this developed organically while other parts were acquired. After a successful decade the firm had some 150 employees and ran activities in several places. Legally, however, they were all in the same limited liability company.

Now the firm encountered severe difficulties for the first time. In order to regain some of the spirit of the young and small firm, entrepreneur X decided to break the firm into smaller, more independent units. He could do this in either of three ways (he chose one of these): a) form a number of wholly-owned but semi-independent, separate legal units that represented the different lines of business under a holding company, which would retain a few central functions; b) like a) but with more complete separate companies, the holding company essentially being only the owner of the brand name and functioning as the group's internal bank; c) like b) but with transfer of majority ownership to the top management in the new units, entrepreneur X only keeping a minority stake via the holding company. In all cases, one new company would represent the group's original core business: software development for business applications.

What is 'the firm' in this story? How much has it grown? In what sense is the resulting company group 'the same' entity as the original part-time business? Do we want it to be regarded 'the same' entity? If so, does that apply regardless of whether entrepreneur X chooses a, b, or c? Is it just the software development company that should be counted, or all business activities that are still under entrepreneur X's ownership control? These questions are not easy, but they need reasonable answers if we are to study 'firm growth' as a process over time.

At a given point in time, it is relatively easy to define or describe what a particular firm 'is'. Important aspects of this description could be what it offers to the market and what assets it controls. Its legal form, its ownership and its established relationships may be other important dimensions. The paradox is that if we try to follow the unit thus defined over time in order to study its growth, the definition will no longer hold. Over time, 'the firm' is likely to change its activities, its assets, its ownership and its legal form, and if something has grown it is *not* 'the firm' as originally defined.

The heart of the problem is that firms are not like biological individuals. There is no question that the pony-size five-year-old Great Dane is the same entity as the little newborn puppy it once was. Not so with firms. Metaphorically speaking, a duckling may really become a swan in the world of firms. The fact that 'firms' are not 'individuals' is a fundamental challenge to any attempt to study business growth at the firm level. An analogy to quantum physics and Heisenberg's uncertainty principle may serve to summarize our point: you cannot uniquely determine 'the firm's' identity and at the same time study its growth.

As shown in Table 3.1, micro-level changes that make the concept of 'firm' problematic are not delimited to cases like entrepreneur X. They are the rule rather than the exception. These data are based on a Swedish data set comprising all commercial, non-government firms that were in existence the entire November 1987 to November 1996 period, and which had an end size of at least 20 employees. By 'firm' is here meant the legal enterprise. Different enterprises that are wholly owned by the same company group appear as separate cases. Constellations of surviving establishments that appear under one company code the first year and another company code the second year are regarded as representing the same, surviving, firm. The table reports only such dynamics that relate directly to the problem of what unit should be regarded as 'the firm'.

The displayed results show that roughly 400 firms annually are probably acquired, as indicated by changes (b) and (f). Are those firms still 'the same' after they were acquired? What if activities that already employed ten people in the acquiring company group are integrated with the acquired firm while activities in the latter employing five people are dissolved – has the latter then grown? Some 200–300 firms annually are likely to represent spin-offs or buyouts (c, e). Were they really 'firms' before they were spun off? If so, are they still 'the same' firms as before? Roughly 150 firms annually change from independent to parent company (a). This probably represents either acquisition of an existing firm or re-organization of a business that was previously run as a single company to becoming a company group. When the growth of these cases is assessed, should not both the parent and the daughters be included in 'year two'? Similar problems with the growth computation apply to firms, which start or terminate activities abroad (g, h).

Over a ten-year period a majority (4779 out of 8562 companies) undergo changes that make it questionable whether they still are 'the same' firm and, hence, the basis for a growth computation ambiguous. While ten years is a long time, it is clear from these data that also analyses with a three- or five-year time frame would be highly problematic in these respects.

Despite all these problems, we hold that firm growth can and should be studied. The above examples clearly illustrate that our interpretation of the growth of the firm depends on our definition of what the firm is, and that this definition has to be made *before* any meaningful discussion of growth can take place. Our alternative to viewing the firm as an unspecified, taken-for-granted entity would be to utilize one or more of the three units of analyses below.

Table 3.1 Category changes over time in 8562 surviving (1987–96) Swedish firms with 20 or more employees in 1996

Year	1988	1989	1990	1991	1992	1993	1994	1995	1996	Entire period
Change governance										
a) indep.→parent	171	192	140	191	102	122	140	112	115	1238
b) indep→daughter	244	238	216	222	237	215	293	290	196	1964
c) daughter→indep.	123	88	123	445	158	205	143	220	228	1559
d) parent→indep.	80	47	56	119	88	87	61	92	113	718
e) daughter→parent	44	44	65	78	46	44	57	48	57	462
f) parent→daughter	100	121	131	131	77	83	152	155	92	1005
Change abroad										
g) started majority-owned activity abroad (from some to none)	91	27	51	95	48	64	159	140	121	754
h) terminated majority-owned activity abroad (from none to some)	18	16	40	27	15	63	53	26	112	356
Any type of change (a through h)	858	766	803	1275	755	853	1033	1049	988	4779 (55.8%)

Note: Entries do not sum up horizontally because some firms undergo the same type of change several times, and not vertically because some firms undergo several different changes.

44

Imagine how different our analyses and interpretations in the above examples would have been, depending on which alternative was chosen:

- All business activities controlled by an individual or group of individuals. The entrepreneur or the entrepreneurial team would be the unit to follow over time. The individual(s) may choose to expand a specific existing legal unit, or place the growth in a new independent firm, or a subsidiary. Existing activities may be expanded, or new, unrelated activities may be added as a result of innovation or acquisition. Thus, the types and number of activities and governance structures controlled by the individual(s) may change over time.
- A particular business activity or a related set of business activities. Here, the unit of analysis would be a particular product or product line, or perhaps entire business concepts as in business format franchising. These activities may, over time, be in different governance structures and controlled by different individuals. They may represent only part of the total operations of a legal entity or, in other cases, all operations of an entire company group.
- A governance structure, which is a decision-making unit, coherently administered and controlled. This unit of analysis could (but does not necessarily coincide with a specific legal or statistical unit that can be found in data registers. In a multi-establishment company group, the unit of analysis could be an establishment, a company, or the whole group. The ownership of a given governance structure may shift over time, and so may its business activities.

Much research to date has implicitly assumed that there is a total overlap between these three units of analysis. When an individual starts and runs one single organization, which expands organically, not diversifying its activities, this is true. In every other route of expansion, these units of analysis will differ from each other. Depending on which unit of analysis the researcher chooses, interpretations and conclusions will differ. The longer the time span over which growth is studied, the more likely is the assumption of total overlap to be wrong. This is an important fact, so far largely overlooked.

FIRM GROWTH THEORY

In order to be able to utilize appropriate units of analysis, and theories in conjunction with these, it is necessary, as noted above, to start with a conceptualization of 'the firm'. In their review of different theories of the firm, Seth and Thomas (1994) identify four different 'theoretical firm' conceptualizations.

These are the firm as 'production function' in neo-classical economics, as 'strategic player' in new industrial organization economics, as 'nexus of contracts' in agency theory, and as 'governance structure' in transaction cost economics.

Unfortunately, none of these 'theoretical firm' conceptualizations was created for the specific purpose of analysing firm growth. That is, they do not provide us with an answer to the question 'What is the unit of our analysis, whose size development we want to study over time?'

The shortcomings of theories which have 'theoretical firm' as point of departure, in giving empirical insights into the growth of the firm, may explain why 'firm growth' researchers have taken a different track. It is more common to utilize some of the theories grounded in real-world firm conceptualizations, called 'empirical firm' theories by Seth and Thomas (1994, p. 168). However, as the above examples and the criticism reviewed in the introduction have illustrated, these conceptualizations are rarely clear or explicit. It is nevertheless possible to infer conceptualizations of firms and theoretical perspectives in previous empirical research into firm growth.

Ardishvili et al. (1998) classified empirical growth studies into (a) factors of growth studies and (b) growth process studies. The former deal with seeking explanations as to why firms grow, that is, antecedents of growth are sought and growth is treated as a dependent variable. The latter are concerned with the changes that take place in an organization as a consequence of growth. Growth is the starting point; the cause.

It is possible to categorize firm growth studies in more detail based on their underlying assumptions. With a focus on general assumptions, concepts, and relationships among concepts, we identified four theoretical perspectives that fall into either of the factor or process categories. These are the resources-based perspective, the motivation perspective, the strategic adaptation perspective, and the configuration perspective (see Wiklund, 1998, for an elaborate treatment of these theoretical perspectives). Three of these are linked to factor studies and one to process studies. As we will later show, each of these theoretical perspectives corresponds in a natural way to the previously introduced units of analysis, viz. a) individual(s), b) activity, or c) governance structure.

In the resource-based perspective, the focus is on the firm as a bundle of resources and the activities it can perform based on these resources. Thus, it is most appropriate for growth studies within the resource-based perspective to use the business activity or related set of business activities as the unit of analysis. Growth in this case would refer to the expansion of related business activities, made possible by the unique combination and/or deployment of resources. This is not to say that this theoretical perspective is entirely incompatible with other units of analysis. Both enterprising individuals and governance structures are associated with certain resources, some of which are so general (for example, financial resources, highly educated staff) that they are of relevance for a wide range of business activities. Therefore, the individual(s) and the governance structure are secondary alternatives for unit of analysis when growth is to be studied from a resource-based perspective.

With its focus on power distribution, structural complexity, and control mechanisms, the conceptualization of the firm in the strategic adaptation perspective relates to the governance structure unit of analysis. Thus, growth studies applying strategic adaptation as the theoretical perspective would benefit from using the governance structure as their unit of analysis. A secondary alternative is the activity, as it is possible to apply different strategies for different 'strategic business units' which encounter different environmental threats. The strategic adaptation perspective is clearly not designed for using the individual unit of analysis. For example, from an enterprising individual's perspective, selling off or closing down entire activities or governance structures may be rational strategic options which still leads to growth of the individual's total business activities. This is not the kind of strategic options that are visible or relevant from 'within' an activity or a governance structure.

In the motivation perspective of firm growth, as in all psychological studies, the focus is on individuals and their actions. Hence, the focus of motivational studies of firm growth corresponds with the individual(s) as the unit of analysis. To investigate the relationship between the individual's motivation and firm growth, the individual's entire business activities need to be followed. It is from this perspective of secondary interest what particular activities under the individual's control expand or not as a result of his/her level of motivation. The same is true for the specific make-up of the governance structure(s) within which the expansion takes place. Therefore, following one legal unit under the individual's control may lead to erroneous results. However, while less central, the motivation of key individuals has a place also in studies using the activity or the governance structure as the unit of analysis.

While the three previously mentioned theoretical perspectives are concerned with factors of growth, the configuration perspective deals with the growth process. The configuration perspective focuses on how managerial problems appear and can be dealt with during a firm's growth through (presumed) typical stages-of-development. This conforms to using the governance structure unit of analysis, which focuses on a particular decision making unit coherently administered and controlled. Product life-cycle theory (for example, Day, 1981) can be regarded as a variety on this theme, more adapted to using the activity as unit of analysis. The configuration theories are clearly not consistent with using the individual unit of analysis. On the contrary, several of the contributors to this perspective address the possibility (sometimes presented as a necessity) of replacing the founder in order to achieve successful further growth of the firm.

MATCHING THEORETICAL PERSPECTIVES WITH CONCEPTUALIZATIONS OF THE FIRM AND DIFFERENTIAL KNOWLEDGE USER INTERESTS

The three possible units of analysis that we have previously identified, and their suitability within the four theoretical perspectives prevalent in growth studies, are summarized in Table 3.2. Our analysis suggests that different units of analysis are 'optimal' for different theories. Further, while the governance structure, and possibly also the activity, as unit of analysis seems to have some compatibility with each theoretical perspective, current formulations of strategic adaptation and configuration perspectives seem ill-adapted for using the individual's entire business activities as the unit of analysis. As we shall see, however, the individual as unit of analysis has other advantages.

Although each of the theoretical perspectives reviewed provides us with valuable insights into the growth of the firm, they address different specific issues. To get a fuller understanding for the antecedents of growth as well as the growth process, it may be beneficial to integrate some or all the theoretical perspectives in a model. Such a model integrating the theoretical perspectives has been suggested by Wiklund (1998). It must be borne in mind, however, that when such integrative models are applied to empirical research, it may become necessary to utilize different conceptualizations of the firm and different units of analysis in parallel.

This – that is, keeping track of the development of different units of analysis when they no longer overlap 100 per cent – would be cumbersome in longitudinal survey studies and virtually impossible in longitudinal studies utilizing secondary data. To some extent, the researcher will have to compromise in the conceptualization of the firm and the unit of analysis. However, the important issue is that these compromises are made consciously, and in ways which are

Table 3.2   Different units of analysis and rankings of their suitability within different theoretical perspectives

Resource-based	Strategic adaptation	Motivation	Configuration
1. Activity 2. Individual or governance structure	1. Governance structure 2. Activity 3. Individual	1. Individual 2. Activity or governance structure	1. Governance structure (2. Activity)

Note: Within each theoretical perspective, the number 1 denotes the most suitable unit of analysis, 2 the second most suitable and so on.

the most appropriate in relation to the theories applied and the specific empirical issues that are investigated. Table 3.2 can serve as an aid when doing such compromises. The alternative, which would be to disregard the fact that the unit of analysis affects empirical results and that different units of analysis are more appropriate for certain theoretical perspectives, is not an acceptable solution. Empirical complexity is a challenge that must be accepted and not disregarded. If not, results and conclusions may be seriously flawed.

The relative merits of these units of analysis are also contingent on the fundamental question *why* we want to study growth. In Table 3.3 we make an attempt to assess the relevance of the different units of analysis to three groups of potential users of research-based knowledge on firm growth: owners, managers and policy-makers.

From an owner's point of view, the totality of her/his business activities is the main interest. Within that totality, what particular activities grow or not is also relevant. Since the organizational framework is also part of the totality, the growth of a particular governance structure is also of some relevance to owners.

A manager is typically the manager of a governance structure, and the causes and consequences of growth of that unit are therefore the main interest. It is also of high relevance to managers what factors contribute to the growth of particular business activities under their control. The growth of individuals' entire business operations is of secondary interest for managers.

Policy-makers may show a keen interest in high-growth firms, but we hold that this interest is misdirected if focused on the growth of governance structures. Policy-makers' positive interest in high-growth firms is, or should be, concerned instead with the growth of activities. It is the emergence and growth of new activities that add value and create genuinely new jobs.

Reading the table column-wise, activity-based growth analysis seems to be of high interest to all three parties. The other two units of analysis are more likely to lead wrong for certain purposes.

This analysis also provides us with an interesting possibility to clarify the differential foci of the overlapping interests of entrepreneurship research,

Table 3.3 Different units of analysis and their relevance for different user groups

	Individual(s)	Activity	Governance structure
Owners	Very high relevance	High relevance	Some relevance
Managers	Some relevance	High relevance	Very high relevance
Policy-makers	High relevance	Very high relevance	Some relevance

management research, and economics. The management discipline is fundamentally about the micro-level in the economy. Its core concerns primarily the performance of established business organizations and what managers can do to influence performance. The fate of the individuals involved is secondary, as is the question whether success of the firm also contributes to the economy-at-large or merely is part of a zero-sum game on the macro-level.

Economics is fundamentally about the macro-level. The performance of the economy-at-large is in focus. The micro-level analysis is there only to give an atomistic rationale for macro-level phenomena. Even if the theorists who at all care about entrepreneurship also theorize (romanticize?) about the entrepreneur (cf. Schumpeter, 1934) the ultimate interest is always with the macro-level effects (Kirzner, 1983).

Entrepreneurship research concerns itself both with micro and macro levels. It takes a clear voluntaristic stance, based on the assumption that individual initiative is a crucial force in the economy-at-large. It takes a genuine interest in the characteristics and behavior of the individuals who take such initiatives. At the same time, entrepreneurship research takes an interest in value creation on the societal level. On this macro-level the main interest in growth studies from an entrepreneurship point of view is the growth of activities – what new activities contribute to GDP and job creation come to the fore, not primarily what particular individuals are behind it, and certainly not the growth of governance structures which may represent mere re-shuffling of existing activities or even unsound concentration tendencies.

For these reasons it is worth considering for entrepreneurship researchers to more explicitly favor the individual(s) or the activity/activities as the unit of analysis. The study of 'entrepreneurial management' is a different story. This is a borderland where the entrepreneurship and management disciplines overlap, and where the governance structure may be the most appropriate unit of analysis.

From a more pragmatic research stance it is also possible to assess how easy or difficult the units of analysis are to work with empirically. We summarize this analysis in Table 3.4.

Obtaining a random sample of enterprising individuals is difficult, and there is certainly no directory of entrepreneurial teams available to the researcher prior to data collection. If companies are sampled with the intention to study owner-managers, those running several businesses will be over-sampled. However, for the purposes of theory construction and testing, the resulting deviations from population representativeness need not always be damaging.

One of the great advantages of using the individual(s) as unit of analysis is that once identified it is a relatively unproblematic unit to collect data from and to follow over time. Teams may be more problematic as members may

Table 3.4   Different units of analysis and their ease of use in empirical research

	Individual(s)	Activity	Governance structure
Sampling	Difficult	Very difficult	Easy, but can be deceptive
Initial data collection	Easy	Easy to difficult	Relatively easy
Longitudinal data collection	Relatively easy	Increasingly difficult (especially in surveys)	Increasingly difficult if done properly

come and go and the distinctions between team member and 'network' or 'employee' may be diffuse. The major problem over time, however, is how to treat retirement. Is the unit now 'dead' or should it be kept? Keeping it means compromising the unit of analysis, while dropping such cases means excluding a phenomenon that may be central to many growth processes. And if kept, is it sensible to use the old owner's dispositions and attitudes as explanatory variables in a growth analysis? The answer is not self-evident (cf. Schein, 1983; Wiklund, 1998).

Activities may be the most difficult units for researchers to study at arms-length distance. There is no way a satisfactory sampling frame could be created beforehand. The sampling unlit would therefore probably have to be something like individuals, establishments or companies, all of which may perform several separate activities. Initial data collection may sometimes be easy, when the total operations are limited and of low complexity. Over time the sampling units would be likely to add new activities, ranging from those very closely related to those completely unrelated. It would then be hard to determine what is and what is not part of the focal 'activity'. Sometimes the studied activity would no longer be associated with the original sampling unit.

It is, however, highly relevant to study the growth of specific activities. Growth often stems from specific activities related to individual innovations. A focus on activities has the potential for studying growth regardless of individuals or organizational context, both of which may change. What at arms length may look like an individual start-up failing after a few years may in fact be an innovation transferred to another organization where it is the great star. Only activity-based growth analysis can handle that sort of phenomenon properly. In the case of the Ericsson group, the activities related to cellular phones (which are spread over a number of different companies) have grown tremendously while other parts of the company group have shrunk almost as dramatically. Using the entire governance structure as unit of analysis apparently leads wrong for many purposes. Therefore, activity-based growth studies are important. Due to the problems of sampling and data collection, however, the growth of activities may best be studied with a case approach.

The governance structure approximated by the establishment, the legal company, or the company group, is by far the easiest to sample. In most countries relatively complete registers can be found for such entities. This is also what is so deceptive. In the example of entrepreneur X above, exactly the same activities may be placed within different governance solutions. Once identified, initial (or cross-sectional) data collection from the unit is relatively easy. An issue which here comes more to the fore than with the individual, though, is whether or not one key informant can adequately represent 'the firm'.

The problems of following the sampled 'governance structure' over time has been illustrated already in Table 3.1 and the associated discussion. Clearly, a serious effort to study firm = governance structure growth over time requires procedures for dealing with a range of qualitative changes that the originally sampled unit may go through.

OPERATIONALIZING GROWTH

Suitable Indicators of Growth

Hoy, McDougall and D'souza (1992) stress that a consensus has been reached among academics that sales growth is the best growth measure. It reflects both short- and long-term changes in the firm, and is easily obtainable. Furthermore, these authors, as well as Barkham et al. (1996), maintain that sales growth is the most common performance indicator among entrepreneurs themselves.

The growth process as such provides further arguments for advocating sales growth. A growth process is likely to be driven by increased demand for the firm's products or services. That is, sales increase first, and thus allow the acquisition of additional resources such as employees or machinery (Flamholtz, 1986). It seems unlikely that growth in other dimensions could take place without increasing sales. It is also possible to increase sales without acquiring additional resources or employing additional staff, by outsourcing the increased business volumes. In this case, only sales would increase. Thus, sales growth has high generality.

On the other hand, there is a widespread interest in the creation of new employment. This makes employment growth another important aspect to capture. In a process of rationalization, it is possible to replace employees with capital investments. In other words, there is to some extent an inverse relationship between capital investment and employment growth. As a consequence, assets are another important aspect of growth. Measuring growth in terms of assets is often considered problematic in the service sector (for example Weinzimmer et al., 1998). This appears to be mainly an accounting problem. While intangible assets indeed may expand in a growing service firm, this is not reflected in the firm's balance sheet. Thus, the problem of studying growing assets in service industries is related to difficulty in data collection rather than lack of relevance.

In the selection of appropriate indicators, theoretical considerations are necessary in addition to these of empirical nature (Weinzimmer et al., 1998). The suitability of utilizing any of these three aspects of growth is contingent on the unit of analysis. The relationship between suitable growth indicators and unit of analysis is displayed in Table 3.5.

For a growth-oriented entrepreneur, the firm is a vehicle to the accumulation of wealth. This implies that when the individual is the unit of analysis, the growth of assets may come to the fore. Since entrepreneurs tend to use sales growth as a performance indicator, this dimension is equally interesting when the individual is the unit of analysis. The growth in terms of employment may however be of secondary relevance in this case. Employment growth is almost never a goal in itself (Gray, 1990; Wiklund, 1998).

When governance structures are studied, managerial problems related to organizational complexity are of particular interest. Organizational complexity is most likely linked to the size and growth of the firm with respect to all three indicators, viz. employment, sales, and assets growth. The need to transform a governance structure from entrepreneurial to professional management will depend on factors such as the number of departments and the number of staff within each department (employment); the number and size of orders (sales); as well as the amount of equipment (assets). This calls for the use of all three indicators in these types of study.

The growth of activities, finally, can be captured mainly in the expansion of sales. Activities have the clearest connection to the market and their growth reflects an increased demand for the products and services provided to the market. While assets and employment may be valuable inputs to any activity,

Table 3.5   The relationship between unit of analysis and suitable growth indicators

	Individual(s)	Activity	Governance structure
Sales	High suitability	High suitability	High suitability
Employment	Low suitability	Limited suitability	High suitability
Assets	High suitability	Limited suitability	High suitability

sales reflect the output of activities. The output volume of activities will depend upon other factors in addition to assets and employment, that is the organization's managerial capabilities.

Others have pointed out that multiple indicators of growth give richer information and may therefore be better than single indicators (Birley and Westhead, 1990; Weinzimmer et al., 1998; Wiklund, 1998). Provided that proper analytical techniques are applied, the present authors support this viewpoint. However, this section attempts to illustrate that not all indicators are equally valid for all purposes and that additional – theoretical – considerations should be taken into account in the selection of proper indicators. It is when the governance structure is the unit of analysis and hence the strategic adaptation, and/or the configuration theoretical approach is applied, that the call for multiple measures is most relevant.

Relative and Absolute Growth

There are two basic approaches to measuring growth: absolute or relative. Measures of absolute growth examine the actual difference in firm size from one observation to another. Growth rates refer to relative changes in size, that is size changes are related to the initial size of the firm, typically by dividing the absolute growth by the initial size of the firm. Both approaches are associated with the problem of the effect of initial size on firm growth. Initial firm size typically has a positive association with absolute growth, but a negative with relative growth rate (Delmar, 1997; Storey, 1994; Weinzimmer et al., 1998).

The fact that size affects growth is conceptually problematic. This is apparent if the size changes of a cohort of firms started a particular year is studied during some later period of time. The vast majority of firms start very small. Over time, the firms that grow more become larger than those that grow less. If all firms, 'larger' or 'smaller', exhibit the same amount of absolute growth during a later time period, the 'larger' firms will get a lower growth rate. This does not overthrow the fact that they have overall grown faster. They are, so to say, 'punished' for having achieved a larger size to use as denominator. Thus, any results concerning the possible influence of size on growth should be interpreted with great care as choices made by the researcher affect results. Not only the measures (relative/absolute), but also the time between start-up and first observation, the growth of the firms up to this point, and the length of the studied time period will influence results.

A wiser decision is to use initial size as a methodological control variable. However, it is probable that many other commonly used antecedents of growth are influenced by size. Thus, the use of initial size as a control variable does not solve the size/growth relationship in a totally satisfactory way. Our recommended solution to the problem is to utilize both absolute and relative measures in parallel.

Some researchers have tried to surpass the inherent problems of absolute and relative growth measures by calculating compound measures containing elements of both types of measures (Birch 1987). Although possibly technically superior, such measures are conceptually empty, since it is impossible to state what dimensions they measure (neither dollars, nor per cent).

Modeling Growth Rates with Two Size Observations

In most studies, growth is calculated from the present size compared with the size some year earlier, that is, from two points of time. When such a calculation is performed, the researcher is actually assuming a particular growth pattern during the time interval between the measurements. Therefore, we will investigate the growth patterns implicitly assumed by three different growth calculations and assess their appropriateness.

The most prevalent measure according to Delmar (1997) and Weinzimmer et al. (1998) has the following mathematical expression:

$$g = (S_{t1} - S_{t0})/S_{t0} \qquad (3.1)$$

g refers to the total growth rate during the whole period, S_{t0} refers to the size at the start of the period and S_{t1} refers to the size at the end of the period.

Equation 3.1 models growth as a quantum size leap at some time during the period studied, that is all sales (or employees or assets) are added at one time. Mathematically, this is explained by the fact that previous size is used in the denominator, that is any new sales or employees are added to the firm at the size it had at the beginning of the period. This model is likely to lead to two types of problems. First, it is not probable that all growth takes place as a quantum leap at one particular point in time, in particular when longer time frames are studied. Second, the model is very sensitive to the initial size of the firm. This measure therefore has a bias in favor of firms that initially had a smaller size. As a result, initial firm size may appear among the strongest explanatory variables for firm growth.

In other contexts, addressing other issues, economists frequently use Gibrat's law, which assumes that the growth rate of a firm is constant. Mathematically, the expression is:

$$S_{t1} = S_{t0}(1 + g)^{t1-t0} \qquad (3.2)$$

g refers to the annual growth rate.

According to this model, an equivalent relative share of new sales or employees is added each year, as with retained compound interest in a bank account. This model is less sensitive to the initial size of the firm. This is advantageous since it reduces the magnitude of the size/growth relationship. The initial size effect is smaller in this case because growth is assumed to be spread over all years of the period.

However, it appears unlikely that a constant growth rate, that is that the growth curve has an exponential shape, would be exhaustive over longer time frames, in particular for firms exhibiting rapid growth.

A third model assumes that an equivalent amount of new sales or employees is added each year. As far as we are aware, this model has so far only been used by Wiklund (1998). When an equal amount is added each year, the mathematical expression becomes:

$$g = 1/N \sum_{n=1}^{n=N} (S_{tn+1} - S_{tn})/S_{tn} \qquad (3.3)$$

$S_{tn} = S_{t1} + S_{tn}(n-1)/N$, and g is the annual growth rate. N refers to the total number of years studied; n refers to any given year. S_{tn} refers to the size at year n and S_{tN} is the size at the end of the period.

This model is similar to model 1, the major difference being that the denominator changes every year. Thus, this model is less sensitive to the initial size of the firm and does not assume one large quantum size leap during the period. but rather smaller, annual size changes.

Regardless of which model we use, we make certain assumptions of the growth curve of the firm and reach different empirical results regarding growth rates. From both a conceptual and empirical standpoint, model 1, which is the most common model, seems to be the *least* appropriate. A constant growth rate, implying exponential growth, would be exhaustive over longer time frames and therefore seems unlikely. This suggests that the linear model 3, assuming that an equal size change takes place each year, would appear to have a lot of merit.

Modeling Growth Rates with More than Two Size Observations

Access to more than two size observations opens opportunities for more elaborated models. In a recent review, only three out of 35 reviewed studies included more than two observations (Weinzimmer et al., 1998). These authors discuss two different approaches to the analysis of longitudinal data; a) fitting a regression line, or b) calculating the average of annual size changes. Fine-grained fluctuations can be taken into account in both these models. The authors advocate the use of the regression line since the effects of outliers can be dampened. However, while better than the two-point models, this model has some weaknesses. It is difficult to utilize multiple indicators of growth, and the model assumes constant growth. A promising alternative is the growth modeling of longitudinal data using latent variables developed by Muthén (Muthén, 1997; Muthén and Curran, 1997). While this modeling technique has to our knowledge not yet been applied to the study of firm growth, it seems to have some clear merit. First, size is a latent variable and any number and type of manifest indicators may be utilized (for example sales, assets, and employment). Second, different growth patterns and growth rates can be modeled during different time intervals of the study. Third, the approach accounts for individual differences between firms as well as similarities among groups of firms.

Organic and Total Growth

A firm could grow organically through the expansion of current activities or by acquiring those already existing. It is likely that the processes underlying these different types of growth are fundamentally different, as are the implications for the economy-at-large. If these two types of growth mechanisms are not separated, results can be confounded, leading to misinterpretations of findings.

Davidsson and Delmar (1997, same database as in Table 3.1 above) is one of the few studies separating organic from acquired growth. Their results show that the difference in interpretation can be quite dramatic depending on which growth criterion is used. They defined firms as 'high-growth' if they were among the top 10 per cent in terms of annual absolute employment growth. Among firms younger than ten years, 58 to 96 per cent of total growth was organic. Among older firms, only 16 per cent was organic. When the analysis was performed across size classes, the difference was even more dramatic. In the smallest size class (0 to 9 employees), 93 per cent of total growth was organic, whereas the largest 'high-growth' firms (2500+ employees) actually shrunk in organic terms.

This example illustrates the differences in empirical results. Theoretical considerations are necessary in order to determine whether organic or total growth is more interesting to the researcher. From an entrepreneurship perspective, concerned with the creation of value and combination of resources, organic growth is most interesting. From a management perspective, on the other hand, the total resources and activities are of greater interest regardless of how they became part of the firm.

CONCLUSIONS

We have argued that despite the increasing number of empirical studies addressing firm growth, there is not much of a common body of well-founded knowledge about the causes, effects or processes of growth. The essence of our argumentation is that gaining such knowledge through empirical research is a much more difficult task than it might first seem. We hold that in order to reach farther, future research on firm growth has to address the following challenges:

- to develop a satisfactory basic research design
- to apply a well-founded conceptualization of growth which in turn requires a well thought-out conceptualization of 'the firm'
- to adequately match this conceptualization with the purpose of the study, the theories used, and the operationalization of growth.

With respect to the first point, our message was straightforward: growth is a process and therefore designs must be longitudinal. We then noted that when growth is studied over time, the conceptualization of the firm becomes problematic. The root of this problem is that 'the firm' is not like a biological individual; 'the firm' can change and transform itself in an indeterminate number of ways. We discussed three alternative micro-level units of analysis: a) an individual's or group of individuals' entire business activities, b) a certain business activity or set of related business activities, or c) a governance structure (often an establishment, a registered legal company, or a company group). We argued that the governance structure, which is the prevalent choice in empirical work, is subject to methodological pitfalls, especially in longitudinal studies. Furthermore, from an entrepreneurship research point of view, the growth of governance structures, which may merely represent ownership shifts of established and not necessarily growing activities, should not be the main interest. The totality of individual entrepreneurs' contributions or the growth of new business activities are alternatives more in line with the core interest of entrepreneurship as academic discipline.

The choice of unit of analysis is also a matter of what theoretical perspective is applied. We argued that the strategic adaptation and the configuration perspectives were most in line with using the governance structure conceptualization of the firm. The motivation perspective clearly points at using the individual as the unit of analysis, while we reason that the resource-based perspective goes well with using the activity as the unit of analysis. Combining several theoretical perspectives may be beneficial in many ways, but the researcher should be aware that this might necessitate compromising with the conceptualization of the firm. Some such compromises may lead to wrong concusions.

We have also discussed many aspects of operationalization of growth. We agree with others that sales turnover may be the most universal growth indicator. Sales alone are not, however, satisfactory for all purposes. Again, it is a matter of matching with the conceptualization of the firm, the theoretical perspective, and the purpose of the study.

Our principal answer to the question whether an absolute or a relative growth measure should be used was to recommend that the analysis be performed with both types of growth measures in parallel. This may help the researcher avoid drawing erroneous conclusions about the 'effect' of initial size and explanatory variables that are correlated with size. We noted that the most common formula for modeling growth – end size minus start size, divided by start size – has several disadvantages. A better formula models a fixed amount of absolute growth annually, which implies a growth rate that decreases with increasing size and age. If the study has more than two data points additional alternatives are available. Finally, we argued that from an entrepreneurship research point of view, organic growth is more relevant than total growth. Empirical evidence suggests that this choice can have a major impact on the results.

Conducting empirical research on firm growth is indeed no easy task. Hopefully the disclosure of the pitfalls and problems associated with such research has not discouraged others from continuing their efforts. It is our solid belief that research on firm growth is possible, valuable, and necessary. Firm growth is a key to economic development and to the creation of wealth and employment. Thus, increased understanding of this phenomenon is of utmost importance. Reviews of the research in the field up to date have been critical in a number of respects. We have presented what we feel are the most important challenges for future research and guidelines to how these challenges can be met. If they are seriously addressed in empirical research, future literature reviews are likely to be more enthusiastic than the previous. If the challenges are not seriously addressed, progress will be limited.

NOTE

1. Previously published as: Davidsson, P. and J. Wiklund (2000), 'Conceptual and empirical challenges in the study of firm growth', in D. Sexton and H. Landstrom (eds), *Handbook of Entrepreneurship*, Oxford, UK: Blackwell, pp. 26-44.

REFERENCES

Aldrich, H. and T. Baker (1997), 'Blinded by the cites? Has there been progress in the entrepreneurship field?', in D. Sexton and R. Smilor (eds), *Entrepreneurship 2000*, Chicago, IL: Upstart Publishing Company.

Ardishvili A., S. Cardozo, S. Harmon and S. Vadakath (1998), 'Towards a theory of new venture growth', paper presented at the 1998 Babson Entrepreneurship Research Conference, Ghent, Belgium, May 21–23.

Barkham, R., G. Gudgin, M. Hart and E. Hanvey (1996), *The Determinants of Small-Firm Growth*, Gateshead, UK: Athenaeum Press.

Birch, D. L. (1987), *Job Creation – in America: How Our Smallest Companies Put the Most People to Work*, New York: Free Press.

Birley, S. and P. Westhead (1990), 'Growth and performance contrasts between "types" of small firms', *Strategic Management Journal*, 2, 535–57.

Brytting, T. (1991), 'Organizing in the small growing firm – a grounded theory approach', dissertation prepared for Stockholm School of Economics, Stockholm.

Cooper, A. C. (1995), 'Challenges in predicting new venture performance', in I. Bull, H. Thomas and G. Willard (eds), *Entrepreneurship: Perspectives on Theory Building*, London: Elsevier Science Ltd.

Davidsson, P. (1989a), 'Continued entrepreneurship and small firm growth', dissertation prepared for Stockholm School of Economics, Stockholm.

Davidsson, P. (1989b), 'Entrepreneurship – and after? A study of growth willingness in small firms', *Journal of Business Venturing*, 4, 211–26.

Davidsson, P. and F. Delmar (1997), 'High-growth firms: characteristics, job contribution and method observations', paper presented at the RENT XI Conference, Mannheim, Germany, November 27–28 (this is an early version of Chapter 8 in this volume).

Day, G. S. (1981), 'The product life cycle: analysis and application issues', *Journal of Marketing*, 45 (Fall), 60–67.

Delmar, F. (1997), 'Measuring growth: methodological considerations and empirical results', in R. Donckels and A. Miettinen (eds), *Entrepreneurship and SME Research: On its Way to the Next Millennium*, Brookfield, VT and Aldershot: Edward Elgar, pp. 190–216, (included as Chapter 4 in this volume).

Delmar, F. and P. Davidsson (1998), 'A taxonomy of high-growth firms', paper presented at the 1998 Babson Entrepreneurship Research Conference, Ghent, May 21–23, later re-written and published as F. Delmar, P. Davidsson and W. B. Gartner, 2003, and included as Chapter 9 in this volume.)

Evans, D. S. (1987), 'Tests of alternative theories of firm growth', *Journal of Political Economy*, 95(4), 657–74.

Flamholtz, E. G. (1986), *Managing the Transition from an Entrepreneurship to a Professionally Managed Firm*, San Francisco: Jossey-Bass.

Foxall, G. (1984), 'Evidence for attitudinal – behavioural consistency: implications for consumer research paradigms', *Journal of Economic Psychology*, 5, 71–92.

Gray, C. (1990), 'Entrepreneurial motivation and the smaller business', paper presented at the 15th IAREP colloquium, Exeter, July 4–7.

Hoy, F., P. P. McDougall and D. E. Dsouza (1992), 'Strategies and environments of high growth firms', in D. L. Sexton and J. D. Kasarda (eds), *The State of the Art of Entrepreneurship*, Boston: PWS-Kent Publishing, pp. 341–57.

Kirzner, I. M. (1983), 'Entrepreneurship and the entrepreneurial function: a commentary', in J. Ronen (ed), Lexington MA: Lexington Books, pp. 281–90.

Muthén, B. (1997), 'Latent variable modeling of longitudinal and multilevel data', in A. Raftery (ed.), *Sociological Methodology*, Boston: Blackwell, pp. 453–80.

Muthén B. and P. J. Curran (1997), 'General longitudinal modeling of individual differences in experimental designs: a latent variable framework for analysis and power estimation', *Psychological Methods*, 2(4), 371–402.

Schein, E. H. (1983), 'Role of the founder in creating organizational culture', *Organizational Dynamics* (Summer), 13–28.

Schumpeter, J. (1934), *The Theory of Economic Development*, Cambridge, MA: Harvard University Press.

Seth, A. and H. Thomas (1994), 'Theories of the firm: implications for strategy research', *Journal of Management Studies*, **3**(2), 165–91.

Sexton, D. L. (1997), 'Entrepreneurship research needs and issues', in D. Sexton and R. Smilor (eds), *Entrepreneurship 2000*, Chicago, IL: Upstart Publishing Company.

Storey, D. J. (1994), *Understanding the Small Business Sector*, London: Routledge.

Weinzimmer, L. G., P. C. Nystrom and S. J. Freeman (1998), Measuring organizational growth: issues, consequences and guidelines', *Journal of Management*, **24**(2), 235–62.

Wiklund, J. (1998), 'Small firm growth and performance: entrepreneurship and beyond', dissertation prepared for Jönköping International Business School, Jönköping.

Wiklund, J., P. Davidsson, R. Delmar and M. Aronsson (1997), 'Expected consequences of growth and their effect on growth willingness in different samples of small firms', in P. D. Reynolds, W. D. Bygrave, N. M. Carter, P. Davidsson, W. B. Gartner, C. M. Mason and P. P. McDougall (eds), *Frontiers of Entrepreneurship Research*, Wellesley, MA: Babson College, pp. 1–16 (this is an early version of Chapter 6 in this volume).

4. Measuring growth: methodological considerations and empirical results*

Frédéric Delmar

INTRODUCTION

Regardless of their sizes, expanding and growing firms are indeed the creators of new jobs and of a healthy economy (cf. Storey, 1995). This is also one of the central issues of entrepreneurship research beside innovation and venture creation. Consequently, it is important to examine the determinants of business growth, and the measurement of growth in new ventures and small businesses presents a significant challenge for scholars. Accurate and appropriate measurement of growth is of central importance to entrepreneurship research. In order to accumulate knowledge about the processes and variables that affect business growth, we have to understand how the choice and construct of the dependent variable of growth will affect the resulting model. Without adequate understanding of the importance of the construct of the dependent variable, theory development will be impeded, results will conflict with each other and will have little practical relevance.

This is not an unknown problem, and some work has been done to guide academics in their choice of performance measures in the quest to assess and model entrepreneurship (for example Brush and Vanderwerf, 1992; Chandler and Hanks, 1993; Murphy, Trailer and Hill, 1996). However, the literature has mainly concentrated on the reliability and validity of different performance measures which are available in that literature. The purpose of these papers has been to compare different performance measures and data collection methods, because data gathering related to performance has been seen as a problem. It is acknowledged here that data gathering can be a problem, but this study goes one step further by focusing on the single performance indicator of growth and how its calculation affects model building and theory development. This is an important issue because, as stated above, expanding firms have a crucial economic importance, and the above mentioned studies found growth to be one of the most reliable and valid measures of new venture performance.

My point of view is that the growth literature has put too little emphasis on the measurement of growth and how this affects the results and theoretical development. The purpose of this chapter is to show that the heterogeneity of different measures is problematic, and that scholars should in the future show more concern for the methodological artifacts that characterize their studies. More specifically, researchers have different concepts of how to measure growth; these differences in measurement affect the relationship among the independent variables and the dependent variable, and consequently the theory development. It is, therefore, important to examine the consequences of different concepts and how they are measured in order to assess recommendations for measuring growth when both the theoretical perspective and data characteristics are taken into account.

This study consists of two parts examining the measurement of business growth: in the first part 55 published research articles using growth as a dependent variable were reviewed and analysed. The articles were sampled from some of the more important entrepreneurship and small business research journals. Each separate article was coded on several relevant parameters. In the second part, data from a sample of small businesses were used to examine the pros and cons of different growth measures. Based on the results from the present study, I shall suggest some steps that will hopefully increase our possibility to further develop entrepreneurship research.

THE GROWTH LITERATURE

Sample and Procedure

In this first part, the empirical growth literature was examined for the years 1989 to 1996, with the exception of four articles which can be considered as classics (Begley and Boyd, 1987; Cragg and King, 1988; Miller and Toulouse, 1986; Miller, 1987). A total of 55 articles were surveyed from journals such as: *Journal of Business Venturing, Entrepreneurship Theory and Practice, Regional Studies,* and *Small Business Economics*. These four journals accounted for 69.1 per cent of the sampled articles. An article was chosen if: (a) it was an empirical study, (b) it included growth as a dependent variable, and (c) the sample was composed of small businesses and/or new entrepreneurial ventures.

Each article was coded for the study. The articles were coded for the used dimensions of growth and how these measurements were calculated. In order to assess the general state of the research area concerning growth each article was also coded for year of publication, journal, sample, response frequency, used analysis method, research perspective, and explained variance. I will start to describe the characteristics of the sample, because the measurement of growth is dependent on several of the mentioned variables.

Sample Characteristics

The sample could be organized in four broad categories depending on the research perspective: strategy (40 per cent), psychology (29.1 per cent), economics (25.5 per cent), and network (5.5 per cent). Thus, the largest group of articles focused on problems concerning the relationship among the environment, business strategies and growth. The second largest groups focused on the behavior of the entrepreneur, and especially his or her stable disposition or biographical data. The third group focused on the role of small businesses for the development of the regional or national economy. This research was mainly concerned with the relationship among the growth, the size, the age of the firm, and industry, and how these relationships can be understood and theorized. The smallest group was represented by the network approach, that is, the importance of social relationships, and comprised more recent articles. The difference in research perspective had an important effect on the choice of research design, where the economic approach stands out as the most homogenous in problem statement and design compared with the other perspectives. Researchers here depended more on large data bases and on time series than others, but they also concentrated their effort on fewer independent variables.

It is of interest to comment upon three variables characterizing the studies, notably the size of the sample used in the analyses, the response frequency for those studies relying on surveys, and the explained variance of the reported models. Table 4.1 shows some statistics for each variable. When a study reported several models, the highest explained variance was coded. It is interesting to note that the correlations among explained variance and sample size, year of publication, and response frequency were insignificant and close to zero, indicating that we have not been able to achieve better estimates over the years. Although perhaps a more reasonable explanation is that many studies did not indicate if adjusted statistics were reported or not. The difference between an adjusted and a not adjusted statistic is more important with small samples and a large number of variables.

An alarming concern was the bias towards sampling only manufacturing industries. High technology and manufacturing represented 49.1 per cent of all studies. The service sector was underrepresented with only 3.6 per cent of the studies dealing explicitly with service firms. The rest of the studies (47.3 per cent) were based on general samples with no specific perspective. The result is problematic because the sample was based on recent research, and we know how relatively more important the service sector has become during the last decade. This knowledge has apparently not led to a greater research interest in the service sector. In the future, we have to focus more on this apparently forgotten area of entrepreneurship research.

Table 4.1   Descriptive statistics for the 55 studies

Variable	n	Mean	Median	Standard deviation	Minimum	Maximum
Sample[a]	49	446	175	841	44	4558
Response frequency	38	35.16	33.00	15.42	8.20	74.00
Explained variance	27	30.37	29.00	14.04	8.00	63.00

Note: [a] An outlier has been here eliminated, because it had a sample of 219,754 cases. The mean would have been 4832 with all cases included.

The Measurement of Growth

The growth measure was coded for three different variables that have an effect on the obtained final results. The three variables were: 1) the choice of growth indicator (for example, employment, market share), 2) the choice of the studied time period (numbers of years studied to determine growth), and 3) the choice of the calculation (as an absolute, relative, or logarithmized figure).

The choice of growth indicator

The different growth indicators and their frequencies of use are included in Table 4.2. Five different indicators were identified in this sample; they assessed different theoretical concepts, but cannot, on a theoretical level, be assumed to be totally commensurable. The most used growth indicators were employment and turnover/sales, probably because they were easily available and because they are seen as non-controversial either from a research point of view or from the respondent's point of view. Furthermore, employment is an important indicator of job creation dynamics. It is an objective measure, as well as sales or assets, compared with indicators such as market share and performance index which are subjective, that is, the respondent is asked to evaluate the business performance relative to the industry, the closest competitors, or his or her goals. Apparently each indicator is unique in some respects, and we shall therefore examine them separately in more depth.

Subjective satisfaction measures of growth or performance, such as the index proposed by Gupta and Govindarajan (1984), have been severely criticized by Chandler and Hanks (1993), who have, in my opinion, rightfully questioned the validity of such measures. They argue that these satisfaction measures are as much a function of the entrepreneurs' personal expectations, as they are of the objective performance. Therefore, it can be questioned what is really measured. Furthermore, different individuals can differ in their satisfaction of the same level of growth or performance. For example, an entrepreneur

Table 4.2   Dimensions of growth and their frequencies

Indicator	Frequency	Per cent
Turnover/sales	17	30.9
Employment	16	29.1
Multiple indicators	10	18.2
Performance	7	12.7
Market share	3	5.5
Assets	1	1.8
Not reported	1	1.8
Total	55	100

can be highly satisfied with a 25 per cent growth, for example, in market shares, because he or she only expected a 10 per cent growth. On the other hand, another entrepreneur can be dissatisfied with 25 per cent growth in market share, because he or she expected a 100 per cent growth. Finally, subjective relative measures are dependent on the entrepreneur's knowledge and perception of the situation. Without having the possibility to control these factors it is difficult to say anything at all about the actual growth performance of a venture. The only thing that can be stated is that the independent variables found to explain the model probably affect the entrepreneur's cognitive and perceptual structure. This is seldom the purpose in the growth literature.

However, the differences were not only restricted to the objective or subjective nature of the indicators, but were also dependent on whether growth was measured in terms of changes in the number of employees, or in sales volume. In other words, depending on the choice of indicator, different stages of the growth processes will be focused upon. Changes in demands for a product or a service will affect the firms in different phases (for example, Anderson and Strigel, 1981). That is, in the first phase, the entrepreneurs will perceive some general changes in demand or a higher interest in the offered product/service from the customer. In the second phase, this higher demand will lead to higher sales. In the third phase, changes in sales volume will lead to changes in the organization in order to adapt to a new level of demand, that is, to hire more personnel or sublet some of the production. Thus, demand can be seen as an anticipatory variable whose expected future constellation forms the basis for business plans. Sales can be seen as an intermediate variable, showing the existent trade-off between the demand and supply forces. Finally, changes in the organization such as hiring more personnel or subletting can be seen as the final adjustment to changes. It is also the variable with the lowest volatility, that is, entrepreneurs will wait until they are sure that the new level of demand will be stable. More precisely, they will refrain from hiring or dismissing an employee until they are sure about the changes. Hence, the number of employees is an instrumental variable planned by the entrepreneur, and it is often lagged compared with the financial development. This difference in volatility will affect the model, because different factors will affect changes in sales, and changes in the number of employees. Changes in sales are probably highly correlated with changes of number of employees, but not necessarily. The entrepreneur can choose to meet changes in demands in different ways, through hiring more personnel, subcontracting, or improving productivity. Thereby, depending on how we assess growth as changes in sales or employees, we assess different phases of the growth process and different responses to external changes.

Changes in assets are not recommended as a growth measure, simply because it is mainly appropriate to use for firms which tend to be capital-intensive. Consequently, it will not be an appropriate measure for the service sector which is relatively less capital-intensive than the manufacturing sector. Another aspect that concerns both changes in assets and in sales is that these are both subjected to changes in inflation. Thereby growth as measured by assets or sales is the effect of real growth plus inflation. On that count, growth in numbers of employees is a better measure if the researcher believes that inflation may play an important role in a given study.

To conclude this section, the empirical literature has used five types of growth indicators. I have argued that subjective measures such as perceived market share and performance satisfaction were not appropriate measures, because they were based on the entrepreneurs' knowledge and expectations. Change in assets is only an appropriate measure for the manufacturing sector, because it is highly dependent on the capital structure. I have also argued that changes in sales and in number of employees assess different processes. First, sales and employees have a different flexibility, with sales changing more rapidly with demands than does the number of employees. Secondly, the entrepreneurs can either hire more people or subcontract. Assuming that growth in broad terms is interesting, then multiple indicators are an option, and also because we can assume that they represent the theoretical concept of growth.

The choice of the calculation of the growth measure
Organizational growth was mainly measured as the difference between two points in time. This change was either seen as an absolute change or as a relative change. Furthermore, the measure was often logarithmized to adjust for skewness in the sample. These calculations affect the final results of a model; and the purpose of this section was to investigate those differences and how they affected the possibilities of comparing results. The results from Table 4.3 indicate that relative measures were the most frequent, and were followed by absolute measures.

Table 4.3   Calculations of growth and their frequencies

Growth measure	Frequency	Per cent
Relative	28	50.9
Absolute	16	29.1
Log absolute	6	10.9
Log relative	3	5.5
Not reported	2	3.6
Total	55	100

The problem with relative and absolute measures is fairly obvious. A relative measure will favor growth in small firms, whereas an absolute measure will bias the results in favor of larger firms. For example, if firm A has started with 1 employee and has after three years 6 employees, its growth is 600 per cent or 5 employees; at the same time, firm B has started with 10 employees and has after the same period 15 employees, its growth is 50 per cent or 5 employees. Both will have the same absolute growth but the former will have achieved a substantially higher relative growth (600 per cent compared with 50 per cent). This exemplifies the problem with relative and absolute measures. Consequently, regardless of the used measure, growth will be dependent of the size of the firm. This is a well-known problem which is often reported in the method section, and thereafter is ignored when the results are discussed and compared with results of other studies. An exception is researchers in economics, who have worked extensively with this problem, which becomes especially clear when testing Gibrat's Law, which states that firm growth rate is independent of firm size (cf. Konings, 1995; Storey, 1989). A possibility to avoid this kind of problem is to work with samples and sub-samples where size is either randomized or preferably controlled for.

Many studies have logarithmized the dependent variable in order to correct a skewed distribution, and thereby fulfilling the assumption of the normal distribution of residuals. Skewness is not a significant problem, because normality is not an important assumption in estimating the most efficient unbiased coefficient, but skewness generates unnecessary outliers. Consequently, skewness compromises the interpretation of the least square fit, because fit is dependent on the distribution around the mean, and the mean is not an appropriate measure for a skewed distribution (Fox, 1991; Tabachnick and Fidell, 1989). Differently stated, whereas the estimates will be correct, we will have a low explained variance. Therefore, the logarithm of the dependent variable is often an option for obtaining both a higher fit and a better use of the data. The problem is the interpretation of the model after a transformation has been made. In other terms, we have to consider how the interpretation of the model is changed by the transformation and how it affects our theoretical conclusions. In a linear (non-transformed) model, the interpretation is pretty straightforward, that is, when x changes with one unit, then y changes with β units. In a log-transformed model the relation is also the same (additive), but we assume an exponential growth function. In other words, we should be careful to compare the effect of a variable that is linear, and in another model exponential, as is the case with a logarithmized model. If different studies use different models we cannot compare their fit to data. Furthermore, the coefficients for the variables are not comparable, but we should assume that variables found statistically different in an additive model, thereby having an influence on the dependent variable, are also significant in an exponential model. What affects y should normally also affect log y. It is consequently possible to compare if the same variables are included in different studies, if the only difference is log transformation; and thereby assess the importance of a variable as a predictor. However, an additive and a log-transformed model assume different theoretical explanations. This is something that was seldom acknowledged in the sampled studies when the results from one study were compared with the results from previous studies

In sum, I conclude that most researchers seem to calculate their measures in order to arrange data in such a way that the highest possible explanation can be achieved, warranting little importance to the possibility of comparing results among studies. The simplest way would be to present several models with the dependent variable calculated differently. To summarize, too much emphasis is probably put on achieving a high explained variance and significant variables, when researchers should perhaps concentrate on making studies more easily comparable, and acknowledge the fact that research can evolve only if it is possible to accumulate findings that are easily comparable, for example, using confidence interval instead of significance. The effect of log transformation will be dealt with more closely in Section 2 of this chapter.

The measurement period
The third choice to be made is the number of years to be included in the measurement period. This choice should be based on the chosen problem of the study, that is, are we more interested in factors determining changes over a longer period of time or over a shorter period of time? Table 4.4 summarizes different time periods chosen and their frequencies.

The most common time periods are periods of five years, of one year and of three years. When reviewing the studies included in the sample little or no information was given why one time period was favored over another. However, we can assume that the measurement period does affect the variables included in the final model, because growth is dependent on both short- and long-term changes.

Table 4.4   The measurement periods in number of years and their frequencies

Years	Frequency	Per cent
5	13	23.6
1	12	21.8
3	9	16.4
2	4	7.3
4	2	3.6
6	1	1.8
7	1	1.8
8	1	1.8
Missing	12	21.8
Total	55	100

Another large group was missing value. This group was composed of three sub-groups: studies using subjective measures without stating the time period (n = 5), studies measuring growth as the difference between the birth year and the measuring year (n = 5), and studies where the time period was not found by the author (n = 2).

Little work has been done on the choice of time period and its consequences on the outcome of an analysis. It is probable that the time period has an effect, because, as stated earlier, some changes in the organization due to a change in demand are lagged. We do not know how these changes are reflected in the choice of time period, and how they affect the resulting model.

The comparability of growth studies
After this review of the growth measures, it is concluded that there was an abundance of different ways of assessing growth in a firm, but were there patterns in growth measurement that allowed comparison of results or was the choice of measures more or less random? A cross-tabulation of the growth indicator based on a) the chosen indicator, b) the chosen calculation, and c) the chosen time period, was performed, yielding an indication on how many researchers have used the same growth indicator, and can therefore be considered to be directly comparable.

The most frequently used combination was relative changes in sales measured over a five-year period. This combination was chosen in six studies. The second most popular combinations were relative changes in number of employees or sales over a three-year period with three studies respectively. In third position, relative changes in numbers of employees, absolute changes in sales over a one-year period, and multiple indicators over a five-year period, were used in two studies respectively. All other combinations scored a maximum of one in each cell.

To conclude, little congruence was found among the used growth measures. This is a somewhat alarming result considering that the differences stemming from working with alternative analytic methods have not even been accounted for. Theses differences can, however, be largely corrected with meta-analytic procedures (Rosenthal, 1991). I am more concerned with how growth measures are apparently chosen in a relatively *ad hoc* manner without any (reported) considerations to the theoretical consequences. The choices that were made were often based on empirical matters.

Summary of result of part 1
This review was based on 55 studies published in some of the major research journals dealing with small business and entrepreneurship. It was concluded that direct comparability among studies was low because a large array of different indicators, time periods, and calculations were used when assessing growth. It was argued that objective measures such as growth in numbers of employees and sales were favorable compared with subjective measures such as perceived performance or market share. Furthermore, the growth indicators were calculated as relative or absolute changes, and sometimes logarithmized. Most researchers were aware of the problems connected with relative and absolute changes, but the differences between an additive and an exponential model was seldom commented upon. Finally, little attention has been given to the importance of the measured time period. It was argued that different time perspectives might yield different results, because organizational changes are lagged relative to each other. In the next section, I will empirically illustrate some of the points made in this section. More precisely, I will test the relationship among number of employees and sales, relative and absolute changes, and the effect of exponential and additive models.

AN EMPIRICAL TEST OF DIFFERENT GROWTH MEASURES

The purpose of section 2 was to empirically test the effects of different growth measures on analysis outcomes. After a first correlation table, data were analysed from a theoretical as well as an empirical perspective. That is, in the first case (the theoretical perspective) the same set of variables was tested on the different indicators. With this design, changes in explained variance were assessed and explained. In the second case (the empirical model), the best model was chosen on the basis of maximum explained variance. The purpose was to focus on the changes in variables found significant and how these changes affect the final conclusions.

The Sample

The tests in this part were performed on data gathered for my dissertation work on growth in small and medium-sized enterprises (Delmar, 1996). Thus, data were not gathered for the prime purpose of testing the use of different growth measures, but they were judged as having a good potential of exemplifying some of the problems related to the specification of the dependent variable of growth.

The sample was taken from Statistics Sweden's register of all Swedish companies. Several restrictions were imposed. First, the sample was restricted to enterprises of between 5- to 49-employees. The 1- to 5-employee class was not included because it contains a large part of part-time enterprises. The classes above 50 employees were not included either, because the actual effect of the entrepreneur's behavior on the business was assumed to diminish with an increasing number of employees. Second, the sample was restricted to certain industries (high tech, manufacturing, services, and professional services). Third, the sample was restricted to independent firms, that is, firms that are not subsidiaries of other firms. Finally, the sample was stratified to ensure equal representation from different size classes and industries.

Of the 730 contacted entrepreneurs, 400 (54.8 per cent) completed the phone interview. The purpose of the survey was to capture data, which according to theory and earlier empirical studies, might explain entrepreneurial and business performance. The first reason to use telephone interviews was the greater probability of a high response rate. The second reason was the large number of questions; the interview and the mail questionnaire contained altogether 261 questions. A split was reasonable to keep up the respondent's attention. The third reason was that the telephone interview afforded a possibility to check that the right person was interviewed. The data were collected during October–December of 1994. Only data from the phone interview were used in this article, because it allowed the use of a larger sample.

The Dependent Variables

Growth was measured as changes in either number of employees or sales over a three-year period. There was no particular reason why I chose three years as the time period, other than that my thesis advisor previously used the same time period in one of his studies. Now afterwards, I could argue that the reliability of the measure is dependent on the memory of the respondent and that most entrepreneurs can remember with some accuracy the sales figures and the employment rate three years back.

However, these data made it possible to test the difference between absolute and relative calculations; between logarithm transformations and non-logarithm transformation; and among employment, sales, or multiple indicators. This gave 12 possible measures of how to assess growth.

Absolute growth was measured as the difference between year one (1991) and year three (1994) in numbers of employees or sales; relative growth was measured by dividing the numbers of employees or sales year three (1994) by the corresponding figures year one (1991); multiple indicators were measured as the sum of changes in employees and in sales; log transformed measures were based on the natural log.

Analysis

All analyses were based on multiple regressions, where in the first case all variables were entered at the same time, and in the second case, stepwise regression was used. Stepwise regression was used because it was the most popular of the regression techniques in the reviewed sample (47.3 per cent of the sampled articles used regression and the single most popular variation was stepwise regression representing 23 per cent of the sample).

RESULTS

Relationship Among the Growth Indicators

The purpose was to examine if there was a pattern of relationships among the different growth measures. Table 4.5 displays the correlation matrix for the 12 different growth measures. All relationships were significant at $p < 0.05$. This does not have any practical meaning in this case, because the significance test would detect a relationship as significant at the $p < 0.05$ level at correlation levels of 0.1 or higher given the size of the present sample.

What is observed in the correlation matrix are sets of measures being highly correlated with each other, but not with other groups. The main result was that relative measures were not comparable to absolute measures (that is, poorly correlated with each other), regardless of the choice sales, multiple indicator, or number of employees, or whether it was logarithmized or not.

Sales and employment correlated highly with each other, which suggests that they were comparable from an empirical point of view. Changes in productivity, the suggested lagged effect, or the possibility to subcontract (discussed in part 1) did not have a substantial effect, at least not over the measured three-year period. It is possible that the chosen time period has

Table 4.5 Correlation matrix of the investigated 12 growth measures (n = 396)

	Abs emplo	Abs multiple	Abs sales	Rel emplo	Rel multiple	Rel sales	Ln abs emp	Ln abs multiple	Ln abs sales	Ln rel emplo	Ln rel multiple	Ln rel sales
Abs empl	1.000											
Abs multiple	0.970	1.000										
Abs sales	0.830	0.941	1.000									
Rel emplo	0.240	0.228	0.190	1.000								
Rel multiple	0.245	0.267	0.270	0.889	1.000							
Rel sales	0.203	0.250	0.291	0.615	0.908	1.000						
Ln abs emplo	0.878	0.792	0.592	0.187	0.192	0.159	1.000					
Ln abs multiple	0.725	0.653	0.488	0.124	0.140	0.127	0.935	1.000				
Ln abs sales	0.768	0.761	0.675	0.158	0.216	0.228	0.896	0.958	1.000			
Ln rel emplo	0.389	0.371	0.309	0.828	0.808	0.632	0.334	0.226	0.277	1.000		
Ln rel multiple	0.345	0.368	0.363	0.748	0.882	0.835	0.289	0.208	0.307	0.919	1.000	
Ln rel sales	0.277	0.333	0.376	0.565	0.811	0.879	0.226	0.175	0.306	0.734	0.935	1.000

erased these effects, because a business adapts faster. Nevertheless, it should be noticed that sales explained 80.3 per cent of the variance at best (Ln abs sales and Ln abs emp), and at worst 37.9 per cent of variance in employees (Ln abs sales and rel empl). The variation in magnitude of the relationships among different growth indicators indicates that the outcome of one model cannot be compared to another. These differences were further investigated by testing a set of variables, focusing on how the different growth measures changed the outcomes. Furthermore, I did not control for if the relationship between sales and employees was altered over time.

Test of the Theoretical Model

Here, the purpose was to examine how the same variables differed in their ability to explain variance in the different growth indicators. Six variables were chosen to be included in this theoretical model. They were chosen because they are well known, and often used as control variables. The six variables were: firm size, start-up year (as indication of firm age), industry, mode of entry (two dummy variables, created and bought), and the age of the entrepreneur (birth year). Table 4.6 displays the results from the analysis, and it was concluded that the same model apparently differed substantially in its ability to explain the variance in the dependent variable. Explained variance for the same applied model ranged from 3 per cent to 45 per cent. The difference was

Table 4.6   Explained variance for different growth measures with the same model

Growth measure	Explained variance	Adj. explained variance	N
Abs empl	0.029	0.014	396
Abs multiple	0.009	–0.007	393
Abs sales	0.032	0.017	393
Rel emplo	0.055	0.040	396
Rel multiple	0.073	0.059	393
Rel sales	0.066	0.052	393
Ln abs emplo	0.326	0.316	396
Ln abs multiple	0.447	0.439	393
Ln abs sales	0.245	0.234	393
Ln rel emplo	0.090	0.076	396
Ln rel multiple	0.100	0.087	393
Ln rel sales	0.098	0.084	393

even greater if adjusted figures were examined and where even a negative value showed up.

Can we conclude that the model was only significant in some and not in other cases? If we should choose a model based on explained variance and significance of the independent variables alone, we should choose the one with logarithmized absolute growth as the dependent variable. However, how bad were the rest of the models and why? This variation in explained variance was mainly a result of the distribution of the dependent variables. All dependent variables departed from the normal distribution assumption (as measured by skewness and kurtosis), therefore generating these large differences in explained variance.

Consequently, the influence of each variable (the expected direction) was the same in almost every case, as suggested in part 1. The normal distribution assumption, as has been stated earlier, is not necessary (but helpful) to produce the best linear unbiased estimator. Even if explained variance is an important factor to consider, we should also focus on the estimator and its confidence interval, if explanation, and not only prediction, is the research goal.

The Empirical Model

In this section, the best model was chosen on the basis of maximum explained variance. The purpose was to focus on the changes in the variables found statistically significant and on how these changes affect the final conclusions. This was achieved by adding another ten variables to the previous set of variables. They were also chosen on the basis of their attributed importance in the literature. These were: type of customers (businesses or consumers), dependence on most important customers, export, present competitive position, intensity of competition, dependence on suppliers, number of board meetings per year, board composition, attributed importance of the board, and planning. A total of 16 variables were tested with a forward stepwise selection procedure. Table 4.7 displays the outcomes of these analyses.

Two main results were obvious from this session. First, all dependent variables based on absolute figures were dependent on size and nothing else. Consequently, a high explained variance is per se not especially interesting. Size was negatively related to all dependent variables except in one model. The interpretation was that small firms grow faster than larger firms when growth was measured as absolute changes, except for growth as absolute changes in sales. For the dependent variables calculated as relative changes, different variables emerged for the different growth variables. However, younger entrepreneurs, that had created their business, had achieved higher levels of growth in their firms than older entrepreneurs. Being in a market where competition was low also led to higher growth rates. Thus, dependent

Table 4.7   Results from the empirical model with 95 per cent confidence interval for B (n = 378)

Growth measure	Variable	B	Lower bound	Upper bound	Adj.R^2
Abs emplo	Constant	3.071	0.345	5.797	0.017
	Size	−0.103	−0.176	−0.030	
Abs multiple	Constant	18.878	2.822	34.933	0.005
	Competition	−3.464	−7.491	0.562	
Abs sales	Constant	2.733	0.761	4.705	0.023
	Size	0.086	0.032	0.141	
Rel emplo	Constant	0.737	0.163	1.311	0.105
	Suppliers	0.020	0.011	0.029	
	Birth year of entrepreneur	0.016	0.007	0.026	
	Create	0.253	0.081	0.425	
	Competition	−0.115	−0.198	−0.032	
Rel multiple	Constant	0.503	−0.348	1.354	0.106
	Suppliers	0.038	0.022	0.054	
	Birth year of entrepreneur	0.040	0.022	0.057	
	Create	0.457	0.140	0.775	
Rel sales	Constant	0.423	−0.063	0.909	0.066
	Birth year of entrepreneur	0.021	0.011	0.031	
	Suppliers	0.017	0.008	0.027	
Ln abs emplo	Constant	5.645	5.633	5.657	0.317
	Size	−0.002	−0.002	−0.002	
Ln abs multiple	Constant	5.872	5.847	5.898	0.434
	Size	−0.003	−0.003	−0.003	
Ln abs sales	Constant	4.522	4.497	4.548	0.230
	Size	−0.004	−0.004	−0.003	
Ln rel emplo	Constant	−0.078	−0.376	−0.221	0.099
	Birth year of entrepreneur	0.009	0.004	0.014	
	Size	−0.002	−0.003	−0.001	
	Competition	−0.071	−0.114	−0.028	
	Create	0.139	0.050	0.228	
Ln rel multiple	Constant	0.499	0.210	0.788	0.088
	Birth year of entrepreneur	0.012	0.007	0.016	
	Create	0.136	0.049	0.222	
	Competition	−0.058	−0.100	−0.016	
Ln rel sales	Constant	−0.035	−0.682	−0.179	0.074
	Birth year of entrepreneur	0.013	0.008	0.019	
	Manufacturing	0.137	0.042	0.232	

variables calculated as relative changes yielded more complex models than dependent variables calculated as absolute changes. Thereby, the same set of variables gave a totally different picture of the processes underlying firm growth. To sum up, it was concluded that choice of growth indicator yielded different results even when tested on the same data.

Second, the high variation in explained variance persisted, which was expected because of the distribution of the dependent variables (that is, the growth indicators). The explained variance was on the average lower for these models than in the sample surveyed in part 1 of the present study. The reason is that the explanatory variables were mainly included in the mail questionnaire, and the purpose of the phone survey was to collect the control and dependent variables.

Summary of Result of Part 2

We have seen that there were large differences between growth calculated as absolute changes and growth calculated as relative changes. The correlations between the two were low, ranging from a minimum of .175 to a maximum of .389. We have also witnessed how the same set of variables drastically differed in their ability to measure growth dependent on how the growth was measured. These differences were attributed to the distribution of the dependent variable which had high values of skewness and kurtosis. It was argued that the estimators were BLUE (best linear unbiased estimator) (Wonnacott and Wonnacott, 1979) and that more emphasis should be put on the estimation of the predictors, rather than on seeking to achieve a high explained variance. Furthermore, we have seen that models based on relative measures gave a totally different result than a model based on an absolute measure. The logarithm of a measure did not significantly alter the included independent variables, but the coefficients changed in amplitude.

CONCLUSIONS AND DISCUSSIONS

The purpose of this study was to examine the effects due to differences in the measurement and calculation of the dependent variable of growth. It was argued that the heterogeneity of different measures impeded theory development. To this end, I have in a first part reviewed 55 recent growth studies, and in a second part used data from a sample of small businesses to examine the effects of different growth measures.

The major findings were that most previous studies were based on samples from manufacturing industries. Furthermore a large array of different measures was used, making direct comparisons among studies very difficult, if not impossible. The growth measures were broken down into three variables: a) used indicator, b) calculation, and c) time period. Most researchers were aware of the effect of growth calculated as relative or absolute changes. However, little attention was given to the choice of indicator, the chosen time period and the consequences of transformations of the dependent variable. It was argued that different phases of the growth process were measured depending on whether changes were measured as changes in, for instance, sales or numbers of employees. This choice had also direct consequences on the chosen measurement period. In the second part, it was concluded that growth measured as relative or absolute changes differed significantly, consequently yielding different models. In other words, the same model differed greatly in its ability to explain growth dependent on the chosen indicator, and different variables explained relative and absolute changes in organizational growth.

It can be concluded that these results depict a poor image of the research field. Apparently little effort has been done to truly understand the pros and cons of different growth measures. Most of the research done in this field was difficult to compare because of lack in agreement on or interest in how the dependent growth variable should be measured and calculated. This automatically leads to confusion as to whether or not an independent variable is significant, and to the nature of its specific influence on growth. The results also indicated that the use of confidence intervals may be more appropriate to use than simple levels of significance. The reason is that significance tests are poor measures of the influence of a single variable (Schmidt, 1996; Cohen, 1994). It is better to consider each separate study as a contribution to research, where questions about a set of variables' assumed importance can be resolved by systematically aggregating findings from different studies. Seldom do we find a single study that has the properties needed to generalize and to finally state the influence of a set of variables. This can probably be better done by using meta-analytical methods. If confidence intervals are reported, then even insignificant results may be regarded as valuable, because they can be combined with other studies.

Research findings can be more easily interpreted if results were reported for several models, not only the one that yielded the highest explained variance. This procedure would lead to a higher level of direct comparability among studies, but also to a higher awareness of the model robustness. Furthermore, if prediction and explanation of organizational growth are the purpose, then multiple indicators should be favored, rather than single indicators such as sales, number of employees, or assets. Multiple indicators have the assumed property of representing a theoretical construct, and in that way the researcher avoids the pitfall of whether or not organizational growth can be seen in different phases, and which indicators are possibly the best indicators of the various phases.

The limitations of the present study is that it deals with only a small sample of the growth literature. Only published articles were reviewed, and other publications were left out of account (such as dissertations and conference proceedings). This may have led to a more negative evaluation of the field, because space limitations in journals may force authors and editors to minimize the method section in favor of other sections. However, it has been shown that more work must be done in justifying how the dependent measures were constructed as reported and why. A qualifier of this study is that the sample was based on recent articles, and therefore can be assumed to give an accurate description of the state of the art. Furthermore, I have systematized and statistically analysed the results from the review. The limitation of the second part was that data were not primarily gathered to test the validity and reliability of different growth measures. This limitation did not allow me to test for the impact of different time periods, or to compare subjective measures with objective measures. Therefore, only a partial test was actually performed. A qualifier was a large sample with a large set of different variables available. For this study as a whole, the advantage was the combination of a literature review of the field and an empirical investigation, which makes it possible to more deeply penetrate the problems related to the definition and measurement of the dependent variable of growth.

Much more work needs to be done on the consequences of the design of the growth measures. However, I will here focus on what I perceive as the most important features. Apparently, there is little knowledge about the two choices made when designing the growth measure: 1) how does the choice of indicator such as numbers of employees or sales, and 2) how does the choice of measurement period affect the final model? I have here presented some arguments that suggest that these two factors may have a higher importance for our models than previously acknowledged. It is therefore important to further investigate the validity of these arguments, because these choices may have a paramount importance for our final models.

To conclude, I truly believe that we will only be able to advance the research frontiers of organizational growth by better systematization of the dependent variables and of our findings. If we are not able to compare and accumulate knowledge about our results, what is the point of research? It merely becomes an academic discussion where the possibility of consensus is small and practical value even smaller. This cannot be the purpose in such an applied research field as entrepreneurship and organizational growth.

NOTE

* Previously published in R. Donckels and A. Miettinen (eds) (1997). *Entrepreneurship and SME Research. On its Way to the Next Millennium* (pp. 199–216). Aldershot, UK: Ashgate.

REFERENCES

Anderson, O. and W.H. Strigel (1981), 'Business surveys and economic research – a review of significant developments', in H. Laumer and M. Ziegler (eds), *International Research on Business Cycle Surveys*, Munich: Springer, pp. 25–54.

Begley, T.M. and D.P Boyd (1987), 'Psychological characteristics associated with performance in entrepreneurial firms and smaller businesses', *Journal of Business Venturing*, **2**, 79–93.

Brush, C.G. and P.A. Vanderwerf (1992), 'A comparison of methods and sources for obtaining estimates of new venture performance', *Journal of Business Venturing*, **7**, 157–70.

Chandler, G.N. and S.H. Hanks (1993), 'Measuring the performance of emerging businesses: a validation study', *Journal of Business Venturing*, **8**, 391–408.

Cohen, J. (1994), 'The earth is round (p<.05)', *American Psychologist*, **49**, 997–1003.

Covin, J.G. (199 1), 'Entrepreneurial versus conservative firms: a comparison of strategies and performance', *Journal of Management Studies*, **28**(5), 439–62.

Cragg, P.B. and M. King (1988), 'Organizational characteristics and small firms' performance revisited', *Entrepreneurship Theory and Practice* (Winter) 49–64.

Davidsson, P. (1989), 'Continued entrepreneurship and small firm growth', doctoral dissertation prepared for Economic Research Institute, Stockholm School of Economics.

Delmar, F. (1996), 'Entrepreneurial behavior and business performance', doctoral dissertation prepared for Economic Research Institute, Stockholm School of Economics.

Fox, J. (1991), *Regression Diagnostics*, Newbury Park, CA: Sage.

Gupta, A.K. and V. Govindarajan (1984), 'Business unit strategy, managerial characteristics, and business unit effectiveness at strategy implementation', *Academy of Management Journal*, **27**, 25–41.

Konings, J. (1995), 'Gross job flows and the evolution of size in U.K. establishments', *Small Business Economics*, **7**, 213–20.

Miller, D. (1987), 'Strategy making and structure: analysis and implications for performance', *Academy of Management Journal*, **30**, 7–32.

Miller, D. and J. Toulouse (1986), 'Chief executive personality and corporate strategy and structure in small firms', *Management Science*, **32**, 1389–1409.

Murphy, G.B., J.W. Trailer and R.C. Hill (1996), 'Measuring performance in entrepreneurship', *Journal of Business Research*, **36**, 15–23.

Rosenthal, R. (1991), *Meta-Analytic Procedures for Social Research*, Newbury Park, CA: Sage.

Schmidt, F.L. (1996), 'Statistical significance testing and cumulative knowledge in psychology: implications for training of researchers', *Psychological Methods*, **1**, 115–29.

Storey, D.J. (1995), 'Symposium on Harrison's "Lean and Mean": a job generation perspective', *Small Business Economics*, **7**, 337–40.

Storey, D.J. (1989), 'Firm performance and size: explanations from the small firm sectors', *Small Business Economics*, **1**, 175–80.

Stuart, R.W. and P.A. Abetti (1990), 'Impact of entrepreneurial and management experience on early performance', *Journal of Business Venturing*, **5**, 151–62.

Tabachnick, B.J. and L.S. Fidell (1989), *Using Multivariate Statistics*, New York: HarperCollins.

Wonnacott, R.J. and T.H. Wonnacott (1979), *Econometrics*, 2nd edn, New York: John Wiley & Sons.

REFERENCES INCLUDED IN THE REVIEW

Arbaugh, LB. and D.L. Sexton (1996), 'New firm growth and development: a replication and extension of Reynolds' research', *Journal of Enterprising Culture*, **4**, 19–36.

Arrighetti, A. (1994), 'Entry, growth and survival of manufacturing firms', *Small Business Economics*, **6**, 127–37.

Audretsch, D.B. (1995), 'Innovation, growth and survival', *International Journal of Industrial Organization*, **13**, 441–57.

Begley, T.M. and D.P. Boyd (1987), 'Psychological characteristics associated with performance in entrepreneurial firms and smaller businesses', *Journal of Business Venturing*, **2**, 79–93.

Binks, M.R. and C.T. Ennew (1996), 'Growing firms and the credit constraint', *Small Business Economics*, **8**, 17–25.

Birley, S. and P. Westhead (1994), 'A taxonomy of business start-up reasons and their impact on firm growth and size', *Journal of Business Venturing*, **9**, 7–31.

Box, T.M., L.R. Watts and R.D. Hisrich (1994), 'Manufacturing entrepreneurs: an empirical study of the correlates of employment growth in the Tulsa MSA and rural East Texas', *Journal of Business Venturing*, **9**, 261–70.

Box, T.M., M.A. White and S.H. Barr (1993), 'A contingency model of new manufacturing firm performance', *Entrepreneurship Theory and Practice*, **18**, 31–46.

Brooksbank, R., D.A. Kirby and G. Wright (1992), 'Marketing and company performance: an examination of medium sized manufacturing firms in Britain', *Small Business Economics*, **4**, 221–36.

Chaganti, R. and J.A. Schneer (1994), 'A study of the impact of owner's mode of entry on venture performance and management patterns', *Journal of Business Venturing*, **9**, 243–60.

Chandler, G.N. and S.H. Hanks (1994), 'Market attractiveness, resource-based capabilities, venture strategies, and venture performance', *Journal of Business Venturing*, **9**, 331–49.

Chandler, G.N. and E. Jansen (1992), 'The founder's self-assessed competence on venture performance', *Journal of Business Venturing*, **7**, 223–36.

Cooper, A.C., F.J. Gimeno-Gascon and C.Y. Woo (1994), 'Initial human and financial capital as predictors of new venture performance', *Journal of Business Venturing*, **9**, 371–95.

Covin, J.G. (1991), 'Entrepreneurial versus conservative firms: a comparison of strategies and performance', *Journal of Management Studies*, **28**, 439–62.

Covin, J.G. and T.J. Covin (1990), 'Competitive aggressiveness, environmental context, and small firm performance', *Entrepreneurship Theory and Practice* (Summer), 35–50.

Covin, J.G. and D.P. Slevin (1990), 'New venture strategic posture, structure, and performance: an industry life cycle analysis', *Journal of Business Venturing*, **5**, 123–35.

Covin, J.G., D.P. Slevin and T.J. Covin (1990), 'Content and performance of growth-seeking strategies. A comparison of small firms in high- and low-technology industries', *Journal of Business Venturing*, **5**, 391–412.

Cragg, P.B. and M. King (1988), 'Organizational characteristics and small firms' performance revisited', *Entrepreneurship Theory and Practice* (Winter) **13**(2), 49–64.

Cressy, R. (1996), 'Pre-entrepreneurial income, cash-flow, growth and survival of startup businesses: model and tests on U.K. data', *Small Business Economics*, **8**, 49–58.

Davidsson, P. (1989), 'Continued entrepreneurship and small firm growth', doctoral dissertation prepared for the Economic Research Institute, Stockholm School of Economics.

Donckels, R. and J. Lambrecht (1995), 'Networks and small business growth: an explanatory model', *Small Business Economics*, **7**, 273–89.

Doutriaux, J. (1992), 'Emerging high-tech firms: how durable are their comparative start-up advantages?', *Journal of Business Venturing*, **7**, 303–22.

Dunne, R. and A. Hughes (1996), 'Age, size, growth and survival: UK companies in the 1980s', *Journal of Industrial Economics*, **XLII**, 115–40.

Dunne, T., M.J. Roberts and L. Samuelson (1989), 'The growth and failure of U.S. manufacturing plants', *Quarterly Journal of Economics* (November), 671–98.

Gales, L.M. and R.S. Blackburn (1990), 'An analysis of the impact of supplier strategies and relationships on small retailer actions, perceptions, and performance', *Entrepreneurship Theory and Practice* (Fall), 7–21.

Ginn, C.W. and D.L. Sexton (1990), 'A comparison of the personality type dimensions of the 1987 Inc. 500 company founders/CEOs with those of slower-growth firms', *Journal of Business Venturing*, **5**, 313–26.

Hansen, E.L. (1995), 'Entrepreneurial network and new organization growth', *Entrepreneurship Theory and Practice*, **19**(4), 7–19.

Kazanjian, R.K. and R. Drazin (1990), 'A stage-contingent model of design and growth for technology based new ventures', *Journal of Business Venturing*, **5**, 137–50.

Kolvereid, L. (1992), 'Growth aspirations among Norwegian entrepreneurs', *Journal of Business Venturing*, **7**, 209–22.

Kolvereid, L. and E. Bullvag (1996), 'Growth intentions and actual growth: the impact of entrepreneurial choice', *Journal of Enterprising Culture*, **4**, 1–17.

Mata, J. (1994), 'Firm growth during infancy', *Small Business Economics*, **6**, 27–39.

McCann, J.E. (1991), 'Patterns of growth, competitive technology, and financial strategies in young ventures', *Journal of Business Venturing*, **6**(3), 189–208.

McGee, J.E., M.J. Dowling and W.L. Megginson (1995), 'Cooperative strategy and new venture performance: the role of business strategy and management experience', *Strategic Management Journal*, **16**, 565–80.

Merz, G.R. and M.H. Sauber (1995), 'Profiles of managerial activities in small firms', *Strategic Management Journal*, **16**, 551–64.

Miller, D. (1987), 'Strategy making and structure: analysis and implications for performance', *Academy of Management Journal*, **30**, 7–32.

Miller, D. and J. Toulouse (1986), 'Chief executive personality and corporate strategy and structure in small firms', *Management Science*, **32**, 1389–409.

Miner, J.B., N.R. Smith and J.S. Bracker (1989), 'Role of entrepreneurial task motivation in the growth of technologically innovative firms', *Journal of Applied Psychology*, **74**, 554–60.

Miner, J.B., N.R. Smith and J.S. Bracker (1994), 'Role of entrepreneurial task motivation in the growth of technologically innovative firms: interpretations from follow-up data', *Journal of Applied Psychology*, **79**, 627–30.

Ming-Hone Tsai, W., I.C. MacMillan and M.B. Low (1991), 'Effects of strategy and environment on corporate venture in industrial markets', *Journal of Business Venturing*, **6**, 9–28.

Morris, M.H. and D.L. Sexton (1996), 'The concept of entrepreneurial intensity: implications for company performance', *Journal of Business Research*, **36**, 5–13.

O'Farrell, P.N., D.M.W.N. Hitchens and L.A.R. Moffat (1992), 'The competitiveness of business service firms: a matched comparison between Scotland and the South East of England', *Regional Studies*, **26**, 519–33.

Ostgaard, T.A. and S. Birley (1996), 'New venture growth and personal networks', *Journal of Business Research*, **36**, 37–50.

Peters, M.P, and C.G. Brush (1996), 'Market information scanning activities and growth in new ventures: a comparison of service and manufacturing businesses', *Journal of Business Research*, **36**, 81–9.

Phillips, B.D. and B.A. Kirchhoff (1989), 'Formation, growth and survival; small firm dynamics in the U.S. economy', *Small Business Economics*, **1**, 65–74.

Siegel, R., E. Siegel and I.C. MacMillan (1993), 'Characteristics distinguishing high-growth ventures', *Journal of Business Venturing*, **8**, 169–80.

Storey, D.J. (1994), 'New firm growth and bank financing', *Small Business Economics*, **6**, 139–50.

Stuart, R.W. and P.A. Abetti (1990), 'Impact of entrepreneurial and management experience on early performance', *Journal of Business Venturing*, **5**, 151–62.

Thwaites, A. and P. Wynarczyk (1996), 'The economic performance of innovative small firms in the south east region and elsewhere in the UK', *Regional Studies*, **30**, 135–49.

Vaessen, P. and D. Keeble (1995), 'Growth-oriented SMEs in unfavourable regional environments', *Regional Studies*, **29**, 489–505.

Wagner, J. (1992), 'Firm size, firm growth and persistence of chance. Testing GIBRAT's law with establishment data form lower Saxony, 1978–1989', *Small Business Economics*, **4**, 125–31.

Wagner, J. (1994), 'The post-entry performance of new small firms in German manufacturing industries', *Journal of Industrial Economics*, **XLII**, 141–54.

Westhead, P. (1995), 'Source and employment growth contrast between types of owner-managed high-technology firms', *Entrepreneurship Theory and Practice*, **20**(1), 5–27.

Willard, G.E., D.A. Krueger and H.R. Feeser (1992), 'In order to grow, must the founder go? A comparison of performance between founder and non-founder managed high growth manufacturing firms', *Journal of Business Venturing*, **7**, 181–94.

Williams, M.L., M. Tsai and D. Day (1991), 'Intangible assets, entry strategies, and venture success in industrial markets', *Journal of Business Venturing*, **6**, 315–33.

Zahra, S.A. (1993), 'Environment, corporate entrepreneurship, and financial performance: a taxonomic approach', *Journal of Business Venturing*, **8**, 319–404.

PART II

Growth Aspirations and Motivation

5. Firm size expectations of nascent entrepreneurs[1]

Frédéric Delmar, Per Davidsson

INTRODUCTION

Business growth and especially early growth is of special importance as it represents one of the major sources of job creation. Several studies have shown that small and medium-sized firms play a very large and/or growing role as job creators (Davidsson, Lindmark and Olofsson, 1996; Davidsson, Lindmark and Olofsson, 1994; Reynolds and White, 1997; Storey, 1994). In Sweden, this is mainly a result of many small start-ups and their incremental expansions. Thus, new employment opportunities are heavily dependent on the number of organizations created and their early growth. New firms can create new job opportunities in two ways: by their start size, and by their subsequent growth. Furthermore, we know that there is a substantial variation among firms with regard to both start size and subsequent growth. While the absolute majority of the firms remain small, some firms choose to engage in growth.

It is therefore interesting to examine more closely the expectations of nascent entrepreneurs with regard to expected start size and expected subsequent growth. These expectations, whether they are realized or not, represent the initial ambitions of a population of nascent entrepreneurs. High growth ambitions should, arguably, also lead to higher rates of realization, that is, larger start sizes and higher growth rates, compared with lower ambitions. Thus, knowledge about the determinants of growth expectations during the venture creation phase may be central if we want to influence and to support the growth of newly founded firms.

This chapter examines what factors affect firm size expectations of nascent entrepreneurs. More precisely, we have used size expectations for the business during the first year of operation and during the fifth year of operation as dependent variables to examine the determinants of growth expectations and performance expectations of nascent entrepreneurs. Hence, our aim is to present and test a decision model of new venture creation where the dependent variable is expected size of the business operation. The model emphasizes the social cognitive process of new venture creation.

PREVIOUS RESEARCH

Early Growth

Previous research on early firm size or growth has traditionally focused on actual size during the first years of operation, normally one to five years after the birth of the venture (Arbaugh and Sexton, 1996; Birley and Westhead, 1994; Chandler and Jansen, 1992; Cooper, Gimeno-Gascon and Woo, 1994; Cressy, 1996; Hansen, 1995). Depending on the adopted perspective on early size variations the literature can be divided into three different theoretical categories. The dominant perspective is related to the individual characteristics of the founder or founders of the business, a perspective which tries to answer the question, 'What personal characteristics affect the early performance of the venture'? Examples of such individual characteristics range from biographical data such as age, sex, and experience (Stuart and Abetti, 1990) to cognitive constructs such as perceived competence (Chandler and Jansen, 1992) and personal goals (Birley and Westhead, 1994). The second class is related to contingency variables and their possible effect on early growth. Examples of contingency variables are industry and geographical affiliation (Bull and Winter, 1991), legal entity, and financial capital (Cressy, 1996). The third and the smallest category in terms of published empirical work is concerned with the network's effect on growth. Here the network size and its composition, as well as the frequency of interactions within it, are of interest (for example, Hansen, 1995).

Regardless of their theoretical point of departure, previous studies share the shortcoming that they are retrospective studies where data on the characteristics of the organization creation process have been gathered after the venture has been launched. The reliance on retrospective data introduces two biases: (a) hindsight biases, that is, memory distortion of what actually happened, and (b) positive selection biases, that is, we have information only about those who are up and running the business. It is possible that those who never realized their start-up plans have other growth or size expectations than those actually starting. For example a nascent entrepreneur could abandon a business idea for the reason that it is not in accordance with his or her growth ambitions.

New Venture Creation

There is in the literature an acknowledged need for studies that try to follow the business creation process and the outcome in real time with a holistic perspective where several dimensions are investigated not separately but jointly (Gartner, 1985; Gartner, Bird and Starr, 1992; Katz and Gartner,

1988). This study has therefore with some modification adopted Gartner's (1985) framework of four dimensions that should be accounted for when the creation of new ventures is studied. Gartner's (1985) original four dimensions are: i) the individual(s) involved in the new venture creation, ii) the activities undertaken by those individuals during the venture creation, iii) the organizational structure and strategy of the new venture, and iv) the new venture's environmental context.

Our model takes off from Gartner's model in that we see the creation process as a process mirroring the nascent entrepreneur(s) own preferences and the willingness to shape the environment in accordance with them. That is, new venture creation is behavior performed by a single person or a limited group of persons trying to evaluate the possibility to establish a venture in accordance with their personal preferences and goals (both personal and business goals) (Shaver and Scott, 1991). This behavior can be seen as a learning experience, where the nascent entrepreneur enters the process with limited knowledge of the outcome and the process leading to the outcome. Because such processes always have a high degree of newness all nascent entrepreneurs enter the venture creation process independently of whether the entrepreneur is really *de novo* or has previous start-up experience. The newness can, for example, be a new business idea or a previously tested business idea to be introduced on a virgin market. The point is that the entrepreneur enters into a process defined only by the willingness to create a business and a relatively high degree of uncertainty as regards the final outcome.

As the process evolves the entrepreneurs will have to make decisions that will shape the future of the business (for example, the optimal size of the firm). However, during the process the entrepreneur will accumulate both information and experience. This accumulated experience and new information might lead to the conclusion that decisions made previously are no longer valid and that they therefore must change. This line of reasoning is close to the idea behind dynamic decision making as well as to Weick's (1979) process of 'enactment'. The former perspective focuses on how the individual interacts with a complex situation in order to understand the information around him or her so actions can be taken. The latter perspective focuses more on how information about the reality is shared and organized among a group of people in order to create a common understanding.

Dynamic decision making research (Brehmer, 1992; Brehmer and Dörner, 1993) focuses on decision making which requires a series of decisions, where the decisions are not independent, where the state of the world changes, both autonomously and as a consequence of the decision maker's actions, and where decisions have to be made in real time. For example starting or creating a business can be seen as a series of small incremental decisions that may be altered along the way as new information is gathered. Moreover, decisions are made in real time and under pressure. There is often a definite time constraint over how long the duration of business gestation may take before the business opportunity disappears. Thus the nascent entrepreneur's decisions and actions are not independent of the changes in the world and the entrepreneur has to adjust. This is a social psychological perspective, where the individual's decision making vis-à-vis the world is the focus.

Weick's (1979) approach focuses on how groups of people interact to create a shared meaning, that is, focusing on the individual's interaction with others in order to form shared reality about what is happening. Shared realities and how theses realities are created is here the focus. This perspective is central as well as it offers an understanding of how nascent entrepreneurs must convince other people around them to share their view of how great the business idea is. What both theories have in common is the assumption that individuals process or filter information about the present situation based on previous experience. This information gathering might lead to old decisions being viewed in new light and that they therefore are altered.

Hence, both perspectives are useful for the understanding of new venture creation. We will here focus on how the individual's own cognitive process in relation to goals and actions taken affects the process. According to the proposed social psychological perspective a new venture creation can be seen as made up by three components: i) time, ii) the individual(s) involved, and iii) the creation of a business concept. By the concept of time we refer to the entrepreneur's time frame as well as to how far he or she is already in the *process* of creating a business. Hence, there is an individual *acting;* those acts are based on decisions, which in turn are based on the individual's motivation and ability to process relevant information. By business concept we here mean everything needed to be *created* or organized in order to legally operate a business in accordance with the demands of the market. Thus the behavior of the nascent entrepreneurs is by definition actions taken to test and perhaps launch a venture.

The process of business creation can therefore best be described as an interaction between the preferences and goals of the individual, the evolvement of the project over time where knowledge is accumulated, and the on-going refinement of the business conceptualization. These three separate components can be further broken down in order to be tested empirically. The individual component can be sub-divided into two components, viz. individual human capital and goals, depending on their stability over time and their theoretical distance from the dependent variable.

The individual human capital is composed of individual characteristics that tend to be distal to the project of creating a venture, and which are stable over time. They represent the set of background variables describing a person's biographical data, such as age, sex, education, and so forth. As they are distal we can only expect them to have low to moderate direct impact on behaviors and goals. However, they are also indicators of social background and therefore work as proxies for preferences and goals.

Personal/business goals, on the other hand, represent a conceptually different component. The variables describe the nascent entrepreneur's intention with the future business. Thus they are proximal to the dependent variable as they are conceptually close. They are assumed have a direct causal impact on size expectations, but also to be relatively easily changed in the light of new information.

Environmental and organizational context represents a group of variables describing the context in which the venture creation takes place. It is here assumed that to a certain degree the nascent entrepreneur has the possibility to create his or her own context. The organizational context is created in relation to the nascent entrepreneur's own goals and his/her perception of what is feasible and needed. The component is proximal to the dependent variable, but the causality is not clear. The question is whether the nascent entrepreneur creates or selects an organizational and environmental context to fit his or her goals, or whether the context determines the goals.

Stage in the gestation process represents both the time and the actual actions undertaken by the nascent entrepreneur in order to create the new venture. Depending on where in the gestation process the nascent entrepreneur is, he or she will accumulate different sorts of information but also different amounts of information. The nascent entrepreneur will either form stronger opinions about certain issues related to business as confirmatory information is gathered, or s/he will reformulate his or her opinions depending on the information and accumulated experience. Thus, this component is assumed to have a direct impact not only on the dependent variables, but also on business and environmental context and personal goals.

The purpose of the proposed model is to make empirical analysis possible while acknowledging the inherent complexity of venture creation. New venture creation is not a linear process involving a finite number of uniform steps that have to be carried out in a predetermined sequence. While we do consider the multitude of influences that shape the process, we will in no way make full justice to the complexity of the processes of starting a new business in our empirical analysis. In an attempt to arrive at meaningful and generalizable simplifications of the real-world complexity we focus in this chapter on an exploration of the extent to which the proposed model, composed of four components, can explain nascent entrepreneur's expected business size and growth.

METHOD

Design

The study was designed to provide population estimates for business start-up efforts and to make it possible to follow a random sample of nascent entrepreneurs during the time period possibly leading to the start of a new business. Because it was estimated that nascent entrepreneurs constitute a relatively small group in society, a very large sample of individuals went through a screening interview aiming at selecting the business starters and a control group (a random 4 per cent of the original sample). As a consequence, the vast majority of the respondents only participated in the screening interview. The individuals in the two groups were then asked if they were willing to participate in a longer telephone interview. The intention is to follow the groups at six-month intervals during at least a two-year period. The interviews reported in this chapter were conducted during the period of May–September 1998.

Sample

Table 5.1 displays the response rate for the present study. Data are based on two samples of randomly selected individuals living in Sweden. The first sample consists of individuals aged between 16–70 years and the second sample consists of individuals aged between 25–44 years. The purpose of the first sample is to get a representative sample of the adult population in Sweden. The purpose of the second sample is to increase the yield of nascent entrepreneurs. We know from earlier statistics that this group has the highest rate of business founders. For all individuals included in the two samples we received information on name, address, and birth year.

Of the 49 979 individuals randomly selected, it was possible to obtain a telephone number for 35 971 (71.9 per cent) of the individuals. The remaining 28.1 per cent did not have a telephone number (secret, unknown or other), had severe disabilities (n = 381), or had moved abroad (n = 289). Of those contacted by telephone, 30 427 individuals (84.6 per cent) agreed to participate.

Nascent Entrepreneur

Out of the 30 427 individuals screened, 961 respondents said that they were at the time of the interview trying to start a business. The longer phone interview was completed by 623 of these. Of the 338 respondents that did not complete the telephone interview, 61 refused or did not have enough knowledge of the Swedish language, and 279 could not be reached again or delayed the appointment for the telephone interview. Of the 623 respondents who completed the phone interview, 128 respondents were defined as nascent intrapreneurs, and another 90 did not meet the upper or the lower bound rule to be defined as nascent entrepreneur. This leaves us with a final sample of 405 nascent entrepreneurs.

The lower bound decision rule is based on 24 so-called gestation activities. Gestation activities are different behaviors associated with starting a new firm (such as earning money on sales, doing market research, saving money to start a business). The respondents were then asked if they had 'initiated' or 'completed' each of the gestation activities. They were also asked what month and year all reported actions were initiated. An individual was considered as a nascent entrepreneur if he or she had completed at least one gestation activity

Table 5.1   Sample and response rates

Category	Men	Women	Total
Individuals randomly sampled			49 979
Individuals with identifiable phone number			35 971
Individuals screened	*15 419*	*15 008*	*30 427*
Percentage			84.6%
Percentage Yes to NE, NI item	4.4%	1.8%	3.2%
No. of 'Yes' answers to nascent entrepreneur or nascent intrapreneur item	*683*	*278*	*961*
Refused to volunteer			−53
Not enough knowledge of Swedish			−6
No contact, not clear if start-up			−147
Started, but did not complete interview, because they were no longer starting a business (misunderstanding, changed situation)			−132
No. who accepted invitation to volunteer and completed long interview	*445*	*178*	*623*
Nascent intrapreneurs			−128
Did not meet the gestation criteria			−90
Nascent entrepreneurs analysed	*294*	*111*	*405*

by the time of the interview. Only two respondents identified as nascent entrepreneurs in the screening interview were excluded because of the lower bound.

The upper bound is concerned with whether the start-up process is already
completed, that is, when a business should be considered started. We consider
the start-up process as completed when the following criteria are fulfilled. A
business is regarded as started if a) money has been invested, b) income has
been made, and c) the firm is already a legal entity. Our definition of a started
business is similar to the one suggested by Carter, Gartner and Reynolds
(1996). They found that nascent entrepreneurs who started a business were
faster at establishing a legal entity, getting finance and investing in facilities
and equipment, getting sales, and devoting full time to the business. A total of
88 respondents were affected by this upper bound.

The Dependent Variable

Growth expectations were measured in numbers of employees (part time and
full time, owner excluded). The time frame is size of the first year of operations
and size after the fifth year of operations. Several options are available regarding the calculation of a growth indicator. Sales has the advantage of being
closely associated to changes in the market and is therefore a good indicator of
market performance. Employment on the other hand is associated with job
creation, not with market performance as different organizational solutions and
industry affiliations will affect its size. Acknowledging that neither indicator is
superior for all purposes we chose employment as the size indicator on the
grounds that it is probably easier at this early stage for the nascent entrepreneur
to state his/her firm size expectations in terms of people rather than money.

As stated previously, a new firm can create employment either by its start
size or by its subsequent growth. In order to acknowledge this fact expected
size after year one and growth until year five (expected size after five years
minus expected size after one year) are used as dependent variables. It was our
original intention to utilize the growth construct developed by Reynolds and
White (1997) and applied by Arbaugh and Sexton (1996). The only difference
is that we used employment instead of sales as our base for calculation.

The purpose of the Reynolds and White growth construct was to develop a
typology of different development trajectories. In order to do that, they
dichotomized their sample on two dimensions: expected start size, and
expected growth after five years. The start size expectations were divided into
a 'high' and a 'low' start-group depending on whether first-year employment
exceeded one employee. Thereafter, the sample was divided into a high and a
low growth group depending on whether the expected growth rate (expected
size year five minus expected size year one) was above or below an increase
of two employees.

Reynolds and White chose to combine the two variables into one variable of four different growth categories (high start–low growth, low start–low growth, low start–high growth, and high start–high growth) with the cases quite evenly distributed in the categories. In our case, the distribution is heavily skewed towards the lower end of the categories: low start–low growth accounted for close to 60 per cent of the valid cases. The practical consequence was that in a multivariate analysis we would obtain cells with too few cases to complete the analysis. Furthermore, an unnecessarily large number of missing values would be introduced in the dependent variable. A third of all cases would have been dropped from the analyses due to missing values for the dependent variable. Missing values are due to a high non-response frequency in size expectations year five. We will come back to this specific problem later.

Instead of using a four-category dependent variable we opted for using two dummy variables (expected start size and expected growth) as dependent variables in separate analyses. Thus we first analyse determinants of expected start size, and secondly we analyse determinants of expected growth. In order to assess the influence of start size ambition on subsequent growth, expected start size is used as a control variable in all analyses of expected growth. The use of two dependent variables in separate analyses provides us with a maximum number of cases and still allows us to investigate different growth trajectories. Table 5.2 displays the distribution of the dependent variables.

However, the problem of missing values remains for the expected growth variable. Missing values are always a problem as they restrict the statistical power of the analysis. Furthermore they may not be missing completely at random and therefore bias our results. In order to control for the later problem separate missing value analyses were run to test if there was a significant

Table 5.2   Distribution of the dependent variables

Dependent variables	Frequency ($n = 405$)	Percentage (100%)
Expected start size		
0–1 employee	306	75.6%
More than one employee	81	20.0%
Missing	18	4.4%
Expected growth		
0–1 employee	208	51.4%
More than one employee	110	27.2%
Missing	87	21.5%

relationship ($p < 0.05$) among the dependent variable's missing values (expected growth) and the exploratory variables. It was found that missing values in the dependent variable are over-represented among those answering that they were starting as a team, those with no previous start-up experience, those reporting a low probability for the business to still be running in five years, and those who are in the beginning of the gestation process (short duration of the gestation period). We therefore concluded that respondents who are at an early stage in the new venture creation process are less likely to be able to give an estimate of the expected size of the business in five years.

Explanatory Variables

Table 5.3 summarizes the constructs used in the chapter. The choice of variables is based on previous literature and most of them do not need any further elaboration. However, the group of variables composed of different variables assessing the nascent entrepreneurs' business start-up activities will be dealt with in more detail. These variables are based on more than 20 different gestation activities the respondents were asked about. For each activity the respondent was asked whether the activity was initiated, completed or not relevant. If the behavior was initiated or completed the respondent was asked when this occurred.

Data thus allowed the construction of variables indicating the number of gestation activities that were either completed or initiated (Carter et al., 1996; Gatewood et al., 1995). Furthermore, using the date for when the activities were initiated, we developed a time frame (measured in months) for the new venture creation process. Three variables were constructed based on the time frame. The duration of the gestation process is measured as the time elapsed between the first initiated gestation activity and the latest initiated activity at the time of the interview. The second variable is the recency of the latest initiated gestation activity measured as the time elapsed between the latest initiated activity and the time of the interview. The last variable is an indicator of efficiency in the gestation work. It is measured as the average time taken to complete an activity.

Analysis

It has been shown that business performance measures rarely fulfill the needed assumptions to perform, for example, an ordinary least square regression and that therefore other, non-parametric techniques are to be recommended instead (Robinson and Hofer, 1997). This study is no exception; the dependent variables are highly skewed. As a consequence, logistic regression was chosen to assess the determinants of expected start size and expected growth. Forward

Table 5.3 The constructs used in the analyses

Construct/dimensions	Measurement	Conceptual definition
Dependent variables		
Expected start size	Dummy	Value 1 = start size larger than 1, 0 = 0 to 1 employee at start
Absolute expected growth	Dummy	Value 1 = adding more than one employee, 0 = adding one or one employee
Initial human capital		
a) Age (birth year)	Scale	A higher score indicates a younger person
b) Education	Ordinal	A higher score indicates a higher education
c) Sex	Dummy	Value 1 = man, 0 = woman
d) Team	Dummy	Value 1 = team start-up, 0 = individual start-up
e) Work experience	Scale	A higher score indicates more experience
f) Management experience	Scale	A higher score indicates more experience
g) Start-up experience	Dummy	Value 1 = start-up experience, 0 = no experience
Business/personal goals		
a) Goals	Two dummy variables, three categories	Value 1 = goal to grow as large as possible, 0 = other Value 1 = manageable size, 0 = other
b) Probability of becoming main source of income	Scale	A higher score indicates a higher probability
c) Probability of survival	Scale	A higher score indicates a higher probability

Table 5.3 (continued)

Construct/dimensions	Measurement	Conceptual definition
Environmental and organizational context		
a) Legal structure	Three dummy variables, four categories	Value 1 = not yet determined, 0 = other Value 1 = sole proprietorship, 0 = other Value 1 = partnership, 0 = other
b) Industry affiliation	Dummy	Value 1 = service, 0 = manufacturing
c) Geographical affiliation	Two dummy variables, three categories	Value 1 = Greater Stockholm, 0 = rest of Sweden Value 1 = Rural Sweden, 0 = rest of Sweden
d) Competition	Scale	A higher score indicates a higher expected competition
Gestation activities		
a) No. of gestation activities initiated	Scale	A higher score indicates a larger number of initiated activities
b) No. of gestation activities completed	Scale	A higher score indicates a larger number of completed activities
c) Duration	Scale	A higher score indicates a longer duration
d) Efficiency	Scale	A higher score indicates a longer average time period needed for each completed activity
e) Recency	Scale	A higher score indicates a longer time period since last activity was initiated or completed

selection with Wald's statistics was used. Due to the complexity of the proposed model and the large number of variables used, a model selection strategy was adopted. Each variable was first tested in bivariate analysis (not reported here). Second, each category of explanatory variables is tested in separate logistic regressions to assess their impact on the dependent variable. Finally, the strongest variables are selected to be tested in a combined model including variables from the different categories of explanatory variables.

RESULTS

The Separate Models

Tables 5.4a and b display the results from the logistic regression analysis for the two different performance measures for each of the four variable categories. The regression coefficients, the base rate, and the predicted correct classification rate are included. Only variables statistically significant ($p < 0.05$) are displayed. The assessment of the model's performance is based on their predictive ability. The predictive ability of the model was here based on the model's ability to correctly classify the cases. The higher the relative increase compared with the base rate, the better is the predictive ability of the model. With no other information than the base rate distribution our best guess is that all cases belong to the largest group. The more a model can beat the base rate the better is the predictive ability of the model. A complication here is that the higher the base rate, the more difficult it becomes to improve the 'blind guess' that every case is a member of the largest group. Therefore, explanatory variables' significant relationships with the dependent variable may be of interest also in the absence of contribution to predictive power.

Two major results can be immediately recognized when examining the regression analyses. Independently of the variable category used it proves difficult to predict with increased accuracy the expected start size. In contrast, the predictive ability is substantially increased when expected growth is used as a dependent variable. As regards expected growth, the strongest contribution of single variable is that of start size. It is clear that those planning to start a larger business from the beginning also expected a higher future growth.

The only variable category that improves predictive ability is 'Environmental and organizational context'. The chosen legal structure and choice of the business location has a small but statistically significant impact. All three dummy variables describing the legal structure are significant ($p < 0.05$) with a negative coefficient, indicating that the nascent entrepreneurs planning to start an incorporated business are more prone to start 'large'. Interestingly, recent results on the relationship between legal form and the actual growth of young firms indicate that this relationship is quite strong (Dahlqvist, Davidsson and Wiklund, 1999). The geographical affiliation is also of importance, with nascent entrepreneurs active in the Greater Stockholm area were more oriented towards larger firms (that is, having more than one employee).

For expected growth it is much easier to enhance prediction with the help of the explanatory variables. Expected start size which is used as a control variable is the single strongest predictor in all four regressions. The models are easy to interpret in the sense that the variables' individual contribution and sign are in the expected direction. When examining the contribution of the 'individual human capital' we can see that men, those with previous start experience, and those expecting larger start size are more prone to expect a higher growth.

The 'personal/business goals' analysis indicates that not only nascent entrepreneurs stating growth as the explicit goal, but also those having harvest as their prime goal, expect more growth. Furthermore, those expecting the future business to become the main income source are also more growth oriented. This is not self-evident, as a substantial share of the nascent entrepreneurs were already business owners before initiating the focal start-up. The picture emerging here is that those nascent entrepreneurs who are most committed to their business venture in terms of an income generator rather than as a part-time effort also expected to grow more, both at an early stage and in a later stage. This picture is even more reinforced when the impact of the 'environmental and organizational context' is examined. We could see that for firms intending to start as an incorporation the growth expectations are higher. This can be seen as an indicator of financial commitment as incorporation is the legal form that requires most initial financial capital.

As regards 'gestation activities' we can see that the further the nascent entrepreneur has come in the gestation process (controlling for start size) the higher are the growth ambitions. The careful reader will note that the number of completed activities has a negative sign, whereas number of initiated activities has a positive sign. This is caused by the two variables' high intercorrelation, that is, the higher the number of initiated activities the higher the number of completed activities. Therefore the model was re-tested with only one of the two variables and then the sign came out as positive for both regressions.

To sum up this section, we conclude that independently of the used variable category it was not possible to satisfactorily predict the variation in expected start size. We found some statistically significant relationships, but their impact on predictive power was very weak. Prediction of expected future growth was more easily improved, due in part to the lower 'base rate' and in part to the strong predictive power of expected start size which was used as a

Table 5.4a   Logistic regression analysis results for separate models of expected start size

Expected start size	Individual human capital, $n = 369$	Personal/business goals, $n = 351$	Environmental and organizational context, $n = 372$	Gestation activities, $n = 382$
Variables included in the model	Constant −2.09 team start 1.12	Constant −0.36 Manageable size −1.39	Constant −0.28 Not yet −1.47 Partnership −1.44 Sole prop −2.29 Reg. Stockholm 0.60	Constant −2.61 No. of initiated activities 0.14
Base rate	294/75 (79.70%)	281/70 (80.06%)	293/79 (78.76%)	301/81 (78.80%)
Correct classification rate	79.70%	80.06%	79.57%	78.80%

Table 5.4b *Logistic regression analysis results for separate models of expected growth*

Expected growth	Individual human capital, n = 307	Personal/business goals, n = 294	Environmental and organizational context, n = 305	Gestation activities, n = 313
Variables included in the model	Constant –2.89 Sex 0.66 Start experience 0.90 Exp. start size 1.91	Constant –1.32 Manageable size –0.87 Main income source 0.01 Exp. start size 2.17	Constant Not yet –1.47 Partnership –2.13 Sole prop. –1.81 Exp. start size 1.76	Constant –2.85 No. of completed activities –0.42 No. of initiated activities 0.54 Exp. start size 2.11
Base rate	204/193 (66.45%)	193/101 (65.65%)	198/197 (64.92%)	206/107 (65.81%)
Correct classification rate	74.27%	73.81%	77.05%	75.72%

control variable in all four regressions. The four variable categories had similar predictive power, but both 'environmental and organizational context' and 'gestation activities' had a somewhat higher predictive power. What came out as the main theme in the different analyses was that the nascent entrepreneurs who are committed to their business, both financially and emotionally, also expected to achieve the larger start size and higher future growth.

The Combined Models

Table 5.5 displays the results of the logistic regression analyses for the combined models. It is concluded that the final models can only offer a relatively small increase in the overall predictive ability. However, they achieve better classification rates within the cells. That is, a model can achieve a high overall correct classification rate either by having a low incorrect classification rate in the largest group, but high incorrect classification rate in the smallest group, or by having an even correct classification rate in all cells.

Two groups of variables are excluded entirely in the combined models, 'initial human capital' and 'gestation activities'. It was expected that the former group would have a weaker impact on the dependent variables as this group represented variables that are supposedly distal according to our proposed model. However, the exclusion of the 'gestation activities' comes as a surprise. In our proposed model it was argued that the stage in which the nascent entrepreneur is would affect the notion of expected size. We do not find any support for this when all variable categories are tested against each other in the combined models.

We find that the 'business and environment context' and 'personal/business goals' are able to predict variation in both dependent variables. These variable groups represent proximal variables, that is, they are conceptually close to the dependent variables. 'Personal/business goals' represent motivational aspects regarding the specific business setting. It was therefore expected that they would have a moderate to high predictive ability. The same line of reasoning is valid for the 'environmental and business context' variable group. These variables are also specific to the situation of the business creation, and it is only natural that the nascent entrepreneur matches his or her size expectations with business and environmental context. Part of the process of venture creation is to construct an organizational context matching the ambitions of the entrepreneurs with the demands of the situation.

More specifically, the results indicate that nascent entrepreneurs expecting a larger start size prefer incorporation as a legal structure for their firm. Furthermore they state the explicit goals of either growing the business as much as possible or get it up and running and then sell it off. The same pattern is repeated (and even magnified in the sense that the model performed better)

Table 5.5   Logistic regression analysis results for combined models

	Expected start size, $n = 370$ Constant 0.73	Expected growth, $n = 291$ Constant 0.22
Variables included in the model	*Environmental and organizational context*	*Environmental and organizational context*
	Not yet determined – 1.51	Not yet determined –1.13
	Partnership –1.46	Partnership –2.21
	Sole prop. –2.25	Sole proprietorship –1.80
	Personal/business goals	*Personal/business goals*
	Manageable size –1.11	Manageable size –0.98
		Main income source 0.01
		Control variable
		Exp. start size 1.67
Base rate	290/80 (78.38%)	190/101 (65.29%)
Correct classification rate	79.73%	80.07%

when expected growth is analysed. Once more expected start size as control variable has a strong influence on the model's predictive ability. Nascent entrepreneurs expect higher growth in their future business if they expect to start 'large' (that is, with more than one employee) and if they choose incorporation as legal structure. Furthermore, a goal with the future business is to represent the main income source. Commitment to the business stands out as the common denominator for the variables which explains differences in size and growth expectations in our sample.

In short, as expected the combined models perform somewhat better than the separate models. However, the increase in predictive ability is marginal compared with the analysis for separate variable categories in Table 5.4a and b. As regards expected start size the model achieves only a marginal improvement over the 'blind guess' that all cases belong to the 'small' (0–1 employee) group. However, when the group sizes are as uneven as in this case it takes a very strong model to beat that naive guess.

CONCLUSIONS

The purpose of this chapter was to examine the factors affecting the firm size expectation of nascent entrepreneurs. This was done by testing a decision model on a unique data set composed of a random sample of nascent entrepreneurs. The proposed model was based on four different components that were tested together and separately to assess their unique and combined effect on size expectations.

The dependent variables used in this chapter reflected the employment growth trajectories that newly founded firms can take. New firms total job creation is a result of their start size or their subsequent early growth, or a combination of the two. It was found that most of the nascent entrepreneurs had low size and growth ambitions. More than 79 per cent did not expect to have more than one employee after the first year, and more than 65 per cent did not expect to have more than one employee after five years of operations.

The prediction of variations in expected start size turned out to be difficult to improve with the explanatory variables used here. When the model's components were analysed separately none of the components offered an increase in the predictive ability compared to the base rate. Even if results were somewhat weak, the significant relationships made sense and were easily interpreted. 'Environmental and organizational context' contributed to the highest number of correctly classified cases. Prediction was only marginally increased when the several variable categories were tested jointly.

Our model for prediction of variations in expected growth was much more successful. However, much of the explained variance was attributed to expected start size which was used as a control variable in the analyses. When the model's separate components were analysed, they all yielded similar increases in correct classification rates compared to the base rate. Prediction was only marginally increased when the combined model was tested.

The emerging picture is that a set of indicators that can be interpreted as reflecting the nascent entrepreneurs' level of *commitment* (incorporation; expectation that the business will become the main source of income; growth as explicit goal; number of gestation activities) to the business start-up at this early stage has some predictive ability with regard to the dependent variables we have used. This reinforces the image one gets from results concerning going from nascent entrepreneur to actual start-up (Carter et al., 1996) and the actual early growth of new firms (Dahlqvist et al., 1999). Thus, 'early stage level of commitment' seems to be a useful concept for discussion and understanding the outcomes of start-up efforts.

Otherwise, the main conclusion from research must be that our ability to predict the subsequent development of business start-ups is very limited. Our results can be interpreted as suggesting that this is to a large extent because the nascent entrepreneurs themselves do not know very precisely at this early stage what they want their firms to become. The strategy to assess a number of presumably relevant 'factors' or 'conditions' at one early point in time in order to 'pick winners' seems to have very limited potential. It is unlikely that increasing the list of explanatory variables or perfecting their measurement would dramatically change that conclusion.

Instead, we would argue that a much more dynamic view is needed in order to further our understanding of business start-ups and our ability to build, as opposed to pick, winners. Both the motivation and the ability to grow the firms are likely to evolve as a consequence of the experiences the (nascent) entrepreneur encounters during the early development. In order to reach further in developing empirical and conceptual knowledge about these important matters we need to find novel ways to collect and analyse real-world data with all its idiosyncratic properties and temporal complexities, without surrendering to saying that all we can learn is that reality is complex, because that we knew from the very beginning. This study has shown that it is possible to study a large random sample of business start-ups in real time. In our continued work we will follow the development of these start-up efforts in the hope that we can find more fruitful ways to analyse and conceptually portray their development over time in ways that really take the process perspective seriously.

NOTE

1. Previously published as: Delmar, F. and P. Davidsson (1999), 'Firm size expectations of nascent entrepreneurs', in: P.D. Reynolds, W.D. Bygrave, S. Manigart, C. Mason, G.D. Meyer, H.J. Sapienza and K.G. Shaver (eds), *Frontiers of Entrepreneurship Research 1999* vol 19, Wellesley, MA: Babson College, pp. 90–104.

ACKNOWLEDGEMENT

This study was financed by Knut and Alice Wallenberg's Foundation, the Swedish Foundation for Small Business Research (FSF), and the Swedish National Board for Industrial and Technical Development (NUTEK). Although funded separately, this research owes intellectually to the Entrepreneurial Research Consortium (ERC) and especially to its initiator and co-ordinator, Professor Paul D. Reynolds, Babson College. The ERC is a temporary, voluntary association of some 30 US and non-US research institutions which have sponsored more than 100 researchers who have taken part in the design and realization of the project.

REFERENCES

Arbaugh, J.B. and D.L. Sexton (1996), 'New firm growth and development: a replication and extension of Reynolds' research', *Journal of Enterprising Culture*, 4(1), 19–36.

Birley, S. and P. Westhead (1994), 'A taxonomy of business start-up reasons and their impact on firm growth and size', *Journal of Business Venturing*, **9**, 7–31.

Brehmer, B. (1992), 'Dynamic decision making: human control of complex systems', *Acta Psychologica*, **81**, 211–41.

Brehmer, B. and D. Dörner (1993), 'Experiments with computer-simulated microworlds: escaping both the narrow straits of the laboratory and the deep blue sea of the field study', *Computers in Human Behavior*, **9**, 171–84.

Bull, I. and F. Winter (1991), 'Community differences in business births and business growths', *Journal of Business Venturing*, **6**, 29–43.

Carter, N.M., W.B. Gartner and P.D. Reynolds (1996), 'Exploring start-up event sequences', *Journal of Business Venturing*, **11**(3), 151–66.

Chandler, G.N. and E. Jansen (1992), 'The founder's self-assessed competence on venture performance', *Journal of Business Venturing*, **7**, 223–36.

Cooper, A.C., F.J. Gimeno-Gascon and C.Y. Woo (1994). 'Initial human and financial capital as predictors of new venture performance', *Journal of Business Venturing*, **9**, 371–95.

Cressy, R. (1996), 'Pre-entrepreneurial income, cash-flow, growth and survival of startup businesses: model and tests on U.K. data', *Small Business Economics*, **8**, 49–58.

Dahlqvist, J., P. Davidsson and J. Wiklund (1999), 'Initial conditions as predictors of new venture performance: a replication and extension of the Cooper et al. study', paper presented at the ICSB World Conference, Naples, 20–23 June.

Davidsson, P., L. Lindmark and C. Olofsson (1994), *Dynamiken i svenskt näringsliv [Business dynamics in Sweden]*, Lund, Sweden: Studentlitteratur.

Davidsson, P., L. Lindmark and C. Olofsson (1996), *Näringslivsdynamik under 90-talet [Business dynamics during the '90s]*, Stockholm: Nutek.

Gartner, W.B. (1985), 'A conceptual framework for describing the phenomenon of new venture creation', *Academy of Management Review*, **10**(4), 696–706.

Gartner, W.B., B.J. Bird and J.A. Starr (1992), 'Acting as if: differentiating entrepreneurial from organizational behavior', *Entrepreneurship Theory and Practice* (Spring), 13–31.

Gatewood, E.J., K.G. Shaver and W.B. Gartner (1995), 'A longitudinal study of cognitive factors influencing start-up behaviors and success at venture creation', *Journal of Business Venturing*, **10**, 371–91.

Hansen, E.L. (1995), 'Entrepreneurial networks and new organization growth', *Entrepreneurship Theory and Practice*, **19**(4), 7–19.

Katz, J. and W.B. Gartner (1988), 'Properties of emerging organizations', *Academy of Management Review*, **13**(3), 429–41.

Reynolds, P.D. and S.B. White, (1997), *The Entrepreneurial Process: Economic Growth, Men, Women, and Minorities*, Westport, CT: Quorum Books.

Robinson, K.R. and C.W. Hofer (1997), 'A methodological investigation of the validity and usefulness of parametric and non-parametric statistical data analysis techniques for new venture research', in P.D. Reynolds, W.D. Bygrave, N.M. Carter, P. Davidsson, W.B. Gartner, C.M. Mason and P.P. McDougall (eds), *Frontiers of Entrepreneurship Research*, Babson Park, MA: Center for Entrepreneurial Studies, Babson College, pp. 692–705.

Shaver, K.G. and L.R. Scott (1991), 'Person, process, choice: the psychology of new venture creation', *Entrepreneurship Theory and Practice*, **16**(2), 23–45.

Storey, D.J. (1994), *Understanding the Small Business Sector*, London: Routledge.

Stuart, R.W. and P.A. Abetti (1990). 'Impact of entrepreneurial and management experience on early performance', *Journal of Business Venturing*, **5**, 151–62.

Weick, K.E. (1979), *The Social Psychology of Organizing*, 2nd edn, New York: McGraw-Hill.

6. What do they think and feel about growth? An expectancy–value approach to small business managers' attitudes toward growth*[1]

Johan Wiklund, Per Davidsson, Frédéric Delmar

INTRODUCTION

In this chapter we investigate how small business managers' beliefs concerning the consequences of growth influence their overall growth attitude. We find this to be an important question. Although previous research has shown that small firm growth is the most important source of new jobs (Davidsson, Lindmark and Olofsson, 1994, 1996; Kirchhoff, 1994; Reynolds and White, 1997), there are also clear indications that many small business managers deliberately refrain from exploiting opportunities to expand their firms. We test the influence of the eight most important perceived consequences of growth on the overall growth attitude in three separate, large-scale surveys of small business managers.

Previous research suggests that there is reason to more carefully assess the role of growth motivation when examining firm growth. Many small business managers are not willing to pursue growth (Davidsson, 1989a, 1989b; Delmar, 1996; Gundry and Welsch, 2001; Storey, 1994). An important implication of this is that many small firms do not realize their full growth potential (Scott and Rosa, 1996), which may constitute a source of great under-utilization of resources. Our knowledge of why small business managers vary so greatly in their growth motivation is still limited. It constitutes an area worthy of further investigation, as research that examines the effect of growth motivation on subsequent business growth finds support for a positive relationship (Bellu and Sherman, 1995; Kolvereid and Bullvåg, 1996; Miner, Smith and Bracker, 1994; Mok and van den Tillaart, 1990).[2]

In this chapter we explicitly assess reasons for differences in levels of growth motivation. More specifically, we focus on the beliefs and attitudes toward expanding a business. Building on the expectancy-value theory of attitudes (Ajzen, 1988, 1991; Ajzen and Fishbein, 1977, 1980; Fishbein, 1967; Fishbein and Ajzen, 1975), we are interested in how the overall attitude toward growth is influenced by specific cognitive beliefs about the consequences of growth. By doing so we are able to tease out the relative importance of different motives underlying small business managers' attitudes to growth. This research is important for two principal reasons. First, in mainstream economic literature the supremacy of the economic motive is taken for granted – people act in ways to maximize their profits. In the small business context, a more diverse view may be relevant. We know that people start and operate their own firms for a variety of reasons other than maximizing economic returns (Davidsson, 1989a; Delmar, 1996; Gundry and Welsch, 2001; Kolvereid, 1992; Storey, 1994). This does not mean that their motives are totally irrational. However, it is important to assess the relative importance of economic and noneconomic motives in order to understand why small business managers exhibit the growth-related attitudes and behaviors that they do.

Second, we believe that this research can have practical implications. People's beliefs are influenced by the persuasive argumentation of others (Ajzen, 1991; Chaiken and Stangor, 1987). Hence, it should be possible to affect small business managers' beliefs about growth through providing them with the relevant information and knowledge. That is, if certain beliefs have a stronger influence on overall attitude, society may be able to take specific actions related to these areas that, in turn, will affect the small business managers' attitudes toward expanding their firms.

The chapter proceeds as follows. The next section introduces the expectancy-value theory of attitudes and shows how previous empirical research regarding the motivation of small business managers can be placed in this conceptual framework in order to explain individual differences in growth motivation. Eight hypotheses concerning how specific expected consequences of growth affect growth motivation conclude the section. Next, the replication design is presented along with the analyses carried out to test the hypotheses. the samples, and the variables. The hypotheses are then tested by means of regression analysis in the following section. A discussion of the results and their implications for future research as well as small business managers concludes the chapter.

THEORY AND HYPOTHESES

Attitudes and Beliefs

Motivation theories are aimed at explaining why individuals choose to act in a certain direction. One of the major concepts in motivation theories is attitude. An attitude is a valuation of an object or a concept, that is, to which extent an object or concept is judged as good or bad. While personality variables such as Need for Achievement or Locus of Control have been extensively researched in psychological studies of entrepreneurial behavior (cf. Stimpson, Robinson, Waranusuntikule and Zheng, 1990), attitudes have received relatively little attention (Robinson, Stimpson, Huefer and Hunt, 1991).

In psychological language, personality variables are distal, that is, weak determinants of specific behaviors. Personality theories are intended to measure general individual tendencies that are stable across a spectrum of different situations (Epstein, 1984). Therefore, general personality variables are likely to have limited predictive power when applied to any specific context (Ajzen, 1991), such as firm growth. Attitudes on the other hand are proximal, that is, more specific and because of their specificity, they are considered to be important determinants of behavior On the other hand, attitudes are less stable over time and across situations, changing through interactions with the environment (Eagly and Chaiken, 1993).

There has been much controversy over the importance of attitudes in predicting behavior. However, research has shown that attitudes can predict behavior if certain conditions are met (Bagozzi and Warshaw, 1992; Kim and Hunter, 1993). Attitudes have been found to be moderately strong predictors of goal-directed behavior ($r = 0.79$ between attitude and behavior when methodological artifacts were removed, cf. Kim and Hunter, 1993). Thus, it would appear that the concept of attitudes is relevant in the present context.

For a long time, there has been an unresolved discussion about whether attitude is a unidimensional construct consisting of the 'amount of affect for or against a psychological object' (Fishbein, 1967, p. 478, citing Thurstone, 1931), or a three-dimensional construct containing an affective, a cognitive, and behavioral/intentional component (*see* Chaiken and Stangor, 1987, for a discussion of these different views).

According to the tripartite view, attitudes can be broken down into three different classes of evaluative responses (Eagly and Chaiken, 1993): 1) *cognitive responses*, also known as beliefs, are thoughts that people have about the attitude object (for example, I believe expanding the business will enhance the possibilities of the business to survive a crisis); 2) *affective responses* consist of feelings, moods, or emotions that people have in relation to the attitude object (for example, I feel happy/anxious about expanding my business); 3) *behavioral responses* are the overt actions or intentions exhibited by people in relation to the attitude object (for example, I turned down the order, because it would have meant expanding the business).

In this chapter, we instead adhere to the view heralded by Ajzen and

Fishbein (Ajzen, 1988, 1991; Ajzen and Fishbein, 1977, 1980; Fishbein, 1967; Fishbein and Ajzen, 1975) suggesting that the cognitive, affective, and behavioral dimensions represent three separate but causally linked constructs termed belief, attitude, and intention. The reason that we chose this approach is that it has been successfully applied to a range of different situations. These concepts are central elements of the Theory of Reasoned Action and the Theory of Planned Behavior, which are validated theories (Locke, 1991) that constitute 'the dominant theoretical framework in the attitude-behavior literature' (Olson and Zana, 1993, p. 131) and 'continue to generate the most research' (Petty, Wegener and Fabrigar, 1997, p. 640).

Embodied in these theories lies the expectancy-value model of attitude (Ajzen, 1991). This model explicitly deals with the relationship between beliefs and attitudes. It has been fruitfully applied in several different areas, such as decisions concerning choice of restaurant, blood donation, detergents, and automobiles and can be considered a paradigm in itself (Bagozzi, 1984). According to this theory, an attitude reflects the degree to which a person likes or dislikes an object, where the term object can refer to any aspect of the individual's world. Importantly, the theory is developed to predict specific attitudes in specific contexts (Ajzen and Fishbein, 1980). In our case we are interested in the specific behavior of expanding a firm. We therefore focus solely on the attitude toward this specific behavior. The individual's attitude toward a behavior can be predicted by the salient beliefs that he or she holds about performing the behavior. It should be noted that the beliefs must correspond to the specific behavior concerning action, target, context, and time in order to permit understanding and prediction of the attitude (Ajzen and Fishbein, 1980). That is, in order to predict the attitudes of expanding the business a certain magnitude (for example, doubling the size) we should explicitly assess the beliefs of the consequences of performing that particular behavior (that is, the expected consequences of doubling the size).

Beliefs associate an object with certain attributes. In the case of behavioral beliefs, the object is the behavior of interest and the associated attributes are the expected consequences of that behavior. Consequences can be good or bad and of varying magnitude. For instance, an individual may believe that expanding the business 100 per cent may lead to a minor increase of profitability but a major decrease in job satisfaction. The strength of an individual's belief is captured by his or her subjective probability that performing a behavior will lead to a certain outcome. Returning to the example above, the individual may be very certain that growth will lead to improved performance (although to a small extent) but less certain that job satisfaction will decrease (although if it does, the decrease will be substantial). According to the original formulation of the expectancy-value model, a person's attitude toward a particular behavior can be predicted by multiplying his or her evaluation of each behavior's expected consequences by the strength of the belief that performing the behavior will lead to that consequence and then summing the product across all beliefs (Ajzen and Fishbein, 1980).

However, empirical tests of this model have revealed that the interaction of evaluation of expected consequences on the one hand and the strength of the belief on the other fails to give significant results (Bagozzi, 1984), leading to a questioning of the multiplicative combination of beliefs and evaluations (Valiquette, Valios, Desharnais and Godin, 1988). More specifically, the strength of the belief dimension has failed to contribute to the prediction of attitude (Pieters, 1988). Tentative analyses of our data supported these findings (Davidsson, 1987). Therefore, we focus solely on expected consequences in our analyses.

Moreover, in the original formulation of the expectancy-value model, salient beliefs are not weighted for their relative importance in determining the attitude (for example, Ajzen and Fishbein, 1980). This approach looses the idiosyncratic dimensionality and uniqueness of the micro beliefs that comprise the attitude (Bagozzi, 1984). Bagozzi (1985) argues that there are in fact several alternative ways of modeling the relationship between beliefs and attitude, some of which estimate the relative importance of individual beliefs. Two of these do not assume a multiplicative combination of beliefs and evaluations. If multicollinearity is severe, latent variable modeling with higher- and lower-order latent variables is necessary. If not, as an alternative the attitude can be regressed over the individual's evaluation of expected consequences as assessed along a positive–negative dimension. We have chosen the latter alternative, because an empirical test shows that multicollinearity is not a problem (cf. footnote 4).

Identifying Relevant Beliefs and Hypotheses

As suggested by the expectancy-value theory of attitudes, we regard expected consequences of growth as evaluations of the behavior's consequences, or beliefs. Based on this logic, we argue that a plausible reason that some small business managers refrain from growing their firms is that they expect some consequences of growth to be negative. If a small business manager believes, for instance, that increased size may jeopardize the firm's ability to maintain the quality of its products or services, such anticipated negative consequences of growth should lead to a negative attitude toward expanding the business. On the other hand, if the small business manager sees expansion as a means to attain personal goals, for example, the possibility of earning more money, such expectations of positive consequences of growth should positively influence his or her growth attitude. In other words, positive expectations of growth are likely to enhance the motivation of a small business manager to expand his or her firm whereas negative expectations of growth are likely to reduce the growth motivation.

In order to establish more precisely small business managers' salient beliefs about growth, a literature review of comprehensive classical works on small business management and motivation was conducted (Bolton, 1971; Boswell, 1972; Deeks, 1976; Smith, 1967; Stanworth and Curran, 1973). This literature review identified eight key areas that are important for small business managers and at the same time likely to be affected (positively or negatively) by growth. These key areas and their sources in the literature are exhibited in Table 6.1. We now detail the arguments concerning each of these areas and formulate the associated hypotheses.

With regard to *workload,* the reasoning is that some managers who are – and intend to stay – involved in all aspects of their business expect growth to increase their workload. Other managers foresee hiring and delegating, and hence reducing their personal load. Thus,

Hypothesis 1: The expectation that increased size would lead to a reduction (increase) of the owner-manager's workload is associated with a more positive (negative) attitude toward growth.

Likewise, regarding *work tasks* some owner-managers define themselves primarily as craftsmen and resist the transition to full-time management that

Table 6.1   Sources for selection of expected consequences of growth that may influence growth motivation

Area affected by growth	Author(s)
Owner-manager's workload	Boswell (1972), pp. 80–81
Owner-manager's work tasks	Deeks (1976), pp. 198–205; Smith (1967), pp. 27–28; Stanworth and Curran (1973), pp. 150–151
Employee well-being, 'atmosphere'	Deeks (1976), pp. 198–205; Smith (1967), pp. 27–28; Stanworth and Curran (1973), pp. 157, 161
Financial outcome	Deeks (1976), pp. 198–205; Smith (1967), pp. 27–28; Stanworth and Curran (1973), p. 98
Control (surveillance)	Bolton (1971), p. 24; Boswell (1972), pp. 80–81; Deeks (1976), pp. 198–205; Smith (1967), pp. 22, 27–28, 45; Stanworth and Curran (1973), pp. 62–63, 152
Independence	Bolton (1971), pp. 23–24; Deeks (1976) pp. 198–205; Smith (1967), pp. 17, 27, 45; Stanworth and Curran (1973), pp. 58, 153
Crisis survival ability	Deeks (1976), pp. 198–205; Stanworth and Curran (1973), p. 58
Quality of products and services	Bolton (1971), p. 23; Deeks (1976), pp. 198–205; Stanworth and Curran (1973), p. 98

expansion may (be perceived to) necessitate. Other managers may be looking forward to letting go of some hands-on work they cannot yet afford to delegate. Thus,

Hypothesis 2: The expectation that increased size would allow the owner-manager to spend more (less) time on favored work tasks is associated with a more positive (negative) attitude toward growth.

Concerning *employee well-being* it has been observed that some managers fear that growth would force formalization and destroy the family-like atmosphere of the small organization, where every member is indispensable. At the same time it has been noted that nongrowing small organizations offer very limited career opportunities for their employees. Again, then, growth may be associated with positive as well as negative expectations. Thus,

Hypothesis 3: The expectation that increased size would make employees enjoy work more (less) is associated with a more positive (negative) attitude toward growth.

It may seem self-evident at first glance that growth should improve the owner-managers *personal income*. However, the literature suggests that this is not universally believed to be the case. For example, the manager may hold that the environment leaves little room for profitable growth. Thus,

Hypothesis 4: The expectation that increased size would increase (decrease) the owner-manager's income and other disposable economic benefits is associated with a more positive (negative) attitude toward growth.

Owner-managers' need for autonomy is heavily stressed in the literature. The relationship between autonomy and growth appears to be complex and possibly involves more than one dimension, which is why we include *independence* and *control* as separate dimensions. On the one hand, a small firm is weak in relation to its environment, not leaving much real independence for the owner-manager. On the other hand, taking additional loans, sharing equity or accepting the dictates of a large, dominating customer may be precisely what is required in order to achieve growth – at the expense of some independence. Similarly, some managers may perceive that increased size would force them away from contact with the day-to-day realities of the firm, reducing their ability to be on top of everything that happens or could happen to it. Other managers may think that the more managerial role in an enlarged firm would reduce myopia and give more time for strategic issues, and thereby increase their control of the firm's long-term destiny. Thus,

Hypothesis 5: The expectation that increased size would enhance (reduce) the owner-manager's ability to survey and control operations is associated with a more positive (negative) attitude toward growth.

Hypothesis 6: The expectation that increased size would increase (decrease) the firm's independence in relation to customers, suppliers, and lenders is associated with a more positive (negative) attitude toward growth.

Also for the last two dimensions, positive as well as negative beliefs can be found in the literature. Some managers may associate increased size with a reduction in flexibility, which would reduce the firm's *crisis survival ability*. Others may associate size with the financial muscles that could cushion a situation of that kind. Thus,

Hypothesis 7: The expectation that increased size would make it easier (more difficult) for the firm to survive a severe crisis is associated with a more positive (negative) attitude toward growth.

With regard to *quality*, some may fear that their own detachment from direct control is a risk, whereas others would see the possibility to introduce formal and systematic quality control of a kind that the very small firm cannot afford. Thus,

Hypothesis 8: The expectation that increased size would make it easier (more difficult) for the firm to maintain the quality of products and services is associated with a more positive (negative) attitude toward growth.

Although we have presented an extensive list of expected consequences of growth, the question arises about whether this list is exhaustive or if small business managers in fact expect additional consequences that affect their growth attitude. Previous expectancy-value research suggests that the domain of salient beliefs could be generated through an open-ended elicitation procedure (Ajzen and Fishbein, 1980; Bagozzi, 1984). In order to identify the beliefs that are salient in a population, a representative sample should be selected for the procedure (Ajzen and Fishbein, 1980; Bagozzi, 1984). Therefore, previous to the first survey, unstructured interviews were conducted with eleven small business managers by one of the authors. The sample was selected to represent as broad a spectrum as possible concerning types of small firms and small firm owner-managers. The interviews first covered general aspects of the business and then issues pertaining to growth. Direct questions about expected consequences of growth were only asked at the very end of the interview and only if they had not previously been spontaneously mentioned by the respondent. These interviews confirmed that the eight dimensions identified in the literature in fact reflected important expected negative and/or positive consequences of growth. Further, the managers did not report any other important consequences of growth either spontaneously or when prompted.

It should be noted that these expected consequences of growth may or may not be well founded. For example, a belief that growth reduces crisis survival ability can be questioned on the basis that research tends to show positive relationships between growth or size on the one hand, and survival on the other (Kirchhoff, 1994). In other words, it is possible that small business managers expect consequences that in fact will not materialize, should their business expand. However, in order to further validate that we have identified relevant expected consequences of growth, we turned to the literature that explicitly deals with the actual consequences of growth. Flamholtz (1986) recognizes ten growing pains, that is, possible negative consequences of growth. While his growing pains are conceptualized in a way that is not directly transferable to our context, it is clear that he identifies similar consequences. Flamholtz identifies possible changes to workload, work tasks, employee well-being, control, and quality. In their study, Hambrick and Crozier (1985) found similar potential negative consequences of growth, but also noted that the very survival of the firm may be threatened. All in all, these studies support that six of the eight consequences we have identified may in fact materialize as a company expands. A reason that these authors do not address changes to personal income and independence in relation to lenders, customers, and suppliers may be that they mainly focus on the negative consequences of growth, whereas they may find positive effects of growth on personal income and independence.

Finally, Ajzen and Fishbein (1980) hold that individuals can only attend to a limited number of beliefs about behavioral outcomes at any given moment and suggest that five to nine would be an appropriate number. Taken together, the above makes us confident that we have identified the relevant range of generally important beliefs about the consequences of growth. This gives us the research model depicted in Figure 6.1.

METHOD

Basic Research Design

This study uses a replication design. As noted by others, small business growth studies are largely incompatible because similar phenomena are studied in isolated research projects using different concepts, models, measures, and methods (Davidsson and Wiklund, 2000; Delmar, 1997; Storey, 1994). As a consequence, our knowledge about small-firm growth is still quite incomplete and incoherent. This lack of replication is shared with the broader domain of business studies (Hubbard, Vetter and Little, 1998). We agree with these authors that 'The goal of science is empirical generalizations or knowledge development. Systematically conducted replications with extensions facilitate this goal.' (Hubbard, Vetter and Little, 1998, abstract; see also Lindsay and

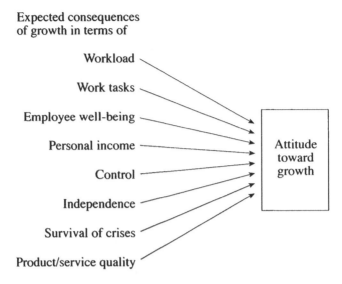

Expected consequences
of growth in terms of

Workload

Work tasks

Employee well-being

Personal income

Control

Independence

Survival of crises

Product/service quality

Attitude
toward
growth

Figure 6.1   Research model

Ehrenberg, 1993). The present study attempts to contribute to cumulative knowledge by means of replication with extension. Three separate studies addressing the same issues with the same measurement instrument in similar samples were carried out during a ten-year period. These three studies are jointly analysed in this chapter.

According to Hubbard, Vetter and Little (1998), replication is a substantial duplication of previous empirical research in order to increase the internal validity of the research design. The aim of replication is typically to determine if the findings from the original study are reproducible. A replication with extension goes somewhat further and aims at increasing the generalizability of research findings by modifying the initial study in some way. If the results reproduce in the modified studies, this would indicate a higher generality of the findings, that is, they extend beyond the specific context of any single study. In the present case, data were collected from three different samples during a ten-year period utilizing the same measurement instrument. The data collections coincided with different phases of the business cycle, and each study used somewhat different sample frames. In this sense, the present research could be regarded as replication with extension. This serves the much-sought-for purpose of generalizing findings beyond what is possible from a solitary study.

However, the fact that the data from all three studies are analysed simultaneously allows us to perform additional analyses. Thanks to the large number of cases provided by the three samples combined, it is possible to split the sample into different subsamples and conduct separate analyses within each of these. It is also possible to analyse all cases in one analysis. Such additional analyses facilitate additional validation of the findings (Campbell and Fiske, 1959).

Taken together, the multiple analyses on different samples and subsamples conducted here reduce the risk of Type 1 errors (erroneous rejections of the null hypothesis). This risk may be substantial in conventional singular analyses, solely relying on the $p < 0.05$ criterion (Cohen, 1994; Hubbard, Vetter and Little, 1998). The separate analyses of multiple samples also reduce the risk of Type 2 errors, that is, failure to reject the null hypothesis when it is false (Cohen and Cohen, 1983).

Sample Characteristics

Over a ten-year period, three independent telephone interview studies were conducted. The two initial studies in 1986 and 1994 were stratified over the Swedish equivalent of ISIC codes. Independent firms from specific manufacturing, service, and retail industries were selected. The samples were also stratified over the standard Swedish size brackets 1–4, 5–9, 10–19, and 20–49 employees. In addition to this, the 1996 sample was stratified over the firms' previous growth rate so that high-growth firms were overrepresented in the sample for all size brackets and industries. The samples had 440, 400, and 630 respondents respectively, totaling 1470 respondents, with corresponding response rates of 83 per cent, 55 per cent, and 75 per cent. The data were collected from the managing director, who in most cases is also the majority owner. The managing director was explicitly asked for at the beginning of the interview.

At the time of the interviews, 40 firms had outgrown the largest size bracket and were omitted. The smallest size bracket was left out of the analyses since only one of the studies included firms of this size. This reduced the number of cases to a total of 1248. The actual number of cases used in the analyses is somewhat lower due to internal nonresponses. There are some statistically significant differences among the three samples (see Table 6.2). The 1986 study reports somewhat younger respondents, smaller firms, and a smaller share of manufacturing firms compared with the two latter studies. The firms of the 1994 sample are on average the youngest. However, for the purpose of this chapter, the differences are unproblematic. Analyses are mainly performed on different subsamples where these differences are controlled; or else these variables are added as control variables.

Variables and Measures

The dependent variable
To measure attitude toward growth, respondents were asked whether a 100 per cent increase in the number of employees in five years' time would be mainly

Table 6.2   Basic characteristics of the three samples

	Full sample $n = 1248$	1986 sample $n = 298$	1994 sample $n = 354$	1996 sample $n = 596$
Mean age of respondent	47	46	48[a]	48[a]
% males	95	95	95	94
% manufacturing	49	40	51[a]	53[a]
% service	30	32	31	27
% retail	21	28[b]	18	20
Mean size (FTE)	17	10	14[a]	21[b]
Mean firm age	33	24[a]	12	30[b]

Notes: One-way ANOVA with Bonferroni test is used in the analysis, except for the sex and industry variables, where chi-2 test is used.
[a]$p < 0.05$ for difference to lowest group.
[b]$p < 0.05$ for difference to lowest and middle group.

negative or mainly positive. Respondents who gave an answer in either direction were then asked to specify whether they perceived such an outcome as 'somewhat', 'rather strongly', or 'very strongly' positive/negative. A seven-point scale ranging from very negative to very positive was thus used to measure this variable. This type of single item bipolar seven-point good/bad scale has been the most often advocated and used variable to measure attitude toward behavior (Ajzen and Fishbein, 1980; Fishbein and Ajzen, 1975). It is suggested to be the most stringent and valid variable, at least in situations where the distinction pleasant/unpleasant is inappropriate, as in our case (Bagozzi, 1984). The explication of a specific amount of growth over a specific time span in the question is important, as the individual's attitude toward growth may vary depending on both amount and time. Individuals may exhibit more positive or negative attitudes toward larger or smaller amounts of growth as well as toward faster or slower growth rates.

Three other possible measures of the dependent variable were also available: 1) whether a 25 per cent increase in the number of employees in five years' time would be mainly negative or mainly positive; 2) the intended ideal size five years ahead regarding sales; as well as 3) regarding number of employees. While it would have been possible to utilize any of these alternative measures of the dependent variable or to compute a global growth motivation index, we prefer to rely on the question concerned with a 100 per cent increase in the number of employees. The reason is that this makes the dependent variable and the independent variables symmetric. That is, they are all anchored in the doubling of the number of employees. This sort of symmetry in independent and dependent variables is deemed important by the expectancy-value theory (for example, Ajzen and Fishbein, 1980).[3]

Table 6.3   Independent variables. How a doubling of the number of employees is likely to affect each area

Workload	Would the small business manager have to work more or fewer hours?
Work tasks	Would he or she be able to spend more or less time on favored work tasks?
Employee well-being	Would employees enjoy work more or less? (The original Swedish word for well-being connotes work atmosphere as well.)
Personal income	Would the small business manager's income and other disposable economic benefits increase or decrease?
Control	Would his or her ability to survey and control operations increase or decrease?
Independence	Would the firm's independence in relation to customers, suppliers, and lenders increase or decrease?
Survival of crises	Would it be easier or harder for the firm to survive a severe crisis?
Product/service quality	Would it be easier or harder for the firm to maintain the quality of products and services?

The independent variables

The eight belief variables derived from the literature review are displayed in Table 6.3. In order to establish validity and reliability, the format of the questions was modeled after the examples given by Ajzen and Fishbein (1980, p. 66). More specifically, respondents were asked how a doubling of the number of employees, regardless of whether this is deemed desirable or possible, would be likely to affect each of the eight areas. A five-point scale, ranging from 'much more negative' to 'much more positive,' was used for measurement (the specific words describing the positive/negative dimension varied across questions, cf. Table 6.3).

The explicit statement 'doubling of the number of employees' was chosen in order to ensure that the beliefs referred to the same behavior as the attitude across variables and respondents. In other words, the context of the belief variables reflected the context of the attitude variable as closely as possible, as recommended in the literature (cf. above and Ajzen and Fishbein, 1980, p. 64).

Control variables

Five variables were used as contingency variables to subdivide the three samples into subsamples and as independent variables in multiple regression analysis. Firm size, firm age, and industry have been shown to affect growth in previous research (Aldrich and Auster, 1990; Audretsch, 1995; Barkham, 1994; Carroll and Hannan, 2000; Davis and Henreksson, 1999; Dunne and Hughes, 1996; Kirchhoff, 1994). The sex and age of the small-business manager have also been associated with differences in growth (Brush, 1992; Davidsson, 1989a; Deaux and Lafrance, 1998; Delmar, 2000). These variables may influence growth directly as assumed in most research, but it is also possible that they have an indirect influence via the attitude toward growth of the entrepreneur. Thus, it is valuable to investigate their influence on attitude toward growth.

Firm size was measured as the number of full-time equivalents. To determine the industry, respondents were asked if the firm's main line of business was manufacturing, service, or retail. Analyses suggest that the Swedish equivalents of ISIC codes are not always updated or relevant. Therefore, we instead relied on the respondents' self-report of main activity as a better indicator of their main industry. Respondents were asked if they knew what year the firm was founded, which was used to calculate the age of the firm. Finally, the respondents' birth year was used for calculating their age, whereas sex in most instances was evident from the interview.

All control variables were recoded into dummy variables. Firms were classified into the standard size brackets 5–9, 10–19, and 20–49 employees. Ten years was the cut-off for being a 'young' or 'old' firm, whereas the mean of 47 years of age was used to discriminate between young and old entrepreneurs.

To make comparison across the three studies more valid, the wording and relative positioning of the questions were the same in all three studies.

Analyses

Multiple linear regression was carried out to test the hypotheses. Two different analysis designs were applied for the control variables. In the first step, the control variables were entered as independent variables to the regression equation, along with the expectancy variables.

In the second step, they were used to divide the sample, since it is possible that the pattern of relationships differs among industries, size brackets, sex, and age groups.

In line with the replication approach, the hypotheses are tested by examining the extent to which results are replicated across the different analyses, rather than relying solely on conventional tests of significance ($p < 0.05$). If substantial and statistically significant effects recur across the analyses, this is taken as evidence that the data support the hypothesis. Conversely, repeatedly small and nonsignificant effects led to the rejection of the hypothesis. When results are mixed, judgment is used to determine if the hypotheses are supported or not. In other words, judgment rather than objective criteria is used to support or reject hypotheses. This is consistent with the research design and not problematic: 'First, do not look for a magic alternative to NHST [null hypothesis significance testing], some other objective mechanical ritual to replace it. It doesn't exist. . . . we must finally rely, as have the older sciences, on replication' (Cohen, 1994, pp. 1001–2).

The skewness and kurtosis statistics of the dependent variable fall well within the boundaries for normality (Robinson and Hofer, 1997; Shapiro and Wilk, 1965). Thus, parametric tests of significance are applicable. Since positive expectations are hypothesized to increase growth motivation and vice versa, directional, single-tailed tests of significance are applied. Forced entry of independent variables and list-wise deletion of missing data are used.

RESULTS

Table 6.4 shows the correlation matrix and summary statistics for the variables used in our analyses (with the exclusion of the nominal variables, sex and industry). All expectancy variables have moderately positive correlations, ranging from 0.14 to 0.41. The model we have chosen, that is, regressing attitude across expected consequences, could be associated with multicollinearity (Bagozzi, 1985). The moderate correlations suggest that this is not the case. However, to ensure that multicollinearity was not an issue, multicollinearity diagnoses were applied to all regression analyses.[4] The strongest correlation with attitude toward growth can be noted for employee well-being ($r = 0.41$). The correlation between firm age and expected workload is moderately negative ($r = –0.17$). The other correlations are weaker.

The hypotheses were tested by first analysing the three samples combined, which is displayed in Table 6.5. The second column of the table shows the results excluding the control variables. The adjusted explained variance of 0.24 indicates that expected consequences have an influence on attitude toward growth and that the proposed model is relevant. Statistically significant effects in the hypothesized direction are obtained for all expected consequences but work tasks. According to the conventional criterion ($p < 0.05$), this supports H1 and H3 to H8. However, the magnitude of the coefficients for variables other than employee well-being are small in magnitude. The large number of cases makes small effects statistically significant. When the control variables are added to the equation, shown in column three, they alter the equation only to a small extent. Albeit statistically significant on three instances, their standardized regression coefficients are generally low and the explained variance is not increased. Comparing the two analyses, it appears that explanatory variables are not dramatically different in different industries,

Table 6.4 Descriptive statistics and correlations

	Mean	s.d.	1	2	3	4	5	6	7	8	9	10	11
Growth motivation	4.58	2.05											
Workload	2.77	0.98	0.22										
Work tasks	3.01	1.26	0.25	0.34									
Employee well-being	2.61	0.96	0.41	0.24	0.35								
Personal income	3.74	0.75	0.22	0.14	0.17	0.20							
Control	2.56	0.90	0.28	0.25	0.27	0.32	0.16						
Independence	3.14	0.94	0.30	0.24	0.31	0.35	0.17	0.28					
Survival of crises	2.41	1.22	0.29	0.20	0.19	0.35	0.20	0.27	0.32				
Product/service quality	2.90	0.99	0.27	0.24	0.25	0.41	0.17	0.27	0.28	0.31			
Firm size (FTE)	16.55	9.95	0.07	0.11	0.00	0.00	0.07	−0.05	0.04	0.12	0.06		
Firm age	22.56	23.85	0.00	−0.19	0.00	0.03	−0.01	−0.01	0.02	0.00	0.01	0.00	
Age of entrepreneur	47.31	9.27	−0.11	−0.09	−0.04	−0.05	−0.05	−0.04	−0.08	−0.08	−0.06	0.04	0.03

Note: With the large size of the combined sample, correlations greater than ± 0.05 are generally significant at the $p < 0.05$ level.

Table 6.5   Linear regression results for the effect of expected consequences of growth on growth motivation for the full sample

	Full sample n = 1158	Full sample with control variables n = 1140
Workload	0.06*	0.05*
Work tasks	0.04	0.05
Employee well-being	0.24***	0.24***
Personal income	0.10***	0.09***
Control	0.09**	0.09***
Independence	0.11***	0.10***
Survival of crises	0.09**	0.08*
Product/service quality	0.06*	0.05*
Manufacturing		–0.05
Service		0.00
5–9 employees		–0.05
10–19 employees		–0.06*
Old Firm		–0.07**
Female		–0.08***
Old entrepreneur		0.00
Adj. R^2	0.24	0.24

Note: Forced entry of independent variables is used. Standardized regression coefficients are displayed in the table. * = $p < 0.05$; ** = $p < 0.01$; *** = $p < 0.001$. Single-tailed test of significance is applied.

size brackets, age groups, or between men and women. Hence, the results appear to have a high degree of generality.

As mentioned earlier, data were collected from three different samples during a ten-year period. There are reasons to analyse the samples separately and compare the results. First, although statistically significant, effect sizes were generally small in the full sample. A comparison of results across samples makes it possible to check the stability of the results. If the results are the same for all three samples, conclusions will be more valid. Second, data were collected during different stages of the business cycle, which may affect the beliefs and attitudes of the respondents and their effects. Different explanatory variables may be important during different phases of the business cycle. A pure trend effect over time is also conceivable.

The results of the analyses of the three different samples are displayed in Table 6.6. Employee well-being is by far the most important explanatory variable in all samples, whereas the magnitude and rank order of all other explanatory variables vary. The joint probability measures illustrate that obtaining

Table 6.6 Linear regression results for the effect of expected consequences of growth on growth motivation for the three different samples

	1986 Sample n = 287	Rank order	1994 Sample n = 338	Rank order	1996 Sample n = 533	Rank order	Joint probability
Workload	0.11*	2	0.04	7	0.02	7	0.0015
Work tasks	0.04	7	0.15**	2	0.00	8	0.0003
Employee well-being	0.27***	1	0.19***	1	0.25***	1	0.0
Personal income	0.07	4	0.08	5	0.12**	4	0.000007
Control	0.10*	3	0.00	8	0.13**	2	0.00003
Independence	0.07	4	0.11*	3	0.13**	2	0.000004
Survival of crises	0.07	4	0.11*	3	0.06	5	0.0002
Product/service quality	0.04	7	0.08	5	0.03	6	0.04
Adj. R^2	0.23		0.20		0.23		

Note: Forced entry of independent variables is used. Standardized regression coefficients are displayed in the table.
$* = p < 0.05$; $** = p < 0.01$; $*** = p < 0.001$. Single-tailed test of significance is applied.

positive coefficients this large for any variable in all three samples is highly unlikely if there were no effects in the population. In all, the relationships are relatively stable overall, but not in detail. No clear cyclical or trend pattern emerges over this time period.

To further validate the findings, we assessed the extent to which results were stable across different contexts. Therefore, the samples from the three studies were combined and the control variables were used to subdivide the sample. This gives us a total of 12 regression analyses in this stage. The results from these regressions are displayed in Table 6.7. The adjusted explained variance ranges from 0.16 to 0.28, indicating that expected consequences have an influence on attitude toward growth in all regressions. The results reveal that noneconomic concerns are very important determinants of attitude toward growth. Personal income is not the most important variable in any regression, suggesting that money is not the most important motivator. A remarkably consistent result across the regressions is that employee well-being is the most important explanatory variable. This holds for 11 out of the 12 regressions, reinforcing the findings from the previous analyses. The exception is found among female entrepreneurs where independence comes out the strongest. The regression for the female subsample, however, is somewhat problematic, since it contains only 61 cases and should be interpreted more restrictively. Due to the small sample size, very large effects are needed in order to achieve statistically significant results even at the 0.05 level. As a comparison, while a regression coefficient of 0.06 is statistically significant among males, a 0.19 regression coefficient is not, among females.

Workload is relatively unimportant in all subsamples as is work-tasks, with the exception of young entrepreneurs and the smallest size bracket. The pattern concerning independence is the opposite; it has a statistically significant effect in all regressions except in the smallest size bracket.

Statistically significant standardized regression coefficients for the remaining explanatory variables have the same signs across all 12 analyses, indicating that the regressions are stable. However, their rank order and magnitude vary, depending on how the sample is divided. Interpretation of these coefficients should be restrictive. Considering the moderate explained variance and the magnitude of the employee well-being coefficient in all regressions, relatively little is explained by other variables in the regressions.

No fewer than 17 regression analyses have been performed to test the hypotheses. A summary of the outcomes of these tests is presented in Table 6.8. This table illustrates that the variables employee well-being, independence, personal income, control, and survival of crises generally receive the largest, and always positive standardized regression coefficients. These variables are also statistically significant on most instances. Thus, it is relatively safe to conclude that the hypotheses concerning the influence of employee

Table 6.7 Linear regression results for the effect of expected consequences of growth on growth motivation dividing the sample based on the contingencies industry, size, firm age, sex, and age

	Manuf n = 571	Service n = 340	Retail n = 246	5–9 emp n = 326	10–19 emp n = 479	20–49 emp n = 353	Old firms n = 771	Young firms n = 372	Male n = 1,096	Female n = 61	Old ent n = 569	Young ent n = 587
Workload	0.07*	0.08	0.00	0.07	0.08*	-0.01	0.07*	0.07	0.06*	-0.10	0.05	0.06
Work tasks	0.04	0.06	0.02	0.13**	0.05	-0.05	0.01	0.10*	0.06*	-0.16	-0.04	0.12**
Employee well-being	0.23***	0.27***	0.23***	0.30***	0.17***	0.29***	0.28***	0.22**	0.25***	0.13	0.24***	0.25***
Personal income	0.10**	0.10*	0.10*	0.11*	0.06	0.13**	0.12***	0.05	0.10**	0.19	0.11**	0.09**
Control	0.08*	0.10*	0.08	0.07	0.12**	0.08	0.10**	0.04	0.09***	0.19	0.12**	0.06
Independence	0.11**	0.09*	0.14*	0.02	0.15***	0.13**	0.10**	0.13**	0.09***	0.30*	0.14***	0.08*
Survival of crises	0.09*	0.10*	0.04*	0.07	0.07	0.13**	0.09**	0.06	0.09**	0.06	0.05	0.12**
Product/service quality	0.06	0.04	0.09	0.06	0.09*	0.00	0.03	0.11*	0.05	0.06	0.06	0.04
Adj. R²	0.22	0.28	0.16	0.26	0.24	0.21	0.25	0.20	0.24	0.16	0.21	0.26

Note: Forced entry of independent variables is used. Standardized regression coefficients are displayed in the table. * = $p < 0.05$; ** = $p < 0.01$; *** = $p <$ 0.001. Single-tailed test of significance is applied.

Table 6.8   *Summary of the results of the hypothesis tests from a total of 17 regression equations*

	Range of the standardized regression coefficient	Total number of regressions with positive regression coefficient (out of 17)	Total number of statistically significant occurrences (out of 17)
Workload	–0.01 to 0.11	15	7
Work tasks	–0.16 to 0.13	14	5
Employee well-being	0.13 to 0.29	17	16
Personal income	0.05 to 0.19	17	12
Control	0.00 to 0.19	17	10
Independence	0.02 to 0.15	17	15
Survival of crises	0.04 to 0.13	17	9
Product/service quality	0.00 to 0.11	17	4

well-being (H3), independence (H6), personal income (H4), control (H5), and survival of crises (H7) on attitude toward growth are supported by the data. Regarding the three remaining hypotheses, results are more mixed and they do not get equally consistent support by the data. Therefore, even if the bulk of the evidence is in favor of the hypotheses, it must be concluded that for most of the respondents, expected consequences of growth concerning workload (H1), work tasks (H2), and quality (H8) do not have an important influence on attitude toward growth.

DISCUSSION

Explaining Growth Attitude

In this chapter, we set out to examine how small-business managers' overall attitude toward growth was influenced by the consequences they expected from growth. In doing that, we used data from three separate survey studies employing the same measuring instruments. This allowed us to come up with many useful comparisons. Some results recur very consistently across subanalyses and can therefore be accepted even if the associated probability of the coefficient is not very low in every analysis. Other results, while 'statistically significant' in one analysis, may be disregarded because the result appears in isolation. The general approach – to repeat the same measurement in several separate surveys – is something we would highly recommend to other researchers. Results from multiple samples are a much better basis for determining one's degree of confidence, than is significance testing alone.

On average, our regression models could explain close to 25 per cent of the variation in attitude toward growth in our different subgroups. This shows that there are substantial, general relationships between expected consequences of growth and attitude toward growth. In other words, small-business managers' feelings about whether the growth of their business is good or bad can, to a reasonable extent, be explained on the basis of the consequences that they expect from growth.

Nonetheless, over three-quarters of the variance is left unexplained by our models, and the reasons for this deserve some discussion. A first possibility is, of course, that important explanatory variables were omitted. Perhaps other expected consequences of growth are important and therefore should have been included. Our selection of explanatory variables was based on a thorough literature review as well as elicited in an open-ended procedure. Consequently, we regard it highly unlikely that any additional more important variables of this kind are to be found. The control variables we have used are also the most important ones in previous research on small-firm growth. Therefore, the 'add variables' route is unlikely to raise explained variance by more than a few percentage points. Further, our results are similar to what have been reported in previous studies (explained variance of 10 per cent to 36 per cent would be typical according to Ajzen, 1991).

The most important reason for the modest explanatory power is instead, arguably, the fact that regression coefficients represent *average* effects. According to expectancy-value theory, there is reason to believe that the true effect for each individual differs from this average (Ajzen and Fishbein, 1980; Bagozzi, 1985). For some managers quality is a great concern, whereas for others their own workload is the top-of-the-mind issue. This fact, that is, that the coefficients represent average effects, is a general problem in this type of research and probably the major reason that explanatory power rarely reaches much higher values than ours even when seemingly all relevant variables have been included. The second major reason is that measurement error is substantial, because the questions do not have exactly the same meaning to each respondent and because people differ in their response styles. Thus, very strong relationships between the independent and dependent variables should perhaps not be expected. We regard our modest explanatory power as a result of these general problems, rather than the omission of important explanatory variables.

Relative Importance of Different Beliefs

Turning to a more detailed assessment of our results, a central finding is that expectation of financial gain is not the outstanding determinant of attitude toward growth. This is clearly contrary to economic theory, but also to normative management theories where the motivation to grow is taken for granted, based on financial outcome being the primary concern of the manager. Our findings suggest that other expected outcomes of growth that are largely noneconomic in nature also influence attitude toward growth. This includes, for example, beliefs concerning the effect of growth on the managers' ability to keep full control over the operations of the firm, the firm's degree of independence in relation to external stakeholders, and its ability to survive crises. The effects are generally not very strong. However, while not always statistically significant according to conventional criteria, they appear very consistently with the same sign across samples, industries, size classes, and age groups. What this means is probably that the effects are real, but they are small because each type of expected outcome has a substantial effect on attitude toward growth only for some managers, whereas it is relatively uninfluential for others. Hence the modest average effect represented by the regression coefficients. This illustrates the strength of our combining data from three studies using the same instruments. In a single and perhaps smaller study, each and every one of these effects may have been disregarded as 'not statistically significant, therefore nonexistent' – a very common practice among social scientists. The same would probably have happened had three different studies used different instruments to assess the same theoretical relationships. With our 'same instrument, multiple samples' approach, we can conclude with confidence that these expectations do have effects on attitude toward growth.

Our most important finding is that expectations concerning the effect of growth on employee well-being is the single most important determinant of overall attitude toward growth. This result stands out with impressive consistency across samples, industries, size classes, and age groups. The important question is, of course, exactly what this means. The very translation of the Swedish original is tricky. While no fully satisfactory translation to English presents itself, the reader might find it informative that the Swedish wording is likely to evoke associations to camaraderie, comfort, atmosphere, and job satisfaction.

Several interpretations are possible. A critical mind would perhaps like to dismiss the result as not really showing that small-business managers' great concern for their employees affects their attitude toward growth. Rather, one might argue, is this variable picked as their scapegoat for less socially desirable reasons to refrain from growing their firms larger. However, additional analyses performed suggest that the variable works both ways. That is, some managers believe that growth will improve employee well-being, and this enhances their attitude toward growth. Another reason for not dismissing the result in this way is that there are other expected outcomes, most notably product/service quality, that would be an equally logical candidate for a social desirability effect.

However, we would agree that it is not unlikely that the managers also have their own well-being in mind when answering the question. A sound interpretation is probably that the result reflects a real concern for the 'soft' qualities associated with small scale, and that this concern is justifiable. There is research to suggest that regarding issues like comradeship, involvement, and job satisfaction, employees and people in general think highly of small firms (Curran et al., 1993; Davidsson, 1993). Even more impressive evidence for the 'soft' advantages of a small scale is presented in the classical study by Barker and Gump (1964; cf. also their extensive references to other studies). Therefore, the small-business manager may have a very real reason to be concerned about the atmosphere of the small firm when faced with expansion opportunities. The generality of our finding in the subanalyses suggests that this concern is a source of a recurrent goal/conflict for many small-business managers.

Limitations and Future Research

The issue of work atmosphere and employee well-being is worthy of further research efforts. One aspect of this would be to assess whether the concern for employee well-being and its effect on attitude toward growth is a cultural peculiarity of Sweden (or perhaps the Scandinavian countries), or if it is more universal. While both outcomes of such an assessment are conceivable, the review of classical works as well as more recent research suggests that a very high concern for employees is not unheard of in other cultures (cf. Kazumi et al., 1996). Future research should also try to capture in more detail what the 'concern for employee well-being' really encompasses; whether it affects real growth and not only attitude toward growth; if managers who have successfully led their companies through a growth phase also felt such concerns before the expansion; whether their expectations were accurate; and what they might have done to counteract the possible negative effects of growth on employee well-being.

Our study has been about attitude toward growth, not actual growth. Whether attitude toward growth – as measured here – has an influence on actual growth or not is an empirical question that remains to be answered. In accordance with previous studies (cf. above), we would hypothesize that such is the case. In order to find out, longitudinal research is needed where attitude toward growth is measured at one point of time and actual growth outcomes are measured later.

A potential limitation to the results presented here has to do with common method variance. While common method variance problems in survey research seem to have been overstated (Crampton and Wagner, 1994), they cannot be neglected (Lindell and Whitney, 2001). The favoring of telephone interviews over mail questionnaires probably reduces common variance, but does not eliminate the risk that reported relationships may be somewhat inflated.

Conclusions and Implications

Beliefs play an important role in understanding why people act the way they do. According to expectancy-value theory, behavior is a function of beliefs relevant to the behavior. Salient beliefs are considered to be the determinants of a person's intentions and actions (Ajzen, 1991). In our research, small-business managers' beliefs about the consequences of growth have provided insights into the reasons that they think that expanding their business is a good or a bad thing. One interesting finding is that noneconomic concerns are more important than the possibility of personal economic gain or loss. Of particular importance is the well-being of the employees, which probably encompasses concerns for the work atmosphere of the small firm in general. Managers who believe that the work atmosphere will improve due to growth tend to have a positive attitude toward growth. Conversely, those who expect that growth will deteriorate the work atmosphere tend to have a negative attitude toward growth.

To some extent, these expectations are probably well founded. The work atmosphere will probably be affected by growth. On the other hand, it is possible for the small-business manager to influence the work atmosphere in order to avoid possible negative consequences. Active measures for introducing newcomers and building a sound company culture can be taken to this effect (cf. Hambrick and Crozier, 1985). If managed correctly, growth can be associated with new challenges and development opportunities for staff rather than loss of direction or alienation.

Like other beliefs, beliefs about consequences of growth can be influenced by the persuasive argumentation of others (Chaiken and Stangor, 1987). If relevant information about the positive consequences of growth – and methods to circumvent negative effects – were made available to small-business managers, this could lead to a more positive attitude toward growth. Information about the positive effects on work atmosphere and ways of mitigating potential negative consequences may affect growth motivation more than would prospects of increased personal income.

NOTES

*   Previously published as: Wiklund, J., P. Davidsson and F. Delmar (2003), 'What do they think and feel about growth: An expectancy-value approach to small business managers' attitudes towards growth', *Entrepreneurship Theory and Practice*, **27**(3), 247–69.
1.   This research was made possible through generous grants by Knut and Alice Wallenberg's Foundation, Jan Wallander's Foundation, Ruben Rausing's Foundation, and the Swedish Foundation for International Cooperation in Research and Higher Education. An earlier version of the chapter received the Best Paper Award at the 1997 Babson College/Kauftman Foundation Entrepreneurship Research Conference and appears in *Frontiers in Entrepreneurship Research*, 1997.
2.   A meta-analysis of the studies finds a weighted average correlation of 0.39 between motivation and growth.
3.   For the purpose of testing the properties of our measure, an index was created. The 'intended ideal size five years ahead' responses and present-size figures were used to calculate intended growth rates of both sales and employees and converted to two seven-point scales. The two items from the 25 per cent and the 100 per cent scales were summed with these two items to form a global growth intention index. The Cronbach's Alpha value of the index was 0.72 and corrected item-total correlations range from 0.47 to 0.55 indicating that the index has acceptable reliability (Nunnally, 1967) and that all items share sufficient variance with the index (Nunnally and Bernstein, 1994). This index was also successfully used in predicting actual growth outcomes in another study (Wiklund and Shepherd, 2003). This suggests that our measure is (1) sufficiently reliable and (2) predictively valid (Nunnally and Bernstein, 1994). We therefore feel confident in relying on this single item measure for our dependent variable.
4.   Due to space limitations, individual figures are not reported. An examination of the variance inflation factor (VIF) suggests that there was no incidence of multicollinearity. Individual figures range from 1.08 to 1.45, which is well below critical values (cf. Hair, Anderson, Tatham and Black, 1998).

REFERENCES

Ajzen, I. (1988), *Attitudes, Personality, and Behavior*, Chicago: Dorsey Press.

Ajzen, I. (1991), 'The theory of planned behavior', *Organizational Behavior and Human Decision Processes*, **50**, 179–211.

Ajzen, I. and M. Fishbein (1977), 'Attitude-behavior relations: a theoretical analysis and review of empirical research', *Psychological Bulletin*, **84**, 888–918.

Ajzen, I. and M. Fishbein (1980), *Understanding Attitudes and Predicting Behavior*, Englewood Cliffs, NJ: Prentice Hall.

Aldrich, H. and E.R. Auster (1990), 'Even dwarfs started small: liabilities of age and size and their strategic implications', in B.M. Staw and L.L. Cummings (eds), *The Evolution and Adaptation of Organizations*, 33–66. Greenwich, CT: JAI Press.

Audretsch, D.B. (1995), 'Innovation, growth and survival', *International Journal of Industrial Organization*, **13**, 441–57.

Bagozzi, R.P. (1984), 'Expectancy-value attitude models: an analysis of critical measurement issues', *International Journal of Research in Marketing*, **1**, 295–310.

Bagozzi, R.P. (1985), 'Expectancy-value attitude models: an analysis of critical theoretical issues', *International Journal of Research in Marketing*, **2**, 43–60.

Bagozzi, R.P. and P.R. Warshaw (1992), 'An examination of the etiology of the attitude-behavior relation for goal-directed behaviors', *Multivariate Behavioral Research*, **27**(4), 601–34.

Barker, R.G. and P.N. Gump (1964), *Big School, Small School*, 1st edn, Stanford, CA: Stanford University Press.

Barkham, R.J. (1994), 'Entrepreneurial characteristics and the size of the new firm: a model and an econometric test', *Small Business Economics*, **6**, 117–25.

Bellu, R.R. and H. Sherman (1995), 'Predicting firm success from task motivation and attributional style. A longitudinal study', *Entrepreneurship and Regional Development*, 349–63.

Bolton, J.E. (1971), *Small Firms. Report of the Committee of Inquiry on Small Firms*, London: Her Majesty's Stationery Office.

Boswell, J. (1972), *The Rise and Decline of Small Firms*, London: Allen & Unwin.

Brush, C.G. (1992), 'Research on women business owners: past trends, a new perspective and future directions', *Entrepreneurship Theory and Practice*, **16**(4), 5–30.

Campbell, D.T. and W. Fiske (1959), 'Convergent and discriminant validation by the multitrait-multimethod matrix', *Psychological Bulletin*, **56**, 81–105.

Carroll, G. and M.T. Hannan (2000). *The Demography of Corporations and Industries*, Princeton, NJ: Princeton University Press,

Chaiken, S. and C. Stangor (1987), 'Attitudes and attitude changes', *Annual Review of Psychology*, **38**, 575–630.

Cohen, J. (1994), 'The earth is round (p < 0.05)', *American Psychologist*, **47**(12), 997–1003.

Cohen, J. and P. Cohen (1983), *Applied Multiple Regression/Correlation Analysis for the Behavioral Sciences*, 2nd edn, Hillsdale, NJ: Lawrence Erlbaum Associates.

Crampton, S.M. and J.A. Wagner III (1994), 'Percept-percept inflation in microorganizational research: an investigation of prevalence and effect', *Journal of Applied Psychology*, **79**(1), 67–76.

Curran, J., J. Kitching, B. Abbott and V. Mills (1993), *Employment and Employment Relations in the Small Service Sector Enterprise – A Report*, Kingston, UK: ESRC Centre for Research on Small Service Sector Enterprises, Kingston Business School.

Davidsson, P. (1987), 'Growth willingness in small firms: entrepreneurship – and after', report no. 224, Stockholm: EFI.

Davidsson, P. (1989a), 'Continued entrepreneurship and small firm growth', doctoral dissertation prepared for the Stockholm School of Economics.

Davidsson, P. (1989b), 'Entrepreneurship – and after? A study of growth willingness in small firms', *Journal of Business Venturing*, **4**, 211–26.

Davidsson, P. (1993), *Folket on företagandet [People on Enterprise]*, FE-publikationer 143, Emeå: Handelshögskolan i Umeå.

Davidsson, P., L. Lindmark and C. Olofsson (1994), *Dynamiken i svenskt näringsliv [Business Dynamics in Sweden]*, Lund, Sweden: Studentlitteratur.

Davidsson, P., L. Lindmark and C. Olofsson (1996), *Näringslivsdynamik under 90-talet [Business Dynamics in the '90s]*, Stockholm: Nutek.

Davidsson, P. and J. Wiklund (2000), Conceptual and empirical challenges in the study of firm growth', in D. Sexton and H. Landström (eds), *The Blackwell Handbook of Entrepreneurship*, 26–44, Oxford, UK: Blackwell (Chapter 3 in this volume).

Davis, S.J. and M. Henrekson (1999), 'Explaining national differences in the size and industry distribution of employment', *Small Business Economics*, **12**, 59–83.

Deaux, K. and M. Lafrance (1988), 'Gender', in D.T. Gilbert, S.T. Fiske and G. Lindzey (eds), *The Handbook of Social Psychology*, Boston: McGraw-Hill, pp. 788–827.

Deeks, J. (1976), *The Small Firm Owner-Manager: Entrepreneurial Behavior and Management Practice*, New York: Praeger.

Delmar, F. (1996), 'Entrepreneurial behavior and business performance', doctoral dissertation prepared for Stockholm School of Economics.

Delmar, F. (1997), 'Measuring growth: methodological considerations and empirical results', in R. Donckels and A. Miettinen (eds), *Entrepreneurship and SME Research: On its Way to the Next Millennium*, Aldershot, VA: Avebury, pp. 190–216 (Chapter 4 in this volume).

Delmar F. (2000), 'The psychology of the entrepreneur', in S. Carter and D. Jones-Evans (eds), *Enterprise and Small Business: Principles, Practice and Policies*, Harlow: Pearson Education, pp. 132–54.

Dunne, P. and A. Hughes (1996), 'Age, size, growth and survival: UK companies in the 1980s', *Journal of Industrial Economics*, **XLII**(2), 115–40.

Eagly, A.H. and S. Chaiken (1993), *The Psychology of Attitudes*, Orlando, FL: Harcourt Brace Jovanovich.

Epstein, S. (1984), 'A procedural note on the measurement of broad dispositions', *Journal of Personality*, **52**, 318–25.

Fishbein, M. (1967), 'Attitude and the prediction of behavior', in M. Fishbein (ed.), *Readings in Attitude Theory and Measurement*, New York: Wiley, pp. 477–92.

Fishbein, M. and I. Ajzer (1975), *Belief, Attitude, Intention, and Behavior: An Introduction to Theory and Research*, Reading, MA: Addison-Wesley.

Flamholtz, E.G. (1986), *Managing the Transition from an Entrepreneurship to a Professionally Managed Firm*, San Francisco: Jossey-Bass.

Gundry, L.K. and H.P. Welsch (2001), 'The ambitious entrepreneur: high growth strategies of women-owner enterprises', *Journal of Business Venturing*, **16**, 453–70.

Hair, J.F., R.E. Anderson, R.L. Tatham and W.C. Black (1998), *Multivariate Data Analysis*, 5th edn, Upper Saddle River, NJ: Prentice Hall.

Hambrick, D.C. and L.M. Crozier (1985), 'Stumblers and stars in the management of rapid growth', *Journal of Business Venturing*, 1(1), 31–45.

Hubbard, R., D.E. Vetter and E.L. Little, 'Replication in strategic management: scientific testing for validity, generalizability, and usefulness', *Strategic Management Journal*, **19**, 243–54.

Kazumi, T., Y. Sato, A. Nishikori, N. Kurose and Y. Sato (1996), 'The entrepeneurial spirit in Japan: a recent assessment', paper prepared for 16th Babson College Entrepreneurship Research Conference, Seattle, WA, 5–7 June.

Kim, M.-S. and J.E. Hunter (1993), ' "Attitude-behavior" relations: a meta-analysis of attitudinal relevance and topic', *Journal of Communication*, **43**(1), 101–42.

Kirchhoff, B.A. (1994), *Entrepreneurship and Dynamic Capitalism: The Economics of Business Firm Formation and Growth*, Westport: CT: Praeger.

Kolvereid, L. (1992), 'Growth aspirations among Norwegian entrepreneurs', *Journal of Business Venturing*, 7, 209–22.

Kolvereid, L. and E. Bullvåg (1996), 'Growth intentions and actual growth: the impact of entrepreneurial choice', *Journal of Enterprising Culture*, **4**(1), 1–17.

Lindell, M.K. and D.J. Whitney (2001), 'Accounting for common method variance in cross-sectional research designs', *Journal of Applied Psychology*, **86**(1), 114–21.

Lindsay, R.M. and A.S.C. Ehrenberg (1993), 'The design of replicated studies', *The American Statistician*, **47**(August), 217–28.

Locke, E.A. (1991), 'Introduction', *Organizational Behavior and Human Decision Making*, special issue, **50**, 151–53.

Miner, J.B., N.R. Smith and J.S. Bracker, 'Role of entrepreneurial task motivation in the growth of technologically innovative firms: interpretations from follow-up data', *Journal of Applied Psychology*, **79**(4), 627–30.

Mok, A.L. and H. van den Tillaart (1990), 'Farmers and small businessmen: a comparative analysis of their careers and occupational orientation', in R. Donckels and A. Miettinen (eds), *New Findings and Perspectives in Entrepreneurship*, Aldershot, VA: Avebury, pp. 203–30.

Nunnally, J.C. (1967), *Psychometric Theory*, New York: McGraw-Hill.

Nunnally, J.C. and I.H. Bernstein (1994), *Psychometric Theory*, 3rd edn, New York: McGraw-Hill.

Olson, J.M. and M.P. Zana (1993), 'Attitudes and attitude change', *Annual Review of Psychology*, **44**, 117–54.

Petty, R.E., D.T. Wegener and L.R. Fabrigan (1997), 'Attitudes and attitude change', *Annual Review of Psychology*, **48**, 609–47.

Pieters, R.G.M. (1988), 'Attitude-behavior relationships', in W.F. van Raaij, G.M. van Veldshoven and K.E. Wärneryd (eds), *Handbook of Economic Psychology*, Dordrecht: Kluwer, pp. 108–42.

Reynolds, P.D. and S.B. White (1997), *The Entrepreneurial Process: Economic Growth, Men, Women, and Minorities*, Westport, CT: Quorum Books.

Robinson, K.C. and C.W. Hofer (1997), 'A methodological investigation of the validity and usefulness of parametric and nonparametric statistical data analysis techniques for new venture research', in *Frontiers of Entrepreneurship Research*, Wellesley, MA: Babson College, pp. 692–705.

Robinson, P.B., D.V. Stimpson, J.C. Huefer and H.K. Hunt (1991), 'An attitude approach to the prediction of entrepreneurship', *Entrepreneurship Theory and Practice*, **9**(4), 13–31.

Scott, M. and P. Rosa (1996), 'Opinion: has firm level analysis reached its limits? Time for a rethink', *International Small Business Journal*, **14**(4) 81–9.

Shapiro, S.S. and M.B. Wilk (1965), 'An analysis of variance test for normality (for complete samples)', *Biometrica*, **52**, 591–611.

Smith, N.R. (1967), *The Entrepreneur and His Firm: The Relationship between Type of Man and Type of Company*, East Lansing, MI: Michigan State University.

Stanworth, M.J. and J. Curran (1973), *Management Motivation in the Smaller Business*, Epping: Gower Press.

Stimpson, D.V., P.B. Robinson, S. Waranusuntikule and R. Zheng (1990), 'Attitudinal characteristics of entrepreneurs and non-entrepreneurs in the United States, Korea, Thailand, and the People's Republic of China', *Entrepreneurship and Regional Development*, **2**, 49–55.

Storey, D.J. (1994), *Understanding the Small Business Sector*, London: Routledge.

Storey, D.J. (1996), *The Ten Percenters*, London: Deloitte & Touche.

Thurstone, L.L. (1931), 'Measurement of social attitudes', *Journal of Abnormal and Social Psychology*, **26**, 249–69.

Valiquette, C.A., P. Valios, R. Desharnais and G. Godin (1988), 'An item-analytic investigation of the Fishbein and Ajzen multiplicative scale: the problem of a simultaneous negative evaluation of belief and outcome', *Psychological Reports*, **63**, 723–28.

Wiklund, J. (1998), 'Small firm growth and performance: entrepreneurship and beyond', doctoral dissertation prepared for Jönköping International Business School.

Wiklund, J., P. Davidsson, F. Delmar and M. Aronsson (1997), 'Expected consequences of growth and their effect on growth willingness in different samples of small firms', in P.D. Reynolds, W.D. Bygrave, N.M. Carter, P. Davidsson, W.B. Gartner, C.M. Mason and P.P. McDougall (eds), *Frontiers of Entrepreneurship Research*, Wellesley, MA: Babson College, pp. 1–16.

Wiklund, J. and D.A. Shepherd (2003), 'Aspiring for, and achieving growth: the moderating role of resources and opportunities', *Journal of Management Studies*, **40**(8), 1911–41.

PART III

Patterns and Determinants of Actual Growth

7. The sustainability of the entrepreneurial orientation–performance relationship

Johan Wiklund

INTRODUCTION

Entrepreneurship is presently a very popular term and there is a tendency to regard entrepreneurship as something inherently good, something firms should always pursue. This may bias us to favor anecdotal evidence in favor of, rather than against, a positive relationship between entrepreneurial activities and firm performance. Dess, Lumpkin and Covin (1997) observe a strong normative bias toward the inherent value of entrepreneurship and suggest that the popular press encourages the belief that entrepreneurship is good. As a result, managers may experience considerable pressures to behave more entrepreneurially in order to improve or maintain the performance of their firms.

Before encouraging wholesale adoption of an entrepreneurial strategic orientation (referred to as EO), more solid empirical evidence on the link between entrepreneurship and performance must be presented. One of the major issues in such an assessment is the sustainability of the EO-performance relationship. Currently, we do not know if EO affects performance over an extended period of time or if it is a 'quick fix' where performance is temporarily affected. This is an important gap in the literature because EO is claimed to be a resource-consuming strategic orientation requiring extensive investments by the firm (Covin and Slevin, 1991). Firms will benefit from knowing whether EO leads to sustained high performance or only has a short-term effect.

Several authors point to the lack of systematic empirical evidence that EO actually leads to improved firm performance (Covin and Slevin, 1991; Sexton and Bowman-Upton, 1991; Zahra, 1991). Hart (1992) sees possible negative consequences of EO and hypothesizes that entrepreneurial and intrapreneurial strategy-making modes are likely to lead to lower rather than higher performance because of role imbalances between top management and organizational members. More recently, however, empirical evidence for an EO to improve company performance has started to mount (for example Brown, 1996; Junehed and Davidsson, 1998; Namen and Slevin, 1993). This evidence is also based on longitudinal evidence (Wiklund, 1998a; Zahra and Covin, 1995). As a result, we may have some confidence in a positive relationship between EO and performance. Still, the sustainability of the relationship remains to be determined.

This study examines the sustainability of the EO–performance relationship. In particular, the study explores the influence of EO on a company using a large, longitudinal data set of small Swedish firms. The study examines this relationship, controlling for company age, size, and industry type. The study also controls for environmental dynamism and capital availability.

THEORY AND HYPOTHESES

The Effect of EO on Company Performance

Although much of the empirical entrepreneurship research has focused on the individual level of analysis, researchers recently have focused on entrepreneurship as firm-level behavior. Much of this research has been based on Miller's work (1983). Miller suggested that firms' degree of entrepreneurship could be seen as the extent to which they innovate, take risks, and act proactively. These were the three 'entrepreneurial' dimensions of strategy out of a total of 11 such dimensions discussed by Miller and Friesen (1978).

A focus on innovation, proactiveness. and risk taking is used in this study to refer to a company's entrepreneurial orientation (EO). This emphasizes the process of entrepreneurship rather than the actors (managers) behind it (cf. Gartner, 1988; Shapero and Sokol, 1982) and has some important implications. First, these proactive, innovative, and risk-taking actions taken by a firm may be affected by any number of actors inside or outside the firm. Second, emphasizing actions taken by the firm puts entrepreneurship in a management framework. By doing so, correlates of entrepreneurship could be sought in a much wider field than that directly related to the individual. The study of EO allows the introduction of traditional management terminology and variables such as strategy, performance. and organizational structure into entrepreneurship research.

Miller (1983) has also developed a scale to empirically measure these dimensions. Covin and Slevin (1986, 1989) have subsequently extended and refined this instrument. Wiklund (1998a) has identified no fewer than 12 studies based on Miller's and Covin and Slevin's instruments. These studies suggest that this measure is a viable instrument for capturing firm-level entrepreneurship.

Despite the success and popularity of Miller's and Covin and Slevin's oper-ationalization, this measurement scale has its weaknesses. Researchers disagree on how to label the scale and what type of concept it really represents (cf., Brown and Davidsson, 1998; Wiklund, 1998a, 1998b). This is probably because the actual items represent a mix of past behaviors and current atti-tudes. However, given the agreement that Miller's conceptualization captures a wide gamut of a company's entrepreneurial activities, this definition and its measures are used in this chapter to gauge EO.

The relationship between EO and performance has inspired discussion in the literature. One important message from past results is the need to control for company and environmental factors in theorizing about this relationship (Covin and Slevin, 1991; Zahra, 1993a, 1993b). There are some empirical as well as conceptual arguments to suggest that EO is not equally suitable in all environ-ments (Covin and Slevin, 1989; Miller and Friesen, 1982; Zahra, 1993b), Therefore, interaction effects should also be investigated. Similarly, an interac-tion effect between EO and capital availability is also possible (cf. Bamford, Dean and McDougall, 1997). However, when such interaction effects were examined in a previous study, none was found (see Wiklund, 1998a). Therefore, only independent effects are investigated in the present chapter.

The thrust of the argument for a positive influence of EO on performance is related to the first-mover advantages and the tendency to take advantage of emerging opportunities implied by EO. Zahra and Covin (1995) hold that firms with EO can target premium market segments, charge high prices and 'skim' the market ahead of their competitors. These firms monitor market changes and respond quickly, thus capitalizing on emerging opportunities. Innovation keeps them ahead of their competitors, gaining a competitive advantage that leads to improved financial results. Proactiveness gives firms the ability to present new products/services to the market ahead of competi-tors, which also gives them a competitive advantage. Further, there is a reason to believe that the relationship between EO and performance may be particu-larly strong among small firms such as those studied here. Most likely, small-ness per se fosters flexibility and innovation but limits competitiveness in other strategic dimensions. Resource constraints may prevent small firms from pursuing cost leadership or differentiation strategies (Porter, 1985). This suggests the following hypothesis:

Hypothesis 1: EO is positively associated with small firm performance.

Some research also suggests that the effect of EO on performance is, long-term, rather than short-term, in nature. Proactive firms can introduce new goods and services ahead of their competitors. As first-movers they can control access to the market by dominating distribution channels. Further, by introducing their products or services ahead of competitors, they can – if successful – establish industry standards. These actions should help first-movers to acquire sustained rather than temporary high performance (Zahra and Covin, 1995). This logic has been supported by empirical findings. For example, Zahra (1991) found a positive and growing correlation between corporate entrepreneurship and performance during three consecutive years. Zahra and Covin (1995) produced more solid findings and were able to show that EO influenced performance during each of the five years studied. The influence of EO on performance in their study increased over time.

These are important findings concerning the long-term effects of EO. However, investments in EO could be evaluated like any other investment: in terms of time to breakeven or total payoff. Thus, in this study it is argued that the compound performance effect of EO (that is, the sustainability) provides more valuable information than does the evaluation of its influence on annual performance. Accordingly, the relationship between EO and performance over a two-year period is compared with the relationship over a one-year period. The long-term, sustainable nature of the EO–performance relationship suggests the following hypothesis:

Hypothesis 2: The EO-performance relationship will increase as the time frame over which performance is studied is extended from one year to two years.

Suitable Indicators of Performance

There is no consensus on the appropriate measures of small firm performance, and prior research has focused on variables for which information is easy to gather (Cooper, 1995). Researchers advocate growth as the most important performance measure in small firms (for example, Brown, 1996; Brush and Vanderwerf, 1992; Chandler and Hanks, 1993; Fombrun and Wally, 1989; Tsai, MacMillan and Low, 1991). It is also argued that growth is a more accurate and easily accessible performance indicator than accounting measures and hence superior to indicators of financial performance. An alternative view is that performance is multidimensional in nature and that it is advantageous to integrate different dimensions of performance in empirical studies (for example, Cameron, 1978; Lumpkin and Dess, 1996). It is possible to regard financial performance and growth as different aspects of performance, each revealing important and unique information. A firm could, for instance, choose to trade off long-term growth for short-term profitability (Zahra, 1991). Taken together, growth and financial performance give a richer description of the actual performance of the firm than each does separately.

The extent to which performance along one dimension affects the other is an empirical question that should be tested. It is important to determine if firms that grow also perform well financially, rather than *a priori* stating that growing firms perform well because performance was defined this way. The degree of correspondence between growth and financial performance determines to what extent they are related.

Hoy, McDougall and D'Souza (1992) stress that a consensus has been reached among researchers that sales growth is the best growth measure. It reflects both short- and long-term changes in the firm, and is easily obtainable. Furthermore, these authors, as well as Barkham, Gudgin, Hart and Hanvey (1996), maintain that entrepreneurs consider sales growth to be the most common performance indicator.

The growth process as such provides further arguments for advocating sales growth. The growth process is likely to be driven by increased demand for the firm's products or services. That is, sales increase first, thus allowing for the acquisition of additional resources such as employees or machinery (Flamholtz, 1986). It seems unlikely that growth in other dimensions could take place without increasing sales. It is also possible to increase sales without acquiring additional resources or employing additional staff, by outsourcing the increased business volumes. In this case, only sales would increase. Thus, sales growth has a high generality.

On the other hand, there is widespread interest in the creation of new employment. This makes employment growth another important aspect to capture. In a process of rationalization, it is possible to replace employees with capital investments. In other words, there is to some extent an inverse relationship between capital investment and employment growth. As a consequence, assets are another important aspect of growth. Measuring growth in terms of assets is often considered problematic in the service sector (for example Weinzimmer, Nystrom and Freeman, 1998), appearing to be mainly an accounting problem. While intangible assets indeed may expand in a growing service firm, this is not reflected in the firm's balance sheet. Thus, the problem of studying growing assets in service industries is related to difficulty in data collection rather than lack of relevance.

When assessing performance, comparisons of competing firms in the market reveal important supplementary information (Birley and Westhead, 1990). Such measures give information on whether firms are simply pulled along by market trends or if they show growth patterns that deviate substantially from their industry in general.

In summary, previous research suggests that performance measures should consider both growth and financial performance. Moreover, performance should also be related to the performance of competitors. When growth is studied, the expansion of sales, employment, and assets all provide important and complementary information. Therefore, in testing the hypotheses, the study will use several indicators of small company performance.

RESEARCH DESIGN AND SAMPLE

Sample

To test the relationships between EO and company performance, data were collected from a large sample of small Swedish firms during three consecutive years. Information on EO was collected the first year and performance data the following two years.

The data for the study were collected in 1996, 1997, and 1998. The first year a telephone interview was followed by a mail questionnaire concerning the independent variables. One year after the initial study, a shorter telephone interview was conducted where performance data were collected. This procedure was repeated the next year. This makes the study longitudinal, and more precisely, a panel study.

The sample was stratified over the Swedish equivalents of ISIC codes. Small firms from specific manufacturing, service, and retail industries were selected. The sample was also stratified over the standard Swedish size brackets of 10–19 and 20–49 employees. Further, the sample was stratified over the firms' growth rate so that the share of high-growth firms was over-represented in the sample for both size brackets and all industries. Data were collected from the firms' managing directors because of their knowledge of the companies' operations.

Out of the 808 firms included in the initial sample, 630 were interviewed by telephone in April and May 1996, resulting in a response rate of 78 per cent. Next, 465 firms (a response rate of 58 per cent) returned completed mail questionnaires. These 465 firms were approached again for a telephone interview one year later. A total of 447 responded, which equals 96 per cent of the remaining firms from the previous year and 55 per cent of the original sample. In 1998, this procedure was repeated, resulting in 420 respondents, equaling 94 per cent of the remaining firms from the previous year and 52 per cent of the original sample. The response rate during the two latter survey rounds was high. Firms where the managing director had been replaced during the studied period were excluded from the analyses since it seems perilous to attribute outcomes of a firm to an individual no longer working there. A total of 34 cases (8 per cent) were excluded because of this reason.

Unfortunately, not all managing directors were able or willing to report complete data during all four surveys. It was difficult to obtain answers to all performance questions. Only those that responded to all questions in all four survey rounds were used in the analyses reported in this chapter. This reduces the effective sample size to 132 cases, corresponding to 16 per cent of the original sample.

Measures

Entrepreneurial orientation. In the present study, Miller's (1983) original scale (see Miller and Friesen, 1982) consisting of eight items is used to measure EO. The Cronbach's Alpha value of the scale is 0.64.

Performance. In order to obtain a multi-faceted performance measure reflecting growth and financial performance, as well as comparisons with competitors, a seven-item scale was developed. The performance construct is made up of three financial performance indicators along with four measures of growth. Despite the breadth of the scale, the alignment among the seven indicators is relatively high. The Cronbach Alpha value for the performance during 1997 was 0.73. The corresponding figure for the compound 1997–98 period was somewhat higher, 0.75.

Four of the items comparing the respondents' firms with competitors are original, developed in collaboration with two colleagues and previously tested on a large sample of firms. The three remaining items are self-explanatory, calculated from size and profit figures. The performance questions were asked in 1997 and repeated in 1998. In order to calculate the compound performance for the two-year period, the annual figures concerning each item were averaged before summation.

Four indicators of growth were utilized: sales growth, employment growth, sales growth compared with competitors, and market value growth compared with competitors. The annual sales growth rate was calculated from present size figures from the two adjacent survey rounds. To capture only organic growth, sales gains from mergers and acquisitions were subtracted from, and sales losses from divestments were added to, the sales growth measure. In order to include growth from the entrepreneur's business activities rather than a single firm, growth in subsidiaries and the entrepreneur's additional firms were added to the sales growth measure. The growth rate was computed for employment growth as it was for sales growth. Unfortunately, additional data on acquisitions and similar activities were not available for employment. To measure growth compared to competitors, respondents rated their own firm on a five-point scale ranging from 'much less than the competitors' to 'much more than the competitors'. The market value item is argued to better capture the 'real' value of the firm than traditional accounting measures such as assets or net worth.

Three questions related to financial performance were asked. Gross profits were divided by current year sales to calculate the gross margin; gross margin is a better performance measure because it is size-neutral. Gross profits, on the other hand, are likely to be leveraged by sales volume, giving a bias in favor of larger firms. Profits and cash flow compared with competitors were measured on scales resembling those measuring growth compared with competitors.

Environmental dynamism. Lumpkin and Dess (1996) claim that the relationship between EO and performance may be more complex than previously assumed. Other variables, in addition to EO, could influence performance directly or may moderate the relationship between EO and performance. This relationship may in particular be contingent upon the characteristics of the environment (Zahra and Covin, 1995). Population ecology models suggest that the environment has a direct effect on firm performance regardless of the strategic choices (Aldrich, 1979; Tsai, MacMillan and Low, 1991). The dynamics of demand, sometimes expressed as market attractiveness, environmental munificence, or dynamism, appears to be the most important variable in the environment to enhance performance. Dynamic environments give rise to abundant opportunities for small firms to take advantage of (Chandler and Hanks, 1994a; Covin and Slevin, 1991; Zahra, 1993a). In particular, market growth is stressed as being important to small firm performance (Chandler and Hanks, 1994b; Lumpkin and Dess, 1996; Sandberg and Hofer, 1987). Lumpkin and Dess (1996) also hypothesize that firms in growing industries may perform better than other firms regardless of their EO and vice versa; that is, market growth and EO have independent, positive effects on performance. Thus, drawing on the above literature, environmental dynamism is an important control variable, likely to have a positive influence on performance. This study used three survey items to capture increases in 'environmental dynamism'. The items were taken from Miller (1987). The Cronbach Alpha's value of the scale is 0.69.

Capital availability. Access to financial capital can influence the performance of small firms. Financial capital provides a buffer against unforeseen difficulties that may arise from environmental changes, poor management, etc. (Castrogiovianni, 1996; Cooper, Gimeno-Gascon and Woo, 1994). Financial capital also provides organizational financial slack, facilitating the necessary response to changing conditions and increasing the willingness of the firm to innovate and change (Castrogiovianni, 1996; Zahra, 1991). A consistent finding across different studies is that access to financial capital affects small firm growth (Storey, 1994). Regarding new ventures, Cooper and Gimeno-Gascon (1992) reported that in six out of eight studies they reviewed, availability of capital was associated with better performance. Further, in a longitudinal study on new firm performance, Cooper, Gimeno-Gascon and Woo (1994) found that capital availability was a predictor of firm performance. Therefore, it is important to control for the influence of financial capital on firm-level performance.

It is difficult to obtain objective measures of whether capital availability for small firms is sufficient or not since it may be that demand for financial capital does not exceed supply. Many small business managers are also reluctant to allow finance to be provided by outsiders (Storey, 1994; Wiklund, 1998b,

Wiklund, Davidsson and Delmar 2003). For this reason, the subjective measure 'capital availability satisfaction' is utilized. This measure is original, measured on a seven-point opposite statement scale ranging from 'insufficient and a great impediment for our development' to 'fully satisfactory for the firm's development'.

Additional control variables. Firm size, firm age, and industry (that is, manufacturing, service, and retail) were included as control variables.

ANALYSIS AND RESULTS

Multiple regression analyses were carried out to test the two hypotheses. The results from the regressions are displayed in Table 7.1. Results of the regression equations predicting performance during 1997 are displayed in the first column of the table and the results for the 1997–98 period are displayed in the second column. In both cases, the adjusted explained variance of the performance variable reaches 0.26, which indicates that the proposed model is relevant.

The first hypothesis states that EO is positively associated with performance. The standardized regression coefficient of EO is positive and statistically significant in the prediction of both dependent variables. Thus, hypothesis 1 is supported by the data.

Table 7.1   Linear regression results for the effect of EO, environmental dynamism, and capital availability on performance during 1997 and during 1997–98

Variables	Performance 1997	Performance 1997–98
Entrepreneurial orientation	0.16*	0.25**
Increased env. dynamism	0.14	0.07
Capital availability	0.38***	0.40***
Firm size	0.13*	0.09
Firm age	–0.11	–0.16*
Manufacturing	–0.17	–0.07
Service	–0.22*	–0.20
Adj. R^2	0.26	0.26
Δ Adj. R^2		0.00

Note: Forced entry of independent variables is used. Standardized regression coefficients are displayed in the table.
* $p < 0.05$; ** $p < 0.01$; *** $p < 0.001$.

A strong test of hypothesis 2 would be to establish if there is a statistically significant increase in the t-statistics of EO between the two regression models. This test did not yield a significant result. However, due to the too-small power of this statistical test (that is the risk of a type II error), such a statistical test cannot be recommended as the only way of assessing the possible increase in the EO–performance relationship (cf. Cohen, 1969). A softer criterion, utilized by Zahra and Covin (1995), is the assessment of the change of the value of the regression coefficient. The standardized regression coefficient of EO is 0.16 in the first column and 0.25 in the second. This indicates that the relationship between EO and performance is indeed stronger during the 1997–98 period than during 1997 alone. Thus, according to this latter criterion, hypothesis 2 is supported.

Environmental dynamism was used as a control variable. Previous research has found that it has an independent positive influence on performance. Although the relationship is positive during both time periods, neither of the relationships is statistically significant. Thus, previous research findings do not receive support by the present analyses.

Based on previous research, a positive association between the availability of financial capital and performance was anticipated. The standardized regression coefficient of capital availability is by far the largest in both regressions, and it increases as the time span is extended from one to two years. In this respect, previous findings are strongly supported.

Upon examining the standardized regression coefficients of firm size, firm age, and the industry control variables, no clear pattern emerges. All control variables have the same sign in both equations, but none of them is significant.

DISCUSSION

A small business manager reviewing the popular press is likely to come across a myriad of stories about the advantages of EO. This, in turn, may influence him or her to change the strategic orientation of the firm in an entrepreneurial direction. Such strategic changes are likely to be both time and resource consuming. Before going through these demanding and costly changes, the manager would benefit greatly from knowing the performance implications of EO.

There are research findings to suggest a positive association between EO and contemporaneous performance. However, as noted earlier, fewer studies have looked into the longitudinal performance implications. The longitudinal results that do exist suggest that EO affects performance during later time periods as well. The present study took a somewhat different approach to examining the performance implications of EO. It sought to investigate the sustainability of the EO–performance relationship. This chapter has argued that assessing the compound performance effect of EO would provide more important information for business managers than would the determination of the performance implications for individual years. To test the compound performance implications of EO, the influence of EO on performance during a two-year period was also compared to the influence of EO on performance during a single year.

The results indicate that there is a positive relationship between EO and performance. This relationship increases over the span of the study's time frame. These results corroborate the findings from previous research and provide additional grounding for statements about the positive effects of EO. Further, and more important, the effects of EO appear to be long-term and persistent rather than short-term and a 'quick fix'. Thus, it appears that investments in EO may be worthwhile for small firms since they pay off not only during the following year, but during the two consecutive years. In light of this, anecdotal evidence about the advantages of entrepreneurship may be beneficial rather than counter-productive to the extent it causes small firms to favor EO (cf., Dess et al., 1997).

Although the influence of EO is consistent with the hypotheses, it is surpassed by the 'financial capital availability' variable, which has the largest influence on performance. According to the literature, financial capital provides a buffer against unexpected events, as well as organizational financial slack, facilitating change (Castrogiovianni, 1996; Cooper et al., 1994; Zahra, 1991). The results indicate that those firms that have sufficient access to capital to perform intended and desired activities perform much better than those that do not. A reasonable interpretation of this result would be that the lack of sufficient resources to perform intended activities, rather than knowledge about appropriate choices, affects performance. Firms having sufficient access to capital carry out certain desired activities. The outcomes of these activities have positive performance implications. On the other hand, those firms that feel restricted to perform desired activities due to their capital shortage perform worse. In other words, firms with action discretion also have the knowledge to perform the correct activities to enhance performance. This would suggest that financial capital rather than lack of management skills is a major resource shortage of small firms.

The performance index is a compound measure, comprising growth and financial performance indicators, as well as performance in relationship to competitors. The results suggest that EO contributes to both growth and financial performance suggesting that it has a 'double payoff' (Zahra, 1993b; Zahra and Covin, 1995). Growth is not a trade-off for economic performance, as suggested elsewhere (Lumpkin and Dess, 1996; Zahra, 1991). On the contrary, growing firms generally exhibit better cash-flow and higher profitability.

Hence, growth may be a suitable strategy for those small firms that wish to do well financially. Further, employment and sales growth are closely related, which indicates that outsourcing does not seem to be very common among small firms. If it were, sales growth without employment growth would be common. Although small business managers may find sales growth but not employment growth desirable, this is not reflected in their growth pattern.

It must be borne in mind that the present study has some limitations and, hence, results should he interpreted with some caution. First, the time period for studying the sustainability of the EO–performance relationship is only two years. A longer time period would of course have been preferred. On the other hand, there is also a problem in extending the time frame too much, since the firm and its environment change. As a consequence other variables would disturb the EO–performance relationship, reducing explained variance and regression coefficients. This relates to the second limitation, viz. the fact that close to three-quarters of the variance remains unexplained in the regression equations. This indicates that other factors (for example, structure, culture, and strategy) influence performance. A third limitation relates to the fact that only a minority of firms revealed full performance information during both survey rounds. This may not be totally surprising. However, there is always a risk that firms with poorer performance are more reluctant to divulge performance information, which in turn may bias the results. Of course, the results may suffer from survivor bias.

In general, however, the present results are encouraging to entrepreneurship scholars as well as small firm managers. Further evidence for the positive effects of EO on performance have been added to the growing body of research in this vein, based on a novel methodological approach. Hopefully, this will spur others to further explore the value of firms' entrepreneurial strategic orientation and to do so utilizing large longitudinal data sets.

NOTE

*   Previously published as: Wiklund, J. (1999), 'The sustainability of the entrepreneurial orientation–performance relationship', *Entrepreneurship Theory and Practice*, **24**(1), 37–48.
1. This research was made possible through generous grants by Knut and Alice Wallenberg's Foundation, Jan Wallander's Foundation and Ruben Rausing's Foundation. An earlier version of this chapter was presented at the 1999 Babson College/Kauffman Foundation Entrepreneurship Research Conference.

REFERENCES

Aldrich, H. (1979), *Organizations and Environments*, Englewood Cliffs, NJ: Prentice Hall.

Bamford, C.E., T.J. Dean and P.P. McDougall (1997), 'Initial strategies and new venture growth: an examination of the effectiveness of broad vs. narrow breadth strategies', in P.D. Reynolds, W.D. Bygrave, N.M. Carter, P. Davidsson, W.D. Gartner, C.M. Mason and P.P. McDougall, *Frontiers of Entrepreneurship Research*, Wellesley, MA: Babson College, pp. 375–89.

Barkham, R., G. Gudgin, M. Hart and E. Hanvey (1996), *The Determinants of Small Firm Growth*, vol 12, Gateshead: Athenaeum Press.

Birley, S. and P. Westhead (1990), 'Growth and performance contrasts between "types" of small firms', *Strategic Management Journal*, **2**, 535–57.

Brown, T. (1996), 'Resource orientation, entrepreneurial orientation and growth: how the perception of resource availability affects small firm growth', unpublished doctoral dissertation, Rutgers University.

Brown, T. E. and P. Davidsson (1998), 'Entrepreneurial orientation versus entrepreneurial management: relating Miller/Covin and Slevin's conceptualization of entrepreneurship to Stevenson's', paper presented at the 1998 Entrepreneurship Research Conference, Ghent, Belgium, 21–23 May. (A developed version of this chapter was published as Brown, T., Davidsson, P. and Wiklund, J. (2001), 'An operationalization of Stevenson's conceptualization of entrepreneurship as opportunity-based firm behavior', *Strategic Management Journal*, **22**(10), 953–68).

Brush, C.G. and P.A. Vanderwerf (1992), 'A comparison of methods and sources for obtaining estimates of new venture performance', *Journal of Business Venturing*, **7**(2), 157–70.

Cameron, K. (1978), 'Measuring organizational effectiveness in institutions of higher education', *Administrative Science Quarterly*, **23**, 604–32.

Castrogiovianni, G.J. (1996), 'Pre-start-up planning and the survival of new small firms', *Journal of Management*, **22**(6), 801–23.

Chandler, G.N. and S.H. Hanks (1993), 'Measuring performance of emerging businesses', *Journal of Business Venturing*, **8**, 3–40.

Chandler, G.N. and S.H. Hanks (1994a), 'Founder competence, the environment, and venture performance', *Entrepreneurship Theory and Practice*, **18**(3), 77–89.

Chandler, G.N. and S.H. Hanks (1994b), 'Market attractiveness, resource-based capabilities, venture strategies, and venture performance', *Journal of Business Venturing*, **9**, 331–49.

Cohen, J. (1969), 'The statistical power of abnormal-social psychological research: a review', *Journal of Abnormal and Social Psychology*, **65**, 95–121.

Cooper, A.C. (1995), 'Challenges in predicting new venture performance', in I. Bull, H. Thomas and G. Willard (eds), *Entrepreneurship: Perspectives on Theory Building*, London: Elsevier Science Ltd., pp. 109–24.

Cooper, A.C. and F.J. Gimeno-Gascon (1992), 'Entrepreneurs, processes of founding and new firm performance', in D. Sexton and J. Kasarda (eds), *The State of the Art in Entrepreneurship*, Boston, MA: PWS Publishing Co., pp. 301–40.

Cooper, A.C., F.J. Gimeno-Gascon and C.Y. Woo (1994), 'Initial human and financial capital as predictors of new venture performance', *Journal of Business Venturing*, **9**(5), 371–95.

Covin, J.G., and D.P. Slevin (1986), 'The development and testing of an organizational-level entrepreneurship scale', in R. Ronstadt, J.A. Hornaday, R. Peterson and K.H. Vesper (eds), *Frontiers of Entrepreneurship Research*, Wellesley, MA: Babson College, pp. 628–39.

Covin, J.G. and D.P. Slevin (1989), 'Strategic management of small firms in hostile and benign environments', *Strategic Management Journal*, **10** (January), 75–87.

Covin, J.G. and D.P. Slevin (1991), 'A conceptual model of entrepreneurship as firm behavior', *Entrepreneurship Theory and Practice*, **16**(1), 7–25.

Dess, G.G., G.T. Lumpkin and J.G. Covin (1997), 'Entrepreneurial strategy making and firm performance: tests of contingency and configurational models, *Strategic Management Journal*, **18**(9), 677–95.

Flamholtz, E.G. (1986), *Managing the Transition from an Entrepreneurship to a Professionally Managed Firm*, San Francisco: Jossey-Bass.

Fombrun, C.J. and S. Wally (1989), 'Structuring small firms for rapid growth', *Journal of Business Venturing*, **4**(2), 107–22.

Gartner, W.B. (1988), ' "Who is an entrepreneur?" is the wrong question', *American Small Business Journal*, **14** (Spring), 11–31.

Hart, S.L. (1992), 'An integrative framework for strategy-making processes', *Academy of Management Review*, **17**(2), 327–51.

Hoy, F., P.P. McDougall and D.E. D'Souza (1992), 'Strategies and environments of high growth firms', in D.L. Sexton and J.D. Kasarda (eds), *The State of the Art of Entrepreneurship*, Boston: PWS-Kent, pp. 341–57.

Junehed, J. and P. Davidsson (1998), 'Small firms and export success: development and empirical test of an integrated model', paper presented at the 10th Nordic Conference on Small Business Research, Växjö, Sweden, 14–16 June.

Lumpkin, G.T. and G.G. Dess (1996), 'Clarifying the entrepreneurial orientation construct and linking it to performance', *Academy of Management Review*, **21**(1), 135–72.

Miller, D. (1983), 'The correlates. of entrepreneurship in three types of firms', *Management Science*, **29**(7), 770–91.

Miller, D. (1997), Strategy making and structure: analysis and implication for performance', *Academy of Management Journal*, **30**(1), 7–32.

Miller, D. and P.H. Friesen (1978), 'Archetypes of strategy formulation', *Management Science*, **24**(9), 921–33.

Miller, D. and P.H. Friesen (1982), 'Innovation in conservative and entrepreneurial firms: two models of strategic momentum', *Strategic Management Journal*, **3**, 1–25.

Namen, J.L. and D.P. Slevin (1993), 'Entrepreneurship and the concept of fit: a model and empirical tests', *Strategic Management Journal*, **14**, 137–53.

Porter, M.E. (1985), *Competitive Advantage*, New York: Free Press.

Sandberg, W.R. and C.W. Hofer (1987), 'Improving new venture performance: the role of strategy, industry structure, and the entrepreneur', *Journal of Business Venturing*, **2**, 5–28.

Sexton, D. and N. Bowman-Upton (1991), *Entrepreneurship: Creativity and Growth*, New York: Macmillan.

Shapero, A. and L. Sokol (1982), 'The social dimension of entrepreneurship', in C.A. Kent, D.L. Sexton and K.H. Vesper (eds), *The Encyclopedia of Entrepreneurship*, Englewood Cliffs: NJ: Prentice Hall.

Storey, D.J. (1994), *Understanding the Small Business Sector*, London: Routledge.

Tsai, W.M.-H., I.C. MacMillan and M.B. Low (1991), 'Effects of strategy and environment on corporate venture success in industrial markets', *Journal of Business Venturing*, **6**(1), 9–28.

Weinzimmer, L.G., P.C. Nystrom and S.J. Freeman (1998), 'Measuring organizational growth: issues, consequences and guidelines'. *Journal of Management*, **24**(2), 235–62.

Wiklund, J. (1998a), 'Entrepreneurial orientation as predictor of performance and entrepreneurial behavior in small firms – longitudinal evidence', in P.D. Reynolds, W.D. Bygrave, N. Carter, S. Menigart, C.M. Mason and P.P. McDougall, *Frontiers of Entrepreneurship Research*, Wellesley, MA: Babson College.

Wiklund, J. (1998b), *Small Firm Growth and Performance: Entrepreneurship and Beyond*, Jönköping: Jönköping International Business School.

Wiklund, J., P. Davidsson and F. Delmar (2005) 'What do they think and feel about growth? An expectancy–value approach to small business managers' attitudes towards growth', *Entrepreneurship Theory and Practice*, **27**(3), 247–70. This is an earlier version of Chapter 6 of this volume.

Zahra, S. (1991), 'Predictors and financial outcomes of corporate entrepreneurship: an explorative study', *Journal of Business Venturing*, **6**, 259–85.

Zahra, S. (1993a), 'A conceptual model of entrepreneurship as firm behaviour: a critique and extension', *Entrepreneurship Theory and Practice*, **16**(4), 5–21.

Zahra, S.A. (1993b), 'Environment, corporate entrepreneurship, and financial performance: a taxonomic approach', *Journal of Business Venturing*, **8**, 319–40.

Zahra, S. and J. Covin (1995), 'Contextual influence on the corporate entrepreneurship–performance relationship: a longitudinal analysis', *Journal of Business Venturing*, **10**, 43–58.

8. High-growth firms and their contribution to employment: the case of Sweden 1987–96[1]

Per Davidsson, Frédéric Delmar

INTRODUCTION

The dynamics of job creation have in recent years attracted increased interest on the part of academics as well as policy-makers. In connection to this, a number of studies carried out in various countries have concluded that small and medium enterprises (SMEs) play a very large and/or growing role as job creators (Baldwin and Picot, 1995; Birch, 1979; Davidsson, Lindmark and Olofsson, 1993; 1994; 1995; 1998a; 1998b; Fumagelli and Mussati, 1993; Kirchhoff and Phillips, 1988; Picot and Dupuy, 1998, Spilling, 1995; for further reference to studies carried out in a large number of countries see also Aiginger and Tichy, 1991; ENSR, 1994; Loveman and Sengenberger, 1991; OECD, 1987; Storey and Johnson, 1987).

While most researchers agree on the importance of SMEs, there is some controversy as regards whether their great role in job creation is mainly a result of many small start-ups and incremental expansions, or if a small minority of high growth SMEs contribute the lion's share of new employment. This is known as the 'mice vs. gazelles' or 'flyers vs. trundlers' debate. Storey and Birch strongly advocate the position that the small group of high growth SMEs are the real job creators in the UK and US, respectively (Birch and Medoff, 1994; Storey, 1994; Storey and Johnson, 1987) whereas, for example, the Davidsson et al. research in Sweden (cf. above) gives more support for the 'mice' hypothesis.

The different views may in part be due to real country differences. It must also be understood, however, that the differential results are to a great extent built into the methodology. As emphasised by Davis, Haltiwanger and Schuh (1993, 1996), the net job creation in the economy-at-large can be attributed to many different sub-sets of firms. Further, some studies follow the development of a group of firms over time while disregarding start-ups that occur during the period. With such a design, if some firms close down during the period and the remaining firms have differential growth rates, it is a given that as the length of the period is extended a small fraction of the original group will account for an ever increasing share of the group's total employment. If, on the other hand, the study includes all annual start-ups, close-downs, expansions, and contractions but does not aggregate the contribution of individual firms over time, the typical result will be that it is the many small contributions that sum up to large aggregate effects.

Further, the employment contribution by 'high-growth SMEs' is heavily contingent on how that category is defined. A definition based on sales growth will, *ceteris paribus,* lead to less employment growth being ascribed to the category, compared with a definition based on employment growth. A definition based on growth rates would favour smaller firms but ascribe less total employment growth to the category than would a definition based on absolute employment growth on the firm level. When reading this and other reports on the importance of high-growth SMEs, it is important to realise that the results are in part an effect of study design and definitions.

At any rate, most researchers and policy-makers are likely to agree on the following:

- A small group of high-growth firms (HGFs) are very important for total employment creation, or at least would be so if the development of a large enough such group could be stimulated.
- The interest in high-growth (small) firms has increased dramatically in recent years, as evidenced by a number of studies on their occurrence and characteristics (Blixt, 1997; Gundry and Welsch, 2001; Johnson, Baldwin and Hinchley, 1997; Sexton and Seale, 1997; Vyakarnam, Jacobs and Handelberg, 1997).
- Nevertheless, our current knowledge about the economic contributions and management practices of high-growth SMEs are at present insufficient for strong theory building as well as for the development of optimal policy measures.

The primary objective of this Swedish study is to make a contribution to the needed knowledge by exploring the dynamics of high-growth enterprises from more of an aggregate level perspective while also tapping into issues of relevance to management. This entails:

- their contribution to employment
- their industry, governance structure, age and size class affiliations
- their (aggregate) development trajectories
- their strategy in terms of organic vs. acquired growth.

In addition, various parts of this chapter will address method issues that are of importance for questions such as those just listed.

METHOD

Sample

A customised data set for the purpose of analysing high-growth firms was developed in close cooperation with experts at Statistics Sweden (that is, the official Bureau of Census). Statistics Sweden's data bases are complete in the sense that all legal commercial activity is represented, whether run as sole proprietorship, partnership, limited liability company or some other legal form. Data originate from different sources such as tax authorities and mandatory surveys. Updating is frequent. Data from four different data bases, and ten annual versions of each, were used in the compilation of our data set.

The unit of analysis in this data set is the firm. These firms may be independent or part of a company group. Each legal company within a company group is a case in the database if it fulfils other criteria for inclusion. A firm may have one or several establishments. A common problem with firm-level analyses with secondary data is the change of the numerical code when a firm changes ownership, industry classification or region. This makes many 'going concerns' appear as closures and corresponding start-ups, which are normally not corrected for. We have overcome this problem by not accepting the numerical identity code as the sole criterion for tracking over time. Instead, we have tracked surviving establishments or groups of establishments, because the identity codes for establishments are more stable over time in the original data bases. When a similar group of establishments appears in two subsequent annual versions of the original data we regard that as a continuing firm, regardless of whether the firm's code is identical for the two years involved.[2] This tracking of establishments associated with the firms is also what makes it possible to separate acquired from organic growth.

In order to create a data set consisting only of high-growth firms, we started with all firms that, in November 1996, were: a) in the private (non-government) sector, b) were commercially active in Sweden, and c) had at least 20 employees. There are 11 748 such firms. We track the development of these firms annually back to 1987, or first year of appearance. Annual data on employment for all firms were compiled for the 1987–96 period. Start-ups during this period are included if they fulfil the size criterion for the final year, as are previous government sector firms that by the final year have been transferred to the private sector. Firms that terminated their operations during the period are excluded regardless of their previous size and growth, as are surviving firms that previously may have had more than 20 employees but do not reach that number in 1996. No upper size limit has been employed, but even though the very smallest firms are excluded the data set is primarily comprised of small- and medium-sized firms.

Sample Description

The firms in the data set employed a total of 1.25 million people in 1996. This represents approximately 60 per cent of total employment in the private sector (cf. Davidsson et al., 1996). The remaining 40 per cent are employed in firms that have fewer than 20 employees. The distribution of employment is rather equal over different size classes, with the exception perhaps of the size class of firms with 250–499 employees. This may be a reflection of the 'Mittelstand' problem, that is, that medium-sized enterprises are relatively under represented compared with the number of small and very large enterprises. However, this is a problem Sweden shares with the majority of European countries (Johansson, 1997). The largest industry sector is (traditional) manufacturing, employing more than 38 per cent of the work force, followed by 'retail, hotel and restaurants' with 23.6 per cent. Because micro firms are excluded, the manufacturing share here is greater than in the private sector at large, whereas the non-manufacturing share is smaller (cf. Davidsson et al., 1996).

Definition of 'High-growth Firm' (HGF)

The most important purpose of this chapter is to examine the contribution of high-growth firms to employment. It was therefore concluded that changes in absolute employment would be the best performance criterion.[3] We define HGF as those 10 per cent of the valid cases (11 748 minus the 233 that only appear in the last year of the data base) that display the highest annual average absolute employment growth.

Being an SME is not part of the HGF definition, so 'high-growth SMEs' will only constitute a sub-set of all HGFs. Compared with a growth-rate, based definition the chosen definition favours larger firms. Compared with a definition based on total employment growth over the entire period, the chosen definition favours younger firms, that is, those that are started during the period. The average annual growth for all firms during the 1987–96 period was 0.1. The 90th percentile, that is, the cut-off point for high-growth firms, was 7.75 new employees annually. This means that we do not demand extreme growth figures for inclusion in the HGF group. The sample has been split into two groups, high-growth firms (HGF) and the rest of the sample (control group).

The firms' initial size does not enter into the growth calculations. An important data correction measure we took in this context is we do not accept zero employees as initial size. That is, when a firm displays a series of employment over the years like 'non-existent–zero–forty-two' we do not accept the increase from 0 to 42 as growth. Instead, we regard the firm as created the next year, with 42 employees as its initial size. Initial analyses strongly suggested this would be the wiser choice, and others have also highlighted the problem as a potential source of highly biased results (cf. Davis et al., 1996).

When assessing the job contributions by different categories of firms, the real interest is normally directed towards genuinely new jobs. For maximum comparability with other studies we have chosen to include total job changes in our growth calculations and hence in our definition of HGFs. The present study has the unique feature of being able to separate organic growth from growth through acquisitions. This was achieved by keeping track over time of the status and size changes of all establishments that are associated with a firm and classifying them into five categories: original, previously acquired, previously created, acquired this year, and created this year. We will comment throughout on what proportion of job creation is organic and what is not. In doing that we calculate annual organic growth as total employment$_{(t)}$ – total employment$_{(t-1)}$ – employment in establishments acquired during this year. Importantly, during subsequent years the development of previously acquired units is included in the firm's organic growth.

Choice of Descriptor Variables

Four different variables were used to break down the analysis into subcategories: firm size (six size classes), industry (16 industries); age (number of years in the data set), and governance, viz. affiliation with a company group (independent, parent, or daughter). In most analyses we collapse data into more aggregate categories than those indicated within parentheses, for example, SMEs vs. large firms.

Firm size was chosen based on its supposed importance for growth and employment creation (Dunne and Hughes, 1996; Storey, 1995; Wagner, 1992). Industry was chosen for two reasons. First, most research on growth firms has been performed on the manufacturing industry only (Delmar, 1997). Second, the importance of the service industry as employment creator has increased drastically during the last decades. Age is a recurrent variable in most studies of growth. Normally, younger firms are more prone to grow than older more established firms (Evans, 1987). Age is also highly correlated to the survival possibilities of a firm, where young firms that grow have twice the probability of survival compared with young non-growing firms (Phillips and Kirchhoff, 1989). Alternative hypotheses could be put forward as regards governance. Although independent firms may enjoy more flexibility and free-dom of action those that are affiliated with company groups are likely to have access.

When interpreting the results presented below, it is important to keep in mind that both the HGF and control groups are moving targets in the sense that for every year from 1987 and onwards, new cases appear in both categories. In the 1987–88 growth calculations 8562 firms are included, while in the 1995–96 calculations 11 515 firms are included. The HGF and control groups are stable, however, in the sense that regardless of a firm's performance during the highlighted year, it is included either as an HGF or as a control firm based on its performance over the entire period it exists in the data set. This is unlike the descriptor variables, where each firm and its associated annual job changes in the longitudinal analyses below have been assigned to the categories the firm was affiliated with during that particular year.

RESULTS

The Categorical Affiliations of High Growth Firms

An important first question is how the HGFs are distributed across size classes, industries, etc. compared with firms in the control group. Table 8.1 summarises these results in terms of what percentage of firms were associated with different categories in 1996.

As regards size classes, we can observe first that HGFs are strongly under represented in the smallest size class but markedly over represented in the 50–249 employee size class, that is, medium-sized firms. While 76 per cent of the HGFs are (still) SMEs (that is, have less than 250 employees) the HGF group has an over representation of large firms (that is, more than 250 employees). This may seem to run counter to widespread beliefs that SMEs are the most important for job creation. However, to some extent this result is a consequence of our HGF definition; a definition based on growth rates would have favoured smaller firms. To a very great extent the over representation of large HGFs is simply a result of their growth. Among the 24 per cent that were large firms in 1996, almost half were classified as SMEs earlier in the period. Hence, a full 87.6 per cent of the HGFs were SMEs at some time during the 1987–96 period.

Concerning industries, the broad picture is that HGFs exist in all kinds of industries, but that they tend to be over represented in young and growing industries and under represented in traditional ones. The over representation is especially pronounced in knowledge-intensive services and in education and health care, that is, precisely those industries that grew the most in absolute and/or relative terms during the period (cf. Davidsson et al., 1996). Blixt

Table 8.1   The distribution of HGFs across categories, 1996 (1995)

	High-growth firms (n = 1153)	Control group (n = 10 595)
Firm size class (No. of employees)		
20–49	29.7%	68.2%
50–249	46.1%	27.6%
250–499	11.0%	2.3%
500–2 499	11.0%	1.7%
2 500+	2.2%	0.2%
Industry		
High-tech manufacturing	4.9%	3.1%
Wood, paper and pulp	2.9%	5.9%
Engineering industries	8.8%	13.8%
Mining and steel	1.1%	2.0%
Other manufacturing	7.4%	11.5%
Knowledge-intensive services; technical	10.2%	4.6%
Knowledge-intensive services; financial	6.0%	3.6%
Knowledge-intensive services; other	5.9%	3.1%
Construction	6.8%	9.0%
Wholesale and retail	16.7%	24.5%
Hotels and restaurants etc.	6.5%	4.8%
Transportation	7.4%	6.5%
Education and health care	10.2%	3.9%
Personal and social services	5.0%	2.7%
Forestry, agriculture and fishing	0.3%	1.0%
Age		
Existed entire 1987–96 period	37.9%	73.0%
Created during period	62.1%	27.0%
Company group affiliation (1995)[a]		
Not part of group	35.0%	38.3%
Parent	12.7%	14.5%
Daughter	52.3%	47.2%

Note: [a] Data for governance were not available for 1996, which is why we use the 1995 data in these cases.

(1997) and Storey (1996), who study Sweden and the UK, respectively, both use sales growth in their definition of high-growth firms and therefore arrive at results that differ in some details, but the general pattern that the occurrence of HGFs is related to the relative growth of industry sectors comes through in their studies as well.

On the age issue, there is a very strong over representation of firms that were created during the period. This is in spite of the fact that we were cautious in our methodology not to favour young firms (that is, the absolute growth criterion and our non-acceptance of zero initial size, cf. the Method section). The message here is very clear: HGFs are to be found primarily among young firms. Blixt (1997) and Storey (1996) also find a clear over representation of young firms among the HGFs, and the same age-growth relationship has been established in a number of other studies as well (cf., for example, Evans, 1987; Storey, 1994).

The last rows of the table make clear that although the difference between the groups is small in this regard, a majority of firms in both groups are affiliated with a company group. This highlights a few important facts. A majority of our HGFs are not independent businesses, and HGF-daughters may well form part of company groups that in their entirety would not be labelled 'high growth'. Conversely, some of the control group 'parents' may head groups that instead would be labelled 'high growth'. While the result makes clear that we are not dealing with an HGF group dominated by independent businesses, it is useful to know that 56 per cent of the HGFs and 64 per cent of the control group were at some time during the period not part of a company group. Neither Blixt (1997) nor Storey (1996) report findings to compare to governance issues.

In sum, while most HGFs are SMEs, almost two-thirds of them form part of company groups that may in some cases in their entirety be 'large firms'. They are markedly younger than the control group, and while present in all industries they are clearly over represented in young and growing ones.

The Contribution of High-growth Firms to Absolute Employment

In this section we will analyse HGFs contribution to new employment, in total as well as broken down by size, region, industry and governance categories. We will for each sub-analysis display a table that gives the job contribution by HGFs and the control group in the final analysis year, from November 1995 to November 1996. This table will be accompanied by a chart, which shows the development over the entire 1987–96 period. In the 'over time' charts, sub-category affiliation is based on data for the actual year in question, that is, except for HGF/control, firms may change categories over the years. The question of organic vs. acquired growth will be dealt with in the next subsection.

When interpreting the data it is important to keep track of the number of cases underlying the analysis. This number is throughout much smaller for the HGF group than for the control group. Furthermore, as one moves back from 1996 towards 1987 the number of cases decreases, and relatively more so for

HGFs than for the control group (because relatively more HGFs were created during the period, cf. Table 8.1). The number of cases in the HGF and control groups over time is given in Table 8.A.1 in the appendix.

Table 8.2 displays the absolute employment and absolute employment changes for HGFs and the control group 1995–96. As can be seen, both groups display positive net employment change figures. However, during this period the much smaller (in numbers) HGF group generated almost 80 per cent of all new jobs, when employing only just over 30 per cent of the total sample's work force. That is an impressive share. But do HGFs contribute a large amount of new jobs in absolute terms? In one sense, yes, the HGFs added almost 40 new employees each on average. However, 45 000 new jobs is a small number compared with concurrent unemployment figures of several hundred thousand. Further, the total figure is of the same magnitude as what is ascribed to the formation of genuinely new firms annually in Sweden (cf. Statistics Sweden, 1995; 1997). According to another source, birth and expansion of small firms, defined as firms with 0–200 employees, contributed with more than 70 000 net new jobs in 1994 (Davidsson et al., 1996). A large share of this is attributable to firms with fewer than 20 employees, that is, a category that is excluded completely from the last year of the present study.

Considering also that we have employed a rather permissive lower bound for HGFs (7.75 new jobs annually on average) and that 1995–96 was their top year (cf. Figure 8.1) the conclusion must be that HGFs as we have defined them are an important source of job creation, but not one that outshines other categories of job creators such as the formation and incremental growth of new and very small firms.

The most important finding in Figure 8.1 from a methodological standpoint is that the HGF group, despite their small numbers and varying business cycle conditions, outperforms the control group in every single year. This is also in spite of the fact that the number of cases decreases more rapidly for HGFs than for the control groups, as one moves from 1996 backwards ($n_{1987} = 437$ and 7736, respectively; cf. Table 8.A.l). A very interesting result is that the performance difference is especially pronounced in the worst recession years, 1992 and 1993. HGFs were apparently much less affected by changes in the general economy. In fact they tended to have a fairly stable development over time, when at the same time the rest of the economy lost a great number of jobs. Thus, high-growth firms seem especially important during a recession period. This is a result we will revert to towards the end of the chapter.

The cumulative total growth of HGFs over the entire period was 185 000 new jobs which is a significant figure but far from making up for the 255 633 net job losses in the control group (plus even more jobs lost via dissolutions not captured by these data; cf. Davidsson et al., 1996). We can safely conclude

Table 8.2   Changes in employment in HGFs and the control group 1995–96

	Employment stock count	Employment stock %	Employment change count	Employment change %	n
High growth firms	400 917	32.0%	45 294	79.7%	11 153
Control group	851 498	68.0%	11 537	20.3%	10 362
Total	1 252 415	100%	56 831	100%	11 515

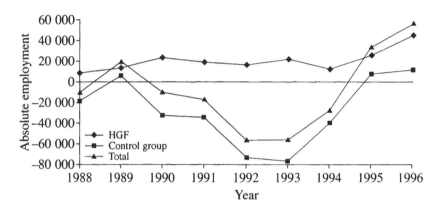

Figure 8.1   Changes in absolute employment by performance category,
1987–96

that high-growth firms have a significant – although not sufficient – impact on employment.

We will now turn to the employment contributions by HGFs in different sub-categories. Perhaps one of the most interesting classifications to do is by size class. Table 8.3 displays the changes in absolute employment by firm size in 1995–96. As a group, small and medium-sized firms (firms with fewer than 250 employees) contributed the majority of jobs (53.8 per cent of net jobs). However, among HGFs large firms were the greater job creators, while in the control group large firms actually lost jobs. This pattern was enhanced when examining the historical development (see Figure 8.2). We can clearly see the difference between the two size classes, where small and medium-sized firms constantly outperformed large firms. Only during the last two years had large firms a non-negative development of employment. During the years of recession, large firms in the control group lost a very large number of jobs. Differently stated, large firms exhibited a greater temporal variance in performance than did small and medium-sized firms during the examined period.

Table 8.4 displays the changes in employment and their distribution by

Table 8.3   Changes in employment firms by firm size 1995–96 (percentage in parenthesis)

	High-growth	Control group	Total
Firms with fewer than 250 employees	13 867 (30.6%) *n* = 874	16 735 (145.1%) *n* = 9 929	30 602 (53.8%) *n* = 10 803
Firms with 250 employees or more	31 427 (69.4%) *n* = 279	−5 198 (−45.1%) *n* = 433	26 229 (46.1%) *n* = 712
Total (*n* = 11 515)	45 294 (100%)	11 537 (100%)	56 831 (100%)

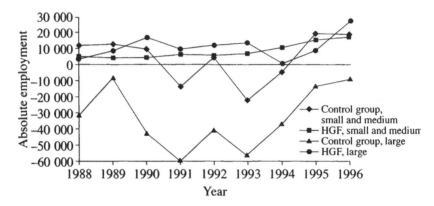

Figure 8.2   Changes in absolute employment by size class, 1987–96

industry 1995–96. We use very broad industry sectors in this analysis, viz. manufacturing (including construction) vs. services (or, rather, 'non-manufacturing'). High-growth firms in the service industry created almost 60 per cent of all new jobs. This is yet another clear indication of the growing importance of the service industry as employment creator. This shows also in Figure 8.3. The high-growth firms in the service industry were steadily above the development of other groups. At the same time, the manufacturing industry control group displays a dramatic decline. In brief, the service industry had the most positive development and this development was largely due to high-growth firms creating the absolute majority of new jobs.

Table 8.1 revealed that most HGFs were by the end of the studied period part of a company group. This comes through also in our employment change analysis. High-growth firms belonging to a company group created more jobs than others. They alone created 60 per cent of all new jobs during the 1995–96 period. The difference between independent high-growth firms and independent firms in the control group was relatively smaller. Also the average growth per firm was higher for HGFs in company groups compared with their independent

Table 8.4   *Changes in employment and their distribution across industry*
1995–96 (percentage in parenthesis)

Industry	High-growth firms	Control group	Total
Manufacturing	11 213 (24.8%) *n* = 288	8 425 (73.0%) *n* = 3 783	19 638 (34.6%) *n* = 4 071
Service	34 081 (75.2%) *n* = 865	3 112 (27.0%) *n* = 6 579	37 193 (65.4%) *n* = 7 444
Total (*n* = 11 515)	45 294 (100%)	11 537 (100%)	56 831 (100%)

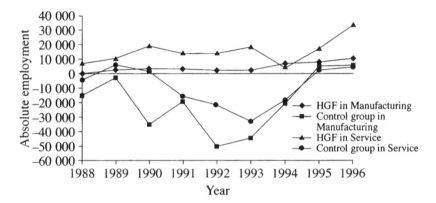

Figure 8.3   *Changes in absolute employment across industries, 1987–96*

counterparts. The changes in absolute employment by type of organisation are
displayed in Table 8.5.

These results hold also for the development over time (see Figure 8.4). On
the whole, firms in company groups performed more poorly than did independent firms. This is in line with results previously obtained by Davidsson et al
(1998a; 1998b). However, HGFs in company groups outperformed all other
firms all years except for 1993. Hence, the variance in changes in employment
was much higher for firms in company groups than for independent firms. In
short, high-growth firms in company groups did generate a large number of jobs,
but the firms in this sub-category's control group lost even more.

To sum up this section, we can conclude that high growth firms were an
important source of new employment in Sweden during the studied period. As
we have defined HGFs the category did not, however, create new jobs at a rate
that looks impressive in relation to concurrent unemployment figures. In
absolute numbers their job contribution was not much greater than what is
annually created by genuine start-ups. An interesting aspect is that high growth

Table 8.5   Changes in employment by type of organisation (independent firm
or part of business group) in 1995–96 (percentage in parenthesis)

	High-growth firms	Control group	Total
Independent firm	11 093 (24.5%)	7 579 (65.7%)	18 672 (32.9%)
	n = 404	n = 3 961	n = 4 365
Part of a business group	34 201 (75.5%)	3 958 (34.3%)	38 159 (67.9%)
	n = 749	n = 6 401	n = 7 150
Total (n = 11 515)	45 294 (100%)	11 537 (100%)	56 831 (100%)

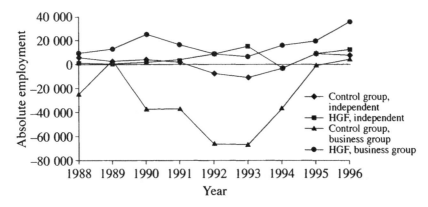

Figure 8.4   Changes in absolute employment by organisation type
(independent or part of a business group), 1987–96

firms were especially important during the recession, moderating the effect of
the recession on the work force. When we more closely examined the characteristics of high growth firms, we revealed several interesting findings.
Relatively large parts of the job creation by HGFs is not attributable to independent SMEs, but to large firms and firms affiliated with company groups.
For example, high growth firms in company groups outperformed all other
firms all years except for 1993. On the other hand, the variance in changes in
absolute employment was much higher for firms in company groups than for
independent firms. High growth firms in company groups did generate a large
number of jobs, but the firms in the company group control group lost even
more.

A Closer Look at Organic Employment Growth in High Growth Firms

It can justifiably be argued that our real interest in this context lies with *genuinely* new jobs, that is, with job changes that would have an effect on employment and unemployment. We will therefore in this sub-section elaborate further on this issue within the HGF group, in order to examine what happens to the above summary results if organic growth is used as the criterion.

The insight that total job contribution of HGFs is modest is reinforced if we deduct growth through acquisitions. The cumulative organic growth of HGFs over the entire period was 60 040 new jobs, that is, less than a third of the HGFs' total growth was organic. If we define the HGFs by their 1996 industry affiliation, we find that for manufacturing HGFs 21.4 per cent represent organic growth. The corresponding figure for service HGFs is 37.3 per cent. Thus, the relative importance of service industry HGFs is reinforced if organic rather than total employment growth is the criterion. Analysis for finer industry categories suggests that the organic share is higher for young and growing industries.

As regards governance we again find quite substantial differences between the categories. For those HGFs that were (still) independent in 1996, the cumulative organic growth was 64.5 per cent of their cumulative total growth. Among the company group HGFs the organic share was much lower, 25.3 per cent. In absolute numbers this means that cumulative organic growth by company group affiliated HGFs still exceeds organic growth by independent HGFs (38 369 vs. 21 671), but the relations look quite different from a comparison of cumulative total growth (151 684 vs. 33 580).

These analyses demonstrate in quite a dramatic way what false conclusions can be drawn because of failure to distinguish between organic growth and growth through acquisition. This distinction is especially crucial with respect to

Table 8.6   Total and organic growth for HGFs of a different age

No. of years existing in data set	No. of cases (n)	Cumulative total employment growth	Cumulative organic employment growth	Per cent organic growth
2	148	3 319	3 191	96.1
3	205	8 865	7 052	79.5
4	137	6 984	6 118	87.6
5	77	7 043	6 619	94.0
6	40	3 912	3 429	87.7
7	42	6 364	4 401	69.2
8	38	3 920	2 992	76.3
9	29	6 919	4 038	58.4
10	437	137 938	22 200	16.1
Total	1 153	185 264	60 040	32.4

firm age and size. Table 8.6 shows that the part of total growth that is organic is much, much higher among those HGFs that were created during the period than among HGFs that were established already in 1987. Evidently, for older firms most of the alleged job creation really reflects restructuring. The shift in the image one gets is quite dramatic. With total growth as the criterion almost three-quarters of HGF employment growth is attributable to older, established firms, while their share of HGF organic growth is little more than one-third. The message is clear: the younger the firm, the more of total growth is organic.

Let us turn next to the issue of firm size. Two analyses are displayed in Table 8.7. We display total and organic growth by initial size for those HGFs that existed the entire 1987–96 period. Since growth is what makes SMEs become large firms, it is useful to look at initial size in order to analyse in what size classes new jobs originate. However, this analysis uses only part of the sample, and all growth is assigned to the initial (small) size class even if most

Table 8.7   Total and organic growth for HGFs of a different size

1987 size class	No. of cases (n)	Cumulative total employment growth	Cumulative organic employment growth	Per cent organic growth
0	30	6 088	4 897	80.4
1–9	35	4 461	4 182	93.7
10–49	91	11 617	7 797	67.1
50–249	188	32 705	17 422	53.2
250–499	37	11 913	2 339	19.6
500–2 499	73	50 492	3 542	7.0
2 500+	13	26 750	-13 082	(48.9)
Total	467	144 026	27 097	8.8

1996 size class	No. of cases (n)	Cumulative total employment growth	Cumulative organic employment growth	Per cent organic growth
20–49	342	8 124	7 963	98.0
50–249	532	44 320	34 208	77.2
250–499	127	22 340	12 497	55.9
500–2 499	127	57 752	15 682	27.2
2 500+	25	52 728	–10 310	(–19.6)
Total	1 153	185 264	60 040	32.4

of it has occurred after the firm has entered a larger size class. For these reasons, we supplement this analysis by reporting also total and organic growth for all HGFs defined by their 1996 size class.

On the most important issue these two analyses are in full agreement. That is, the smaller the firm, the larger is the part of total employment growth that is organic. The shift of image one gets is even more dramatic in this case than with firm age, as both analyses show that the HGFs with more than 2500 employees actually shrink in organic terms. This is our perhaps most dramatic demonstration that if genuinely new jobs are what we are really interested in, analysing total job creation may lead to completely false results.

The size class that stands out as the primary HGF job creator is instead the medium-sized firm, with 50–249 employees. This is quite ironic, since there are widespread beliefs that this is precisely what Sweden is lacking: growing, medium-sized firms. Our results suggest that among firms that have reached this level we do find a substantial group of HGFs that also grow organically for the most part. Now, the absolute numbers of jobs created by medium-sized HGFs are tiny compared with concurrent unemployment figures, so from a policy-maker's point of view one would, of course, like to have more of those firms. It is rather there that the real problem is. While the absolute number of firms in the economy-at-large is much greater in the <50 size class than in the 50–249 size class, the number of HGFs in the sub-50 category is relatively small. The fact that most employment growth in this category is organic does not make up for the fact that there simply are too few HGFs in this size class.

In summary the analyses of organic growth show that some categories of high-growth firms may have a much higher relative importance for genuine employment growth than an analysis of total job growth suggests. Young, small and independent firms in young and growing industries come much more to the fore when the analysis excludes acquisitions, which arguably represent restructuring rather than job creation.

DISCUSSION AND CONCLUSIONS

Major Results

In this chapter we have analysed high-growth firms in non-government enterprises across all industry sectors in Sweden during the 1987–96 period, using a high-quality data set that has been carefully developed for this purpose. We have restricted the study to the firm level, and to firms that had a minimum size of 20 employees in the final year, 1996. No upper size bound was used. As our primary interest is in employment creation, we defined high-growth firms as those 10 per cent of all firms that contributed most in annual average absolute employment growth.

It turned out that firms that had an average annual employment increase of 7.75 people qualified as high-growth firms. This we may also regard as a first result: it did not take extreme growth figures to be among the top 10 per cent growth firms in Sweden during the studied period. Their average contribution during the last year in our analysis (1995–96) appears more impressive. During this top year, the high-growth firms added close to 40 new jobs each on average. However, even this does not look very impressive in the aggregate. It is a contribution of the same magnitude as that annually provided by genuine start-ups, and even doubling the contribution by high-growth firms would not have meant a quick solution to the unemployment problem of the time.

We found that there was an over representation of high-growth firms in certain sub-categories. Importantly, young firms are much more likely to be high-growers than are older firms. As regards industries, we found an over representation of high-growth firms in young and growing industries, in particular knowledge-intensive business-to-business services, education and health care. A slight majority of our high-growth firms are company group daughters, and another 13 per cent are the parent company of a group. Stand-alone independent firms are thus a minority both among high-growth firms and in the control group, and firms that by the end of the period are still stand-alone independents account for less than 20 per cent of the total high-growth firm job contribution during the period.

The above results all concern total employment growth on the company level. A very important contribution by this study is that we are able to analyse also organic growth, that is, to disregard growth via acquisitions and focus on that part of job growth that really has a direct effect on employment and unemployment figures.

When organic growth is focused some of the above results are further emphasised, whereas others are changed. The most dramatic changes occur for firm age and firm size. Among HGFs five years or younger 80 per cent or more of the total growth is organic and presumably reflects genuine job creation. By contrast, only 16 per cent of the growth of HGFs ten years or older is organic. For firm size the effect is even more dramatic, with HGFs in the largest size class actually shrinking in organic terms.

The overall picture that emerges from our data is that young and small firms, often in young and growing industries, create genuinely new jobs to a great extent. Large, established firms, often in mature industries, account for relatively more of total job changes, but the net result tends to be negative in terms of number of jobs. The latter categories do comprise, however, a group of growing firms that account for a relatively large share of total net job creation, but most of this represents restructuring rather than the creation of genuinely new jobs. Apparently, as firms are young and small, if they grow at all they often do so in organic terms. When getting older and larger they are more likely to develop by acquiring existing activities and by closing down or selling some of their units that are getting obsolete. Importantly, both of these roles are crucial to economic development; the organic growth of genuinely new activity where young and small firms play a big role, and the restructuring for more efficient use of resources which on the company level is dominated by large, established firms.

Implications

One of our main results is that there is a shortage of high-growth firms in Sweden (or at least there was one during the 1987–96 period). This gives reason to examine if and how the institutional framework in Sweden that is politically controlled affects both the number of high-growth firms and their ability to achieve high-growth over time (cf. Davidsson and Henrekson, 2002).

Although over represented in young and growing industries our analysis shows that HGFs appear also in stagnant or declining industries. This suggests to the policy-maker that there is opportunity for selection and targeting. For the business manager the lesson is that growth niches can be found even in difficult environments. A striking feature of our 'over time' analysis of high-growth firms reinforces this latter conclusion: their relatively stable development over time. This is in spite of the fact that the economy has been through, during the analysed period, the most dramatic business cycle shifts since the Great Depression. This is, as we see it, a highly suggestive result that in a way gives some input to the population ecology vs. strategic adaptation debate (Child, 1972; Hannan and Freeman, 1977; Hawawini, Subramanina and Verdin, 2003). That is, do firms shape their destiny, or are they powerless victims of changes in their environment? In our analyses, the high growth-firm very much appears as a category of firm, which is capable of shaping its own destiny. One can infer, arguably, that their aggregate development is a result of proactiveness, goal-directedness and opportunity-orientation as described in the entrepreneurship literature. When the economy turns down, they continue to develop much as before. When it turns up, they do not necessarily (on a per firm basis) start to grow much more. It is as if regardless of the environmental situation, they find ways to achieve their goals. In the toughest years organic growth may be hard to achieve, hence their growth-by-acquisition is somewhat higher instead. This suggests that at least some business managers are capable of controlling the destiny of their firms.

Our analyses of organic vs. acquired growth should highlight for researchers the crucial importance of definitions and measurement. The results also indicate that growth is not a homogenous phenomenon. Firms achieve growth in different ways, which in turn give different effects on the economy at large. The political interest in firm growth is often related to job creation. Our results clearly show that many high-growth firms do not create any new jobs, but achieve growth by acquiring already established firms. The distinction between organic and acquired growth leads us to question whether the political interests at all should be directed towards growth on the firm level. Our results support the idea that the political interests should instead be directed towards renewal, in the form of a large number of entries of new firms in young, growing industries. High-growth firms are over represented among these firms and industries, and at the same time the share of organic growth is higher. This clearly indicates that renewal leads to organic growth and to growth in the economy at large.

The Limitations of the Study

There are two important issues that we have not been able to deal with satisfactorily. First, many firms may choose to pursue growth not by expanding the original firm (only), but by creating a company group. In our total sample, 1672 firms (14.2 per cent) were parent companies in 1996. A full 1372 firms (11.7 per cent) actually turn into parent companies from something else during the ten-year period. Clearly, this may hide some high-growth business activities. Second, many firms may pursue growth in sales but not in employees, and handle this by increased outsourcing or sub-contracting. An employment-based definition would not capture these firms, yet they create new employment outside the boundaries of their own organisations. Data on the company group level, as well as sales data, were appended to our data set after the analyses in the present manuscript were performed. Analyses of these additional data suggest that our main conclusions are not artefacts caused by the limitation to firm level employment data (Davidsson and Delmar, 2003; Delmar, Davidsson and Gartner, 2003).

It is conceivable that the time period has affected our results. The analysis periods include a very deep recession when large firms cut back, and a period when more generally the trend among large, established firms was towards outsourcing rather than internal growth. We acknowledge that this may have made old and large HGFs display an even greater preference for acquisition growth over organic growth than would be the case during other time periods. However, the pattern with organic growth turning to increased acquisition growth as the firm grows older and larger makes theoretical sense from a variety of perspectives, We therefore feel confident that the essence of our results are not due to peculiarities of the studied period.

APPENDIX

Table 8.A.1 Development of sub-panel sizes over time

Count (pct of 1996 figure)	1987	1988	1989	1990	1991	1992	1993	1994	1995	1996
HGF	467	509	547	591	658	760	942	1 103	1 153	1 153
	(40.5)	(44.1)	(47.4)	(51.3)	(57.1)	(65.9)	(81.7)	(95.7)	(100)	(100)
Control group	8 095	8 501	8 870	9 195	9 487	9 800	10 110	10 310	10 493	10 595
	(76.4)	(80.2)	(83.7)	(86.8)	(89.5)	(92.5)	(95.4)	(97.3)	(99.0)	(100)

NOTES

1. Previously published in French as: Davidsson, P. and F. Delmar (2002), 'Les entreprises à forte croissance et leur contribution à l'emploi: le cas de la Suède 1987–1996', *Revue Internationale PME*, **14**(3–4), 164–87 (also reprinted in *Revue Gestion 2000*, **5**, 167–90).
2. More specifically, for us to accept at t1 that firm A_{t0} is the same unit as firm B_{t1} the following has to apply: i) at least 50 per cent of the former employment in A is now found in B; and ii) this same employment constitutes at least 50 per cent of B's total employment. This criterion is programmable and can establish unique links in the great majority of cases. Because of mergers and splits the above criteria do not always lead to a unique and satisfactory solution. In these cases the two foremost business data experts at Statistics Sweden used a manual procedure for deciding, according to their best collective judgment, which of several links should be used, or neither. For any individual year 0.7 per cent was the maximum fraction of cases for which a link was accepted on the basis of manual inspection rather than fulfilling both of the '50 per cent' criteria.
3. It should be noted that if performance were calculated as relative growth, this would have an important impact on the results. The correlation between changes in absolute employment and changes in relative employment for each year varies between 0.002 and 0.30, indicating a very modest relationship. Sales data are available only for about 50 per cent of the firms in the data set.

REFERENCES

Aiginger. K. and G. Tichy (1991), 'Small firms and the merger mania', *Small Business Economics*, **3**, 83–102.
Baldwin, J. and G. Picot (1995), 'Employment generation by small producers in the Canadian manufacturing sector', *Small Business Economics*, **7**, 317–31.
Birch, D. (1979), *The Job Generation Process*, final report to Economic Development Administration, Cambridge, MA: MIT Program on Neighborhood and Regional Change.
Birch, D.L. and J. Medoff (1994), 'Gazelles', in L.C. Solomon and A.R. Levenson (eds), *Labor Markets, Employment Policy and Job Creation*, Boulder, CO, and London: Westview Press.
Blixt, L. (1997), 'Tillväxtföretag i Sverige' [Growth companies in Sweden'], NUTEK working paper, Stockholm.
Child, J. (1972), 'Organizational structure, environment and performance: the role of strategic choice', *Sociology*, **6**, 1–22.
Davidsson, P. (1995), 'SMEs and job creation in Sweden', manuscript prepared for the OECD Secretariat/working party on SMEs/the Ad Hoc Group on SME Statistics.
Davidsson, P. (1997), 'High-growth SMEs: feasibility analysis for the Swedish study', mimeo prepared for the OECD Working Party on SMEs, Paris, and the Jönköping International Business School, Jönköping, Sweden.
Davidsson, P. and F. Delmar (2003), 'Hunting for new employment: the role of high growth firms', in D. Kirby and A. Watson (eds), *Small Firms and Economic Development in Developed and Transition Economies: A Reader*, Aldershot, UK: Ashgate, pp. 7–19.
Davidsson P. and M. Henrekson (2002), 'Institutional determinants of the prevalence of start-ups and high-growth firms: evidence from Sweden', *Small Business Economics*, **19**(2), 81–104.
Davidsson, P., L. Lindmark and C. Olofsson (1993), 'Business dynamics in the Swedish economy: a regional perspective', report submitted to the EC Commission.

Davidsson, P., L. Lindmark and C. Olofsson (1994), *Dynamiken i svenskt näringsliv* |*Business Dynamics in Sweden*|, Lund: Studentlitteratur.

Davidsson, P., L. Lindmark and C. Olofsson, (1995), 'The trend towards smaller scale during the 1980s: empirical evidence from Sweden', paper presented at ICSB's 40th World Conference, Sydney, June.

Davidsson, P., L. Lindmark and C. Olofsson (1996), *Näringslivsaynamik under 90-talet* |*Business Dynamics in the 90s*|, Stockholm: NUTEK.

Davidsson, P., L. Lindmark and C. Olofsson (1998a), 'The extent of overestimation in small firm job creation – an empirical examination of the regression bias', *Small Business Economics*, **10**, 87–100.

Davidsson, P., L. Lindmark and C. Olofsson (1998b), 'SMEs and job creation during a recession and recovery', in Z. Acs, B. Carlsson and C. Karlsson (eds), *SMEs, Entrepreneurship, and the Macro Economy*, Cambridge, MA: Cambridge University Press.

Davis, S.J., J. Haltiwanger and S. Schuh (1993), 'Small business and job creation: dissecting the myth and reassessing the facts', National Bureau of Economic Research working paper no. 4492, Cambridge, MA.

Davis, S.J., J. Haltiwanger and S. Schuh (1996), *Job Creation and Destruction*, Boston, MA: MIT Press.

Delmar, F. (1997), 'Measuring growth: methodological considerations and empirical results', in R. Donckels and A. Miettinen (eds), *Entrepreneurship and SME Research: On its Way to the Next Millennium*, Aldershot, Avebury, pp. 190–216, Chapter 4 in this volume.

Delmar, F., P. Davidsson and W. Gartner (2003), 'Arriving at the high growth firm', *Journal of Business Venturing*, **18**(2), 189–216, Chapter 9 in this volume.

Dunne, P. and A. Hughes (1996), 'Age, size, growth and survival: UK companies in the 1980s', *Journal of Industrial Economics*, **XLII**(2), 115–40.

European Network for SME Research (ENSR) (1994), *The European Observatory for SMEs, Second Annual Report*, Zoetermeer: EIM Small Business Research and Consultancy.

Evans, D.S. (1987), 'Test of alternative theories of firm growth', *Journal of Political Economy*, **95**, 657–74.

Fumagelli, A. and G. Mussati (1993), 'Italian industrial dynamics from the 1970s to the 1980s: some reflections on the entrepreneurial activity', *Entrepreneurship and Regional Development*, **5**, 25–37.

Gundry, L.K. and H.P. Welsch (2001), 'The ambitious entrepreneur: high growth strategies of women-owned enterprises', *Journal of Business Venturing*, **16**, 453–70.

Hannan, M.T. and J.H. Freeman (1977), 'The population ecology of organizations', *American Journal of Sociology*, **82**(5), 929–64.

Hawawini, G., V. Subramanina and P. Verdin (2003), 'Is performance driven by industry- or firm-specific factors?', *Strategic Management Journal*, **24**(1), 1–16.

Johansson, D. (1997), 'The number and the size distribution of firms in Sweden and other European countries', licentiate thesis prepared for the Stockholm School of Economics, Stockholm.

Johnson, J., J. Baldwin and C. Hinchley (1997), 'Successful entrants: creating the capacity for survival and growth', catalogue no. 61-524-XPE, Statistics Canada.

Kirchhoff, B. and B. Phillips (1988), 'The effect of firm formation and growth on job creation in the United States', *Journal of Business Venturing*, **3**, 261–72.

Loveman, G. and W. Sengenberger (1991), 'The re-emergence of small scale production: an international Comparison', *Small Business Economics*, **3**, 1–37.

OECD (1987), 'The process of job creation and job destruction', *Employment Outlook*, 97–220.

Phillips, B.D. and B.A. Kirchhoff (1989), 'Formation, growth and survival: small firm dynamics in the US economy', *Small Business Economics*, **1**, 65–74.

Picot, G. and R. Dupuy (1998), 'Job creation by company size class: the magnitude, concentration and persistence of job gains and losses in Canada', *Small Business Economics*, **10**, 117–39.

Sexton, C. and F. Seale (1997), *Leading Practices of Fast Growth Entrepreneurs*, Kansas City, MO: National Center for Entrepreneurship Research.

Spilling, O. (1995), 'Do small firms create jobs?', paper presented at the 6th ENDEC World Conference on Entrepreneurship, Shanghai, December.

Statistics Sweden (SC13) (1995), 'Nyföretagandet i Sverige 1993 och 1994 |New firms in Sweden 1993 and 1994|, in *Statistiska Meddelanden F 15 SM 9501*, Örebro: SCB Publishing Service.

Statistics Sweden (SC13) (1997), 'Nyföretagandet i Sverige 1995 och 1996 |New firms in Sweden 1995 and 1996|, in *Statistiska Meddelanden F 15 SM 9701*, Örebro: SCB Publishing Service.

Storey, D.J. (1994), *Understanding the Small Business Sector*, London: Routledge.

Storey, D.J. (1995), 'Symposium on Harrison's "Lean and mean": a job generation perspective', *Small Business Economics*, **7**(5), 5–8.

Storey, D.J. (1996), *The Ten Percenters – Fast Growing SMEs in Great Britain*, London: Deloitte and Touche.

Storey, D.J. and S. Johnson (1987), *Small and Medium-Sized Enterprises and Employment Creation in the EEC Countries: Summary Report*, Programme of Research and Actions on the Development of the Labour Market, study no. 85/407, EC Commission.

Vaessen, P. and D. Keeble (1995), 'Growth-oriented SMEs in unfavourable regional environments', *Regional Studies*, **29**(6), 489–505.

Vyakarnam, S., R.C. Jacobs and J. Handelberg (1997), 'Formation and development of entrepreneurial teams in rapid growth businesses (summary)', in P.D. Reynolds, W.D. Bygrave, N.M. Carter, P. Davidsson, W.B. Gartner, C.M. Mason and P.P. McDougall (eds), *Frontiers of Entrepreneurial Research 1997*, Wellesley, MA: Babson College, pp. 86–7.

Wagner, J. (1992), 'Firm size, firm growth and persistence of chance. Testing GIBRAT's law with establishment data from Lower Saxony, 1978–1989', *Small Business Economics*, **4**, 125–31.

9. Arriving at the high-growth firm[1]

Frédéric Delmar, Per Davidsson, William B. Gartner

EXECUTIVE SUMMARY

The focus of this research is to offer a variety of ideas, measures, and empirical facts on how organizations grow. This chapter presents evidence that organization growth can be achieved in a number of different ways, and the pattern of firm growth, over time, can look very different across all growth firms. We use a data set that covers all firms in Sweden with more than 20 employees in 1996 tracing their development back to 1987. The data allow us to assess growth in sales as well as in employment, separate organic from acquired growth, identify new entrants, compare independent firms with firms in company groups, and track their subsequent growth over time. In addition, the article explores the differential representation of these growth patterns for firms of different demographic affiliation in terms of firm size, firm age, industry, and ownership/governance.

A review of prior academic scholarship on firm growth suggests substantial heterogeneity in a number of factors that characterize this phenomenon. Failure to recognize this heterogeneity appears to have led to some confusion and conflict in current theory and research findings. There is variation in the kinds of growth measures used in previous research studies on firm growth. Comparison between studies is difficult as the time frame, the growth indicator, and the growth formula often differ. There is heterogeneity in the choice, validity, and reliability of different growth measures as determined from theoretical and methodological perspectives. Different growth measures and calculations affect model building and theory development differently. Scholars have recognized this as an important issue, and have suggested that research should strive towards one single, or a few possible ways, of calculating growth. We believe that the goal of a 'one best way' of measuring growth has diverted researchers from acknowledging that firm growth is fundamentally a multidimensional rather than unidimensional phenomenon. All high-growth firms do not grow in the same way. This implies that researchers should measure different forms of growth with different growth measures. We believe that a single growth measure would likely provide knowledge about only one form of organizational growth. We provide evidence that indicates the growth patterns exhibited by organizations are highly heterogeneous, and that multiple measures and methods for exploring organizational growth are important for an understanding of firm growth processes.

Data for this study were created by combining several of Statistics Sweden's (that is, the official 'Bureau of Census') registers, in close cooperation and advice from Statistics Sweden experts. All legal commercial activity is represented, whether run as sole proprietorship, partnership, limited-liability company (LLC), or some other legal form. The unit of analysis is the firm. These firms may be independent or part of a company group. Each firm within a company group is a case in the database if it fulfills other criteria for inclusion.

We started with all firms that, in November 1996, were: (a) in the private (nongovernment) sector, (b) were commercially active in Sweden, and (c) had at least 20 employees. There are 11 748 such firms in Sweden, all of which appear in this data set. Annual data on employment for all firms were compiled for the 1987–96 period. Start-ups during this period are included if they fulfill the size criterion for the final year. Firms that failed during the period are excluded regardless of their previous size and growth. While the very smallest firms are excluded, the data set is primarily comprised of small- and medium-sized firms. In order to be selected as a high-growth firm, a firm had to be among the top 10 per cent of all firms in terms of an annual average in one or more of six categories: 1) absolute total employment growth, 2) absolute organic employment growth, 3) absolute sales growth, 4) relative (that is, percentage) total employment growth, 5) relative organic employment growth, and 6) relative sales growth. There were 1501 firms that met these selection criteria. In order to examine different growth patterns, cluster analysis procedures were utilized to develop a taxonomy of growth patterns. The demographic characteristics of the clusters were then explored. This could be seen as testing the external validity of the clusters, that is, if the clusters do not differ on variables not used in the cluster analysis, they are unlikely to represent distinct empirical categories.

We arrived at a seven-cluster solution. Based on the cluster means from the K-means clustering, the clusters were labeled as follows: *Super absolute growers*, representing 13.5 per cent ($n = 202$) of the high-growth population, exhibited impressive absolute growth both in employment (total and organic) and in sales. *Steady sales growers*, representing 12.8 per cent ($n = 193$) of the cases, exhibited negative development in terms of employment, but a strong positive development in absolute sales. *Acquisition growers*, representing 10.0 per cent ($n = 150$) of the cases, had a strong positive development in absolute sales and total employment, but negative development in organic employment.

This indicates that growth in employment was mainly achieved by acquiring other firms. *Super relative growers*, representing 16.3 per cent (*n* = 244) of the cases, had the strongest development in relative terms. Firms in this cluster had the highest share of high-growth years. Growth was rapid and concentrated for these firms. *Erratic one-shot growers* represented 16.7 per cent (*n* = 250) of the cases. These firms were characterized by negative development in absolute sales and employment (total and organic), even though they were included in the high-growth population. These firms exhibit positive relative growth, on average, because of an artifact of how average relative growth was calculated. *Employment growers*, representing 16.0 per cent (*n* = 240) of the cases, were characterized by having negative development in absolute sales and weak positive development in numbers of employees. *Steady overall growers*, representing 14.8 per cent (*n* = 222) of the cases, were characterized by a relatively strong development in absolute sales and employment growth (total and organic), but had weaker relative (percentage) development.

An important aspect of this study concerns cluster differences in demographic affiliation. We found that firm size and age, and industry had a strong relationship to differences among the clusters and that ownership (governance) had a moderate relationship to the seven growth patterns.

We believe that this study shows that high-growth firms exhibit different growth patterns. These growth patterns are not random. Instead, the patterns of high firm growth are empirically distinct, conceptually comprehensible, and systematically related to demographic affiliation. There is no such thing as a typical growth firm. Rather, there are many different types of growth firms with different growth patterns. Recognizing that 'high growth' is multidimensional in nature, and that 'high growth' occurs in a variety of ways, is an important insight for researchers and practitioners.

INTRODUCTION

The topic of organizational growth as a focus of entrepreneurship scholarship has attracted considerable attention (Collings and Porras, 1994; Gundry and Welsh, 2001; Kirchhoff, 1994; Mata, 1994; Ostgaard and Birley, 1995; Siegel et al., 1993; Welbourne, 1997). However, research in this area has largely failed to generate cumulative results. One explanation for the failure to achieve a cumulative body of knowledge is that researchers use different firm growth measures (Brush and Vanderwerf, 1992; Chandler and Hanks, 1993); Davidsson and Wiklund, 2000; Delmar, 1997; Murphy et al., 1996; Weinzimmer et al., 1998). We offer a different explanation. Previous empirical research on organizational growth has failed to recognize the heterogeneous nature of this phenomenon. Recognizing that researchers have used different measures and methods for analysing firm growth is just one aspect of the need for a more complicated and comprehensive view of this issue.

We argue that firms grow in many different ways and that these patterns of growth, over time, can vary significantly and have different causes. Implicit in this view is a belief that the search for an explanation for why firms grow without knowledge of how firms grow leads to conflicting theories about the causes of firm growth. We argue that firm growth patterns are related to the demographic characteristics of these firms. The view that a firm's growth pattern is dependent on its age, its size, and its industry affiliation has been acknowledged in previous theoretical work (Penrose, 1959; Stinchcombe, 1965), but this view has received little empirical research.

The primary focus of this chapter is to provide empirical evidence on firm growth using a variety of firm growth measures and measures of firm demography, such as firm age and size, industry affiliation, and governance (independent firm or part of a larger corporation). Providing more heterogeneous and longitudinal empirical evidence on this topic is important for several reasons. First, if firms grow in different ways we can also assume that the reasons leading to growth and the outcome of growth may also be different. Second, expanding the evidence to include information about the demographic profile of each growth firm suggests that these characteristics affect the probability of the type of growth that occurs and how the firm will expand. Third, firm growth is not static in nature. Previous research (often cross-sectional in design) appears to have focused on the occurrence of growth, not on the dynamic evolution of changes, over time, within these growing firms. Cross-sectional evaluation of growth firms is, therefore, problematic. Such analyses preclude the examination of the ordering of the development of each firm, which is important for accurate estimation of how a firm actually achieved growth.

LITERATURE REVIEW

The study of firm growth is, itself, heterogeneous in nature. The variation in measures used in organizational growth studies, the variation in growth indicators, the variation in the measurement of firm growth over time, the variation in the processes by which firm growth occurs (for example, organic vs. acquisition), and the variation in the characteristics of these firms and their environments are all important features of organizational growth as a phenomenon. Some of these problems have been identified in previous reviews of the organizational growth literature (Brush and Vanderwerf, 1992; Chandler and Hanks, 1993; Delmar, 1997; Murphy et al., 1996; Weinzimmer et al., 1998;

Wiklund, 1998). This section of the article will attempt to address, in a systematic way, how all of these issues affect the study of firm growth.

Heterogeneity In Firm Growth Measures

A number of scholars have noted that the diversity of measures used in organizational growth studies severely impairs the ability of scholars to accumulate and compare results (Delmar, 1997; Murphy et al., 1996; Weinzimmer et al., 1998). For example, some studies might rely on measuring growth as absolute sales growth measured over a time period of five years (Dunne and Hughes, 1996; McCann, 1991; Merz and Sauber, 1995; Miller, 1987), whereas other studies rely on relative employment growth over a time period of three years (Cooper et al., 1994; Donckels and Lambrecht, 1995, Peters and Brush, 1996; Vaessen and Keeble, 1995; Zahra, 1993). The choice of absolute or relative growth is especially important for the relationship between size – and anything correlated with size – and growth. Absolute measures tend to ascribe higher growth to larger firms whereas smaller firms more easily reach impressive growth in percentage (that is, relative) terms. The implications of the choice between relative and absolute measures is much discussed in the literature and seems to be reasonably well understood by researchers when designing their studies, but frequently forgotten when results are compared with other studies. The issue of time frame has achieved even less attention (Delmar, 1997). Comparison between studies is impossible or misleading when the time frame, the growth indicator, and the growth formula differ.

Heterogeneity in the Appropriateness of Specific Firm Growth Indicators

The second, partly overlapping problem concerns the choice, validity, and reliability of different growth measures as determined from theoretical and methodological perspectives (Chandler and Hanks, 1993; Weinzimmer et al., 1998). Based on extensive reviews of the literature, Ardishvili et al. (1998) and Delmar (1997) arrive at almost identical lists of possible growth indicators: assets, employment, market share, physical output, profits, and sales. This article focuses on sales and employment only, for the following reasons. First, the use of sales and employment measures are the most widely used in empirical growth research (Delmar, 1997). Second, these growth indicators are the only ones available in the present study for all of the firms of interest. Finally, other indicators have some obvious shortcomings that limit their applicability outside of very special contexts. For example, such indicators as market share and physical output can only be compared within industries for firms with a similar product range. Using an indicator such as total asset value is highly related to the capital intensity of the industry and sensitive to changes over time. And, while profits are an important indicator of success, the relationship of profits to size is only evident in aggregates of firms or over long periods for individual firms.

There seems to be an emerging consensus that if only one indicator is to be chosen as a measure of firm growth, the most preferred measure should be sales (Ardishvili et al., 1998; Hoy et al., 1992). It is relatively easily access- ible, it applies to (almost) all sorts of firms, and it is relatively insensitive to capital intensity and degree of integration. It has been argued that sales are a highly suitable indicator across different conceptualizations of the firm (Davidsson and Wiklund, 2000) and that it is also the indicator favored by entrepreneurs themselves (Barkham et al., 1996). This is related to another argument, namely that demand and, therefore, sales is a precursor of growth in other indicators, that is, the nature of the growth process itself points to sales as a natural choice (Delmar, 1997; Flamholtz, 1986).

Sales are not, however, the perfect indicator of growth for all purposes. Sales are sensitive to inflation and currency exchange rates, while employment is not. It is not always true that sales lead the growth process. For high-tech- nology start-ups and the start-up of new activities in established firms, it is possible that assets and employment will grow before any sales will occur. Arguments have been offered for employment as a much more direct indica- tor of organizational complexity than sales, and may be preferable if the focus of interest is on the managerial implications of growth (Churchill and Lewis, 1983; Greiner, 1972). The same line of reasoning about the value of employment-based measures of growth applies for resource and knowledge- based views of the firm (Penrose, 1959; Kogut and Zander, 1992). If firms are viewed as bundles of resources, a growth analysis ought to focus on the ac- cumulation of resources, such as employees. Furthermore, when a more macro-oriented interest in job creation is the rationale for the study, measuring growth in employment seems the natural choice (Schreyer, 1999). Obvious drawbacks of employment as a growth indicator are that this measure is affected by labor productivity increases, machine-for-man substitution, degree of integration, and other make-or-buy decisions. A firm can grow considerably in output and assets without any growth in employment.

Using Multiple Growth Indicators for Measuring Heterogeneity in Firm Growth

Because no universally superior growth indicator seems to exist, some schol- ars advocate composite measures using multiple indicators (Davidsson, 1989a) while other scholars advocate using the same explanatory model on several growth measures (Delmar, 1997). The reasoning behind multiple-indicator measures is that different indicators of growth (such as change in employees, sales, or market share) are attributes of the same underlying theoretical concepts of growth and therefore tend to be correlated. The underlying causes of growth are assumed to be the same, but situational and idiosyncratic factors that cannot be included in the research model may determine the specific form of growth a firm engages in. A multiple-indicator measure can capture this variety of responses to common, underlying causes of growth. The implication of this view is that growth research would only be investigating the overall concept of organizational growth. A drawback of this perspective is that the assumption of common causes may be incorrect. Furthermore, relations among dimensions must be well specified in order for a multidimensional construct to work. This is not the case when organizational growth is studied (Law et al., 1998).

Although there appear to be few theoretical arguments to guide the selection of the best model and/or best growth measure, a recommendation to use an array of measures may divert attention from ascertaining whether a measure is suitable given the purpose and theoretical background of the study (Davidsson and Wiklund, 2000). Different growth measures and calculations affect model building and theory development differently. Scholars have recognized this as an important issue, and have suggested that research should strive towards one single way, or a limited number of ways, of calculating growth (Chandler and Hanks, 1993; Delmar, 1997; Weinzimmer et al., 1998). We disagree.

Since there appears to be no one best measure of firm growth, as well as no one best composite measure of firm growth, it would be advantageous to explore the use of many different growth measures in a study of firm growth. The use of multiple measures of firm growth would likely provide a more complete picture of any empirical relationships as well as provide a way to test the robustness of any theoretical model to misspecifications in the dependent variable. The use of multiple measures also offers the opportunity to use a measure optimized to the study's specific purposes while allowing comparisons with the results of previous studies using other growth measures.

Heterogeneity in the Regularity of Growth Over Time

One neglected issue in the growth literature has been the issue of regularity (or irregularity) of growth over time. Empirical research has usually studied size differences between two points in time (Delmar, 1997; Weinzimmer et al., 1998). This approach ignores the development in-between (and outside of) these two points in time. This in turn creates two potential problems. First, the amount of growth, as measured, may be greatly influenced by stochastic variation (Davis et al., 1996). For this reason, Weinzimmer et al. (1998) recommend multiple-period assessment of size, and using the regression beta-weight as the measure of a firm's growth rate. The tendency of this measure to smooth out irregularities is an advantage relative to the problem of stochastic influence. A clear drawback of a betaweight estimate is that a minimum of 15 observations is required to properly fit the regression line to time-series data properly (Weinzimmer et al., 1998).

Furthermore, smoothing out the growth pattern is in direct conflict with solving the other problem with comparing size at two points in time, namely that the regularity or irregularity of growth over time may be an important topic to study in itself. It is likely that total growth achieved through monotonous, gradual expansion vs. large-chunk and oscillating size development may have different causes. These different patterns almost certainly have different implications for management, and possibly also for the long-term performance of the firm. Regularity in firm growth has been largely ignored in empirical growth studies. It has been observed empirically that growth measures tend to have moderate serial correlation over time (Dunne and Hughes, 1992; Kumar, 1984) and, therefore, 'high-growth firms' are a temporally unstable population – its members are constantly exchanged (Blixt, 1998). Finally, while the literature on firm growth that focuses on 'stages-of-development' recognizes that growth patterns are irregular over time, little systematic empirical support has been offered (for example, Greiner, 1972). The study of Chandler and Baucus (1996) is one of the few empirical studies that explicitly focus on the variability of firm growth over time.

Heterogeneity in Organic Growth vs. Acquisition Growth

Another neglected aspect of how firms grow is the issue of whether these firms grew by organic growth, growth through acquisition, or a combination of both. This is surprising, as the distinction has crucial implications at the firm as well as at the societal level. The two types of growth are likely to place different types of demands of managers that try to pursue them, and these paths to growth may also have a differential impact on firm performance. At the societal level, organic growth is more likely to represent genuine job creation than is growth through acquisition, where existing jobs are shifted from one organization to another. Penrose's (1959) book is one of the few places where a more elaborate treatment of these two types of growth can be found. Penrose relates the issue of organic growth vs. acquisition to the previous issue about (ir)regularity of growth over time, suggesting that firms that grow organically will show a smoother growth pattern over time compared with firms that grow mainly through acquisitions (Penrose, 1959). She also suggests that organic growth should be more associated with smaller firms, younger firms, and emerging industries whereas acquisition growth is more likely in older and larger firms, and in mature industries (Penrose, 1959). Some support for such relationships is found in a few empirical studies (Levie, 1997; Wiklund and Davidsson, 1999).

Heterogeneity In Firm Demographics

We believe that one possible reason for the conflicting results among firm growth studies is that many theoretical explanations of firm growth and most research designs fail to account for differences in firm size, firm age, type of industry, and type of governance among the firms that are studied. We believe that these four demographic variables are likely to influence how firm growth occurs.

Theories and research on firm size and its relationship to growth had been developed in the economic literature in the context of analyses of firm size distribution (Carroll and Hannan, 2000). Most well known is Gibrat's (1931) law, which holds that growth is proportional to size and that the magnitude of the proportion is random. Gibrat's law has generated a substantial amount of research. Some studies have indicated that growth rates are independent of size, other studies have indicated that Gibrat's law is applicable only to large organizations (but not to small organizations), and some studies find that growth rates diminish with increasing size (Dunne and Hughes, 1996; Evans, 1987; Storey, 1995; Sutton, 1997; Wagner, 1992). Even if we still cannot determine the direction in which firm size affects growth, we can conclude that size may have an effect on growth. A firm will expand differently, dependent on its size.

A more clear relationship is to be found between firm age and growth, where firm growth rates tend to decline with the age of the firm. This result stands out independently of whether the sample of firms studied comes from multiple industries or from a single industry (Barron et al., 1994; Sutton, 1997).

Industry affiliation is not assumed to be related to firm growth per se, but to the nature of the growth process. Organizational ecologists argue that populations (that is, industries) are so unique that they can only be studied one at the time (Carroll and Hannan, 2000). They indicate that there are a number of industrial and institutional covariates that are unique to each industry and they affect the development of the firms in the studied population. Given this line of reasoning, we would assume that the industry affiliation of a firm would affect its growth pattern.

Regarding ownership, it appears that independent firms are more flexible whereas firms affiliated with a group had access to different and more resources (Barney, 1991; Morris and Trotter, 1990). Implications for growth are therefore mixed. It is possible that increased flexibility related to independence leads to a higher probability in identifying opportunities, but a lower probability of exploiting them due to the lack of resources. For firms affiliated to a company, the logic would be the reverse. The increased availability of resources leads to a higher probability of exploiting opportunities, but a lower probability of identifying them due to the lack of flexibility.

In summary, previous theory and empirical evidence on the topic of high-growth firms depicts substantive variation in how they achieve growth and how research has investigated the phenomenon. The goal of empirical exploration of high-growth firms, then, is to demonstrate how recognition of the issues described above will likely identify different types of growth firms by describing how high-growth firms grow in different ways.

METHOD

Sample

A customized data set for the purpose of analysing high-growth firms was developed in close cooperation with experts at Statistics Sweden (that is, the official 'Bureau of Census'). Data from four different registers[2] and ten annual versions of each were used in the compilation of our data set. All legal commercial activity is represented, whether run as sole proprietorship, partnership, LLC, or some other legal form.

The unit of analysis in this data set is the firm. These firms may be independent or part of a company group. Each legal company within a company group is a case in the data base if it fulfills other criteria for inclusion. A firm may have one or several establishments. A common problem with firm-level analyses with register data is the change of the numerical code when a firm changes ownership, industry classification, or region. This makes many 'going-concerns' appear as closures and corresponding start-ups, which are normally not tracked. We have overcome this problem by not accepting the numerical code as the sole criterion for tracking over time. Instead, we have tracked surviving establishments or groups of establishments, because the numerical codes for establishments are more stable over time in the original registers. When a similar group of establishments appears in two subsequent annual versions of the original register, we regard that as a continuing firm, regardless of whether the firm's code is identical for the two years involved.[3] This tracking of establishments is what makes it possible to separate acquired from organic growth.

We started with all firms that, in November 1996, were: a) in the private (nongovernment) sector, b) were commercially active in Sweden, and c) had at least 20 employees. There are 11 748 such firms in Sweden. We track the

*Table 9.1   The distribution of the (sub)population of firms across firm size
classes and industries*

	Percentage of the entire population ($n = 11\ 748$) (%)	Percentage of the subpopulation with sales data available ($n = 5\ 540$) (%)
Firm size class (number of employees)		
20–49	64.4	41.8
50–249	29.4	47.5
250-499	3.1	5.5
500–2 499	2.6	4.6
2 500+	0.4	0.6
Industry classification (number of firms)		
Manufacturing	43.9	57.7
Service	56.1	42.3

development of these firms annually back to 1987. Start-ups during this period
are included if they fulfill the size criterion for the final year. Firms that terminated their operations during the period are excluded. Although the very smallest firms are excluded the data set is primarily comprised of small- and
medium-sized firms (see Table 9.1).

Annual data on employment (full-time equivalents in November) were
compiled for all firms. Data on sales were also gathered, but these were not
complete for all firms in the data set. For manufacturing firms with more than
20 employees, and service firms with more than 50 employees, there are no
missing values. The problem for our purposes, then, is missing data for
nonmanufacturing firms in the size brackets of up to 20–50 employees. As
Statistics Sweden collects sales data on samples of that subpopulation, we
have satisfactory data for parts of it: 7472 firms had information on sales.
From this group of firms with sales information, 5540 firms fulfilled the
following criteria and were kept for further analysis:

a) Balanced data on both employment and sales changes, that is, the same
    number of observations for each single case for sales and for employment.
b) Fewer than four missing values over time for sales data. This was an ad
    hoc judgment, but it was judged that analysing time-series with more than
    three missing values would lead to a higher than acceptable level of uncer-
    tainty. If a missing value appeared between two values, it was replaced by
    the average value of the two known values, based on the observation that

sales (level) measures showed high serial correlation (varying between 0.8 and 0.9). If a missing value appeared in the beginning or at the end of the time-series, the value was estimated as the average sale per employee for the years with complete data.[4]

c) The company had been registered for at least three years (earliest start in 1994). As a consequence, all firms exhibited at least two time-periods of change.

As can be seen in Table 9.1, the subpopulation fulfilling these criteria tended to be larger and in the manufacturing industry compared with the population of all firms.

For this chapter, the focus was on the 'high-growth' part of this population of 5540 firms (cf. Penrose, 1959, p. 7). In order to be selected as a high-growth firm, we set the criterion that a firm had to be among the top 10 per cent (cf. Storey, 1998) of all firms in terms of 'annual average' on one, or more, of six growth indicators: 1) absolute total employment growth, 2) absolute organic employment growth, 3) absolute sales growth, 4) relative (that is, percentage) total employment growth, 5) relative organic employment growth, and 6) relative sales growth. Absolute growth refers to annual change in numbers of employees or monetary units, whereas relative growth refers to annual percentage change in employees or sales. Organic growth is total growth minus the additions that came with units that were acquired by the firm this particular year. Our data allow dividing total growth into its organic vs. acquisition parts only for employment and not for sales.

The selection criteria were met by 1501 firms. The distribution of firms and how many criteria they fitted are displayed in Table 9.2. The correlations among the six growth categories are displayed in Table 9.3.

The absolute majority (66.9 per cent) fit only one or two criteria. While

Table 9.2   Number of 'high-growth' criteria met by firms included in the final data set

Number of 'high growth' criteria fitted	Frequency	Percentage of firms in sample (%)
1	621	41.4
2	367	25.5
3	249	16.6
4	138	9.2
5	88	5.9
6	38	2.5
Total	1501	100.0

Table 9.3 Correlations of growth measures

Variable	Mean	S.D.	1	2	3	4	5	6
1. Absolute total employment growth	6.10	59.83	1.00					
2. Absolute organic employment growth	2.26	41.71	0.68 (0.00)	1.00				
3. Absolute sales growth (in thousand SEK)	40 954.54	232 624.14	0.09 (0.00)	-0.08 (0.00)	1.00			
4. Relative total employment growth (%)	146.30	249.11	0.06 (0.03)	0.086 (0.00)	-0.036 (0.17)	1.00		
5. Relative organic employment growth (%)	143.76	247.93	0.05 (0.056)	0.09 (0.001)	-0.04 (0.14)	0.99 (0.00)	1.00	
6. Relative sales growth (%)	532.74	6 410.82	-0.01 (0.887)	0.01 (0.984)	-0.01 (0.758)	-0.01 (0.97)	-0.01 (0.98)	1.00

Pearson correlations ($n = 1\,501$).

191

more than one-third (34.2 per cent) of the firms included in the final data set fit at least three of the six criteria, only 2.5 per cent of the high-growth firms fulfill all six criteria. The results from these tables indicate that we are dealing with a heterogeneous group of expanding firms. As has been noted in previous organizational growth studies (Chandler and Hanks, 1993; Davidsson and Delmar, 1997), the growth measure most commonly celebrated in the popular press (for example, in the *Inc. 100* and *Inc. 500*), relative sales growth, is not correlated to any of the other organizational growth measures!

Variables

Growth Variables
The first group of variables is the growth measures needed to fulfill the main purpose of the study. A description of the 19 variables in six different classes that were computed to examine different growth patterns is provided in Table 9.4.

The first growth category (Category 1 in Table 9.4) is composed of the six variables previously used as the criteria to form the population of high-growth firms studied in this work. These are indicators of the average pace of growth. As this is measured separately for sales, total employment, and organic employment, a firm's profile across these six measures is indicative not only of how fast it grows, but also of how it grows. The original variables were rescaled into monotonously increasing ten-point scales.

Categories 2–5 (a total of 11 indicators) concern aspects of the regularity (or consistency) of growth over time. The reason for forming several different categories of variables reflecting this aspect is that different original variables (absolute vs. relative) lend themselves to different types of transformations. Category 2 measures the number of growth years and high-growth years achieved during the period, in relation to the numbers of years in existence in the data set. Our goal was to distinguish between modest continuous growth vs. rapid and concentrated growth. Category 3 measures the variation around the mean growth for the individual firms. The standard deviations show whether the growth pattern is uniform or erratic (comprising large positive and negative changes in relation to the mean). Category 4 addresses the duration of a firm's growth development. A high value here indicates frequent changes in the growth trend. Category 5 captures more extreme forms of irregularity in growth, as when the bulk of the growth over the period was achieved during a single year. These variables were constructed as the highest growth achieved during a single year compared with the maximum size achieved by the firm during the measurement period. Maximum size was used because using end size led to extreme values in cases where the firm has subsequently shrunk considerably.

Table 9.4   Variables used in the cluster analysis

Category	Description	Interpretation
1.	*Average growth rate measures*	
	Average annual change in . . .	A large value indicates the firm achieved a high absolute growth (scaled 1–10)
(a)	absolute total employment	
(b)	absolute organic employment	
(c)	absolute sales	
	Average annual change in . . .	A large value indicates the firm achieved a high relative growth (scaled 1–10)
(d)	relative total employment	
(e)	relative organic employment	
(f)	relative sale	
2.	*Regularity of growth 1: The relative number of growth and high-growth years*	
	The relative share of years that can be characterized as either growth years or high-growth years in relation to the total measurement period. It is measured as:	A large value indicates the firm exhibited either growth or high growth during most of the measurement period
(a)	growth years in relative total employment	
(b)	growth years in relative sales	
(c)	high-growth years in relative total employment	
(d)	high-growth years in relative sales	

193

Table 9.4 (continued)

Category	Description	Interpretation
3.	*Regularity of growth II: Standard deviation of growth over time* Standard deviation of relative change. It is measured as:	A large value indicates high dispersion around the mean, i.e., the growth pattern is highly disruptive or volatile
(a)	Standard deviation of relative total employment	
(b)	Standard deviation of relative sales	
4.	*Regularity of growth III: Duration of development* The relation between the number of both positive and negative changes in growth in relation to the numbers in existence in the data base. It is measured as:	A high value indicates tendency of frequent changes in growth rate
(a)	absolute employment	
(b)	absolute sales	
5.	*Regularity of growth IV: One-shot growth* The share of the highest single growth in relation to the maximum size achieved during the period. It is measured as:	A large value indicates that the firm's total growth was mainly achieved during one period. Maximum size is used as the denominator as it diminishes problems with size dependency and a smaller end size compared with the maximum size.
(a)	absolute total employment	
(b)	absolute organic employment	
(c)	absolute sales	

194

6.	*Dominant type of growth: Ranking total employment growth to organic employment growth or sales growth*	
	The relation between sales and employment growth when ranked	A large value indicates high growth in sales in relation to growth in total employment (scaled 1–10)
	The relation between organic employment and employment growth when ranked	A large value indicates high organic growth in relation to growth in total employment (scaled 1–10)

The purpose of the variables in Category 6 was to describe different types of growth. It was noted in the literature review that it is possible for a firm to achieve growth in sales without a matching growth in the number of employees and that a growing business can choose to expand organically or via acquisitions. After ranking all firms on their absolute sales growth, total employment growth, and organic employment growth, we computed two indicators: a) rank for sales growth relative to rank for total employment growth and b) rank for total employment growth relative to rank for organic employment growth. It may appear that having just two indicators for dominant type of growth could be too little. However, what type of growth dominates for each firm is reflected also in each firm's relative position on other growth indicators, especially those in Category 1.

Method of Analysis

Cluster analysis procedures were utilized to develop a taxonomy of growth patterns. Since these procedures are not based on probabilistic statistics, there is rarely one single best solution to a clustering problem. Furthermore, one does not have specified test characteristics to guide selection of particular sets of clusters from several alternative solutions. Issues concerning the validity and stability of cluster solutions are of great importance (Hair et al., 1995; Milligan, 1996; Punj and Stewart, 1983).

In the light of these issues, we used a four-step approach to the cluster analysis. The first step consisted of the selection of the variables to be included in the cluster analysis. Based on the arguments presented previously, we selected the 19 growth variables as our clustering base. As cluster methods are sensitive to outliers, we reduced the variation in the variables (for example, dividing the variance into ten equal groups or censoring the variation). Standardized variables were used (z scores).

The second step was to divide the population into a try-out sample and a hold-out sample. The try-out sample was used to assess the optimum number of clusters. The hold-out sample was used to validate the results from the try-out sample (cf. Hair et al., 1995; Milligan, 1996). To determine the number of clusters, we used hierarchical clustering with Ward's method and Euclidean distances. The number of clusters can either be assessed: a) empirically by examining the changes in the agglomeration schedule or b) theoretically by paying attention to ease of interpretation. Based on the agglomeration schedule from this initial clustering, the optimal number of clusters should be in the range from four to seven. However, we extended the maximum number of groups for further consideration to nine clusters. The centroids from this range of cluster solutions were then saved to be used in the validation phase.

The purpose of the third step was to find and validate the most stable solution. The holdout sample was used and a K-means clustering was performed using the centroids from the try-out sample as a base. A second clustering using hierarchical clustering with Ward's method was then performed. The first clustering was then compared with the second clustering. The lambda statistic was used in a cross-tabulation to assess the level of agreement between the two cluster solutions. The highest stability was achieved with a seven-cluster solution, generating a lambda of 0.73. We concluded that this seven-cluster solution was optimal from both theoretical and empirical standpoints. The cluster solution was stable across samples and easy to interpret.

Finally, in the fourth step, the seven-cluster solution was extracted on the complete high-growth population. It was first extracted by hierarchical clustering with Ward's method and the centroids were saved. The centroids were then used to extract the K-means clusters, which were used as the final results and the basis for the interpretative analysis.

The overall purpose of the four steps was to find a stable cluster solution and thereby secure its internal validity. The demographic characteristics of the clusters were used to test for the external validity of the clusters. That is, if the clusters do not differ on variables outside of the cluster analysis, they are unlikely to represent distinct empirical categories. Bivariate analyses were used for the demographic contrasts. We chose to use and report significance tests, although the analyses are on a slightly biased census (due to incomplete sales data – see Table 9.1) rather than on a probability sample. Interpretations focus on the size of the differences, not on significance.

RESULTS

Cluster Analysis

As noted above, the most satisfactory cluster solution identified seven different clusters. This solution exhibited the highest stability (measured here as maximizing lambda) and internal validity and was also the most easily interpretable. A final seven-cluster solution on the basis of all cases ($n = 1501$) was then developed. The means for each cluster on the 19 growth indicators are displayed in Table 9.5.

Based on the cluster means from the K-means clustering and the cluster sizes the clusters were labeled as follows:

1. *Super absolute growers*, representing 13.5 per cent ($n = 202$) of the high-growth population. These firms exhibited very high absolute growth both in employment (total and organic) and in sales. They also have strong

Table 9.5 Means describing the characteristics of the different clusters

Variable	Cluster							Total
	1	2	3	4	5	6	7	
1. Average growth rate measures								
(a) Absolute employment change	25.43	−37.45	29.49	11.29	−6.87	4.03	21.73	6.10
(b) Absolute organic employment change	21.46	−33.73	−10.32	11.11	−2.09	5.83	15.89	2.26
(c) Absolute sales change (SEK)	86.04	117.10	93.33	10.82	−3.52	−41.86	71.16	40.95
(d) Relative employment change	1.39	0.98	1.13	2.50	1.01	1.89	1.08	1.46
(e) Relative organic employment change	1.34	0.98	1.02	2.46	1.01	1.89	1.07	1.44
(f) Relative sales change	1.48	1.27	1.30	4.58	22.48	1.13	1.13	5.33
2. Regularity of growth I: The relative number of growth and high-growth years								
(a) Share growth years in relative employment	0.72	0.25	0.39	0.67	0.41	0.58	0.56	0.52
(b) Share growth years in relative sales	0.69	0.63	0.61	0.57	0.48	0.38	0.70	0.57
(c) Share high-growth years in relative employment	0.40	0.03	0.17	0.48	0.11	0.35	0.13	0.25
(d) Share high-growth years in relative sales	0.32	0.06	0.17	0.43	0.27	0.12	0.05	0.21
3. Regularity of growth II: Standard deviation of growth over time								
(a) Standard deviation of relative employment	0.69	0.12	0.39	2.90	0.22	2.00	0.17	1.00
(b) Standard deviation of relative sales	0.85	0.70	0.71	7.92	63.17	0.75	0.17	12.23

4. Regularity of growth III: Duration of development

(a) Trend duration of employment change	0.29	0.46	0.43	0.42	0.47	0.46	0.32	0.41
(b) Trend duration of sales change	0.28	0.34	0.37	0.37	0.44	0.41	0.28	0.36

5. Regularity of growth IV: One-shot growth

(a) One-shot growth in employment	0.29	0.04	0.20	0.36	0.14	0.30	0.14	0.22
(b) One-shot growth in organic employment	0.47	−16.16	0.25	0.34	5.19	0.29	6.68	−3.60
(c) One-shot growth in sales	0.32	0.17	0.24	0.45	0.37	0.09	0.17	0.27

6. Dominant type of growth: Ranking total employment to organic employment and sales

(a) Rank sales vs. employment	0.91	39.18	1.01	0.70	2.02	0.57	1.02	5.96
(b) Rank organic employment vs. employment	1.01	1.67	0.45	1.03	1.36	2.57	1.16	1.37

relative development. The cluster does not stand out markedly in either direction as regards the regularity of growth.

2. *Steady sales growers*, representing 12.8 per cent ($n = 193$) of the cases. This cluster exhibited strong positive development in absolute sales, but negative development in terms of employment. It gets the highest rank when development in total sales is put in relation to development in employment. The low relative growth indicates that this group consists of large firms. The development over time in sales was characterized by slow positive development with few high-growth years.

3. *Acquisition growers*, representing 10.0 per cent ($n = 150$) of the cases. The development of this cluster resembles that of Cluster 1 (steady absolute growers), with the distinctive exception of growth in organic employment. More precisely, the firms in this cluster had strong positive development in absolute sales and total employment, but negative development in organic employment. This indicates that growth in employment was mainly achieved by acquiring other firms, so they were not great creators of genuinely new jobs. Furthermore, the growth momentum for this group, in relative figures, was slower compared with Cluster 1, which is reflected also in the numbers of growth years and high-growth years.

4. *Super relative growers*, accounting for 16.3 per cent ($n = 244$) of the cases. This group of firms represents (along with Cluster 1) those that most consistently appear as 'high-growth firms' across different growth criteria. If Cluster 1 represented the highest growth in absolute figures, this cluster represents the highest growth in relative terms. Firms in this cluster had the highest share of high-growth years. Furthermore, they had a high standard deviation in sales growth indicating an uneven development compared with the other clusters reported so far.

5. *Erratic one-shot growers*, representing 16.7 per cent ($n = 250$) of the cases. Even though they qualified for inclusion in the high-growth population, these firms are characterized by having negative development in absolute sales and employment (total and organic). The reason is that they exhibit positive relative growth, on average, because of an artifact of how average relative growth was calculated. Relative growth was calculated as an average growth rate over the period. This measure could, therefore, identify as 'high-growth firms' those firms that have a year with strong positive development and a following year with an equally dramatic negative development.[5] Oscillating development around a relatively low minimum level, then, is likely to characterize many of the firms in this cluster. This is also revealed in a large one-shot increase and a high standard deviation in sales.

6. *Employment growers*, representing 16.0 per cent ($n = 240$) of the cases. This cluster is characterized by showing relatively more growth in

employment than in sales. According to some indicators the development of sales may even be negative. This is a surprising pattern. There is probably more than one explanation behind it. First, we find that many of these firms appear to be 'receivers' of the outsourcing efforts of other large firms. Hence, these firms may be subcontractors or service providers who take over more and more operations from their large customers while at the same time being subject to pricing pressures. Another group of firms that would end up in this cluster are those that engage in backward integration. They then decrease their purchases through increasing internal employment, making employment growth without sales growth possible. A third explanation is temporal. Some firms that first grew rapidly in sales and employment may later face severely failing demand. If the cutting of personnel lags the decline in sales, the annual average growth would still be high for employment but not for sales.

7. *Steady overall growers*, representing 14.8 per cent ($n = 222$) of the cases. This cluster is characterized by relatively strong development in absolute sales and employment growth (total and organic), but weaker relative development. From that perspective, this cluster was quite similar to Cluster 1 (super absolute growers), but with weaker development. Growth in numbers of employees was mainly achieved organically, and in many cases during a short period as this cluster had the highest value on one-shot growth in organic employment. This group was further characterized by relatively few high-growth years, despite a large share of growth years. In combination with low standard deviations and low duration values, these factors indicate a smooth and stable development over time in total growth despite the irregular development of organic employment growth.

As previously noted, this clustering solution is satisfactory since it is easily interpretable and exhibits a high degree of stability, consequently satisfying the criterion for internal validity. In line with our suspicion, the high-growth population was highly heterogeneous, even concealing firms that had contracted during the measurement period after first achieving substantial growth. We found differences in growth patterns related to absolute vs. relative growth; growth in sales and employment; but also the duration of growth, that is, if it was achieved over a longer or shorter time period and if changes in growth rates were frequent or not. Only two of the seven clusters (Clusters 1 and 4) could be labeled as 'high-growth firms' according to most of the criteria commonly used to describe 'high-growth firms.' We believe that these results demonstrate the importance of definitions and measurements for understanding and explaining firm growth.

Table 9.6 provides additional insights into the character and contributions of the different groups of firms that the clusters represent. It should be noted

Table 9.6   Size in number of employees and number of firms included in the different clusters, 1987–96

	Cluster							Total
	1	2	3	4	5	6	7	
Mean employment size of firms								
1987	145	1 196	477	29	135	78	373	390
1996	283	815	735	80	64	66	513	326
Relative change (%)	196	68	154	280	48	84	138	115
Median employment size of firms								
1987	43	592	159	17	44	28	146	80
1996	132	415	272	48	40	44	233	91
Relative change (%)	307	70	171	282	91	157	160	114
Total employment								
1987	15 207	185 375	61 038	2 053	25 501	8 363	67 867	365 404
1996	57 233	157 302	110 271	19 445	16 050	15 763	114 072	490 136
Relative change (%)	376	85	181	947	63	188	168	134
Mean sales of firms (KSEK)								
1987	119 378	1 397 472	453 950	43 948	197 159	144 895	442 148	451 326
1996	736 666	2 368 413	1 223 263	98 873	136 291	88 822	1 042 223	733 037
Relative change (%)	617	170	270	225	69	61	236	162
Median sales of firms (KSEK)								
1987	37 785	684 605	149 162	10 323	28 862	32 366	170 195	87 233
1996	205 665	1 132 519	547 245	39 674	59 742	34 042	468 157	143 981
Relative change (%)	544	175	366	384	206	105	270	165

Number of firms								
1987	105	155	128	72	189	108	182	939
1996	202	193	150	244	250	240	222	1 501
		37						
Relative share of firms created during the period (%)	48	20	15	71	24	55	18	

Note: Eight SEK corresponded to one USD in 1996.

that this information has to be interpreted with some care, as the differences between 1987 and 1997 are compounds of growth and entry effects. It should also be noted that the distributions within Clusters 5 (erratic one-shot growers) and 6 (employment growers) were highly skewed. That is, the means of these clusters were severely affected by outliers. To report only the mean would therefore distort the descriptions of these clusters.

As Clusters 1, 3, and 7, that is, super absolute growers, acquisition growers, and steady overall growers stand out in this respect both on a per firm basis and in the aggregate, it is safe to conclude that these three clusters are by far the categories that add most to increases in employment. Each of these categories increased their employment base by over 40 000 people. However, while the growth of Clusters 1 and 7 was more balanced, it is reasonable to assume that the role of acquisition growers in the economy is that of restructuring rather than genuine job creation. This illustrates the importance of matching the definition and measurement of 'high growth' with corresponding theory and policy. For example, if policies aimed at job creation were based on studies of firms that are acquisition growers, the decisions taken are very likely to be suboptimal for increasing total growth in employment.

Is also interesting to note that firms in Clusters 2 (steady sales growers) and 5 (erratic one-shot growers) actually decreased in total numbers of employees during this period. This is particularly notable as we are dealing only with surviving firms that are defined as high-growth firms according to at least one of the six growth criteria, and as we also allow entry during the period. As noted previously, these two clusters were characterized by sales expansion. Their growth patterns suggest substantial gains in efficiency at the firm level, but losses in employment at the macro level. Whereas the sales growth of steady sales growers is impressive in comparison with other clusters, the median sales growth of erratic one-shot growers is high only in relation to their own shrinking employment base.

Demographic Contrasts

The demographic characteristics of the clusters were used to test the external validity of the clusters. That is, if the clusters do not differ on variables outside of the cluster analysis, they are unlikely to represent distinct empirical categories. In addition, organizational growth patterns are likely to be the outcome of different strategies and different environmental constraints. That is, associations between demographic affiliations on the one hand, and type of growth pattern on the other may explain what caused the firms to follow different growth paths. In terms of theoretical development as well as sample construction and measurement, our study is more ideal for identifying and validating types of growth firms than for explaining why firms end up with a particular type of growth. While suggestive, our results concerning the latter issue should be regarded as tentative.

We cross-tabulated all demographic variables against cluster membership, which was regarded as the dependent variable. The magnitude of the relationship was measured with the lambda statistic when the independent variable was measured with an ordinal scale and with the eta statistic when the independent variable was measured with an interval scale. Four different demographic control variables are present in the data set: size (6 size classes), industry (14 industries), firm age (number of years in the register, consorted at 10 years), and governance (affiliation with a company group vs. independent). In most of the analyses, we chose to collapse data into more aggregate categories than those indicated within the parentheses above (that is, SMEs vs. large firms). As noted earlier, the primary role of the demographic variables is to provide an external criterion for assessing whether the types of growth firms that we identified earlier are meaningful categorizations.

As small- and medium-sized firms (having fewer than 250 employees) dominate the data set, the firms were divided into size classes. When combining the information from the central tendency measures, as well as from the cross-tabulation, it was concluded that size was significantly related to cluster membership (cross-tabulation for 1987: eta = 0.20, sign = 0.000, and for 1996: eta = 0.24, sign = 0.000). Examining the effect of size for the first year (1987) and for the last year (1996), we found that Cluster 2 (steady sales growers) was dominated by very large firms. Clusters 3 (Acquisition growers) and 7 (Steady overall growers) also had a substantial share of larger firms. Note that these three groups had the highest increase in total employment (cf. above). All other clusters were dominated by small- and medium-sized firms, having fewer than 50 or fewer than 250 employees, respectively. These clusters had a median size below 50 employees during the first year. Overall, this analysis indicated a clear relationship between firm size and the type of growth pattern. High-growth firms of different sizes tend to grow in different ways.

The age of the firm was significantly related to cluster membership (eta = 0.10, sign = 0.000). This was indicated in Table 9.6 by the differential share of firms created during the measurement period. A majority of the firms (63 per cent) included in this sample were created before or during 1987. There were large variations among the clusters. In Cluster 4 (super relative growers), 71 per cent of the firms were created during the measurement period, whereas in Cluster 3 (acquisitions growers) only 15 per cent of the firms were created during the same period. We conclude that age had a substantial impact on the different growth patterns. However, clusters dominated by small firms also had a high share of new firms, so there is some risk of confounding.[6]

Substantial differences were also found when we investigated industry affiliation (lambda = 0.086, sign = 0.000). Clusters 1 (super absolute growers) and 4 (super relative growers) resembled each other in that they were both found in knowledge-intensive industries. Cluster 1 had an overrepresentation of manufacturing industries (for example, high-technology and technology-oriented manufacturing), while Cluster 4 was more dominated by professional services (for example, business and information technology consultants, advertising, education, and health care). These industries are new or growing. These firms appear to be the outcome of newly created markets (such as information technology) or were previously state monopolies being deregulated (education and health care). Clusters 2 (steady sales growers) and 3 (acquisition growers) had a high representation of firms in traditional industries such as pulp, steel, and other manufacturing. Cluster 3 also included many construction and retail firms. Traditional, low-technology, and stagnant industries characterize these two clusters. Their growth patterns are either characterized by acquisitions or sales growth without employment growth, pointing to outsourcing and a growth in the concentration of firms in these industries. Firms in Clusters 5 (erratic one-shot growers) and 6 (employment growers) were predominantly found in low-technology service industries such as retail, hotel and restaurants, and other services. Firms in Cluster 7 (steady overall growers) were primarily found in manufacturing industries. In summary, there were differences among clusters regarding industry affiliation. These differences appear to be explainable in terms of knowledge intensity, newly created markets vs. traditional industries, and manufacturing vs. service sectors.

For independent vs. company group status, the directional measures indicated small differences (lambda = 0.034, sign = 0.071), whereas association measures pointed to significant differences (chi-square = 134.7, sign = 0.000). Clusters 2 (steady sales growers), 3 (acquisition growers), and 7 (steady overall growers) were heavily dominated by firms in company groups (93 per cent, 87 per cent, and 86 per cent, respectively, to compare with the overall proportion of 75 per cent). The largest share of independent firms, 39 per cent (overall percentage: 25), was found in Cluster 4 (super relative growers). Hence, while there seems to be some relationship between company group affiliation and growth pattern, none of the clusters was dominated by independent firms.

Table 9.7 offers a descriptive summary of the growth patterns of the seven different clusters as well as their demographic characteristics. We found that the seven clusters differed not only in their growth patterns, but also in their demographic affiliation. Furthermore, firm size and age, industry, and ownership (governance) had significant relationships with growth patterns. Some of the differences are of considerable magnitude, supporting the meaningfulness of dividing the sample of high-growth firms into the different categories identified in the cluster analysis. In relation to previous research, these results largely support a view that organic growth is more associated with young and

Table 9 Summary descriptive of the seven growth patterns

Cluster	Name	Growth pattern	Demographic characteristic
1.	Super absolute growers	Exhibited high absolute growth both in sales and employment	Dominated by small- and medium-sized firms. Found in knowledge-intensive manufacturing industries
2.	Steady sales growers	Rapid growth in sales and negative development in employment	Almost totally dominated by large firms Found in traditional industries such as pulp, steel, and other manufacturing. Dominated by firms affiliated with company groups
3.	Acquisition growers	Resembles Cluster 1 but has negative organic employment growth. Growth is achieved by acquiring other firms	Large firms are over represented Dominated by older firms (that is, firms created before 1987). Found in traditional industries such as pulp, steel, and manufacturing. Dominated by firms affiliated with company groups
4.	Super relative growers	Has a very strong but somewhat erratic development of both sales and employment	Dominated by small- and medium-sized firms Seventy-one per cent of the firms created during the period of observation. Found in knowledge intensive service industries. A high representation of independent firms
5.	Erratic one-shot growers	Has on average negative size development, with exception of one single very strong growth year	Dominated by small- and medium-sized firms. Found in low-technology service industries
6.	Employment growers	Growth is relatively stronger in employment than in sales	Dominated by small- and medium-sized firms Found in low-technology service industries
7.	Steady overall growers	Resembles Cluster 1, but has weaker development	Larger firms are over represented. Found in manufacturing industries. Dominated by firms affiliated with company groups

small firms, and that acquisition growth is more common among larger and older firms, and firms in stagnant or low-tech industries.

DISCUSSION AND CONCLUSION

The primary finding is that high-growth firms do not grow in the same way. Recognizing the heterogeneity that exists in measures of firm growth, how firms grow, and the demographic characteristics of these growth firms, is an important conclusion for scholars and practitioners. Based on the very low correlation among the six growth measures and the finding that few firms meet more than one high-growth criterion, we conclude that what a 'high-growth firm' is, conceptually and operationally, is very dependent on the growth measure used.

Among firms that can be labeled high-growth firms, their growth patterns differ not only in pace, but also in content and regularity. However, when different aspects of growth are combined systematically, a finite number of empirically distinct and conceptually meaningful growth patterns can be identified (out of an infinite number of theoretical possibilities). Firms do not end up with particular growth patterns at random. Instead, 'how firms grow' is systematically related to characteristics of these firms and their environments: such as their age, size, and industry affiliation. We have empirically demonstrated that the phenomenon of the high-growth firm is heterogeneous. There appears to be some kind of order in how a firm grows, and therefore, a potential for gaining a deeper understanding of how high firm growth occurs.

Theoretical Implications

We believe that the primary value of this study is the insight that future firm growth research would benefit by recognizing differences in firm growth patterns: firm growth is not a unidimensional but a multidimensional phenomenon. Recognizing this insight will require future research to construct appropriate samples and measures. It is our belief that researchers who want to contribute to an understanding of the nature of firm growth may follow either of two research strategies. The first research strategy would be to continue to focus on a narrow aspect of growth, using a single measure of growth, or a population of high-growth firms defined by a single criterion. Relative to past research, however, such efforts would have to be much more careful and consistent in their design and execution. The purpose of these studies and their theoretical perspective needs to be matched with the sample and growth indicator, and – importantly – the generalizations and implications have to be restricted to the domain to which they actually apply. Yet, there is the risk that a reduction to a single aspect of growth will not suffice. The nonstudied aspects of growth may blur the results, or the domain to which the results can be generalized may be too narrow to be practically meaningful. To the extent that different forms of growth have common underlying causes, using a composite measure or a multidimensional construct of growth may be an improvement.

The causes and consequences of growth may also be different for different forms of growth. Different forms of growth, then, have to be analysed separately. Yet, with the exception of historical studies, it is not possible at the design stage to know exactly what aspects of growth firms are going to exhibit. This points to the other main strategy for future research on firm growth, which would be to openly acknowledge the complexity of the phenomenon to be studied, and to accept the challenge such an insight implies. It is very likely that factors such as strategies, entrepreneurial motivation, management team composition, organizational form, financial structure, and various aspects of relative environmental munificence are differentially related to different forms of growth. This calls for comprehensive studies of firm growth, using an array of theoretical tools and an adequate spectrum not only of growth measures, but also measures of potential causes and consequences of growth. Designing and executing such studies is no doubt challenging, but to continue to pretend that growth is a simple and unidimensional phenomenon is not a productive way to deal with that challenge.

Practical Implications

We believe this study should have some value for practitioners. For managers, the results of the cluster analysis suggest that there are many different ways that a firm might pursue growth, dependent (more or less) on its demographic characteristics. Yet, the far-from-deterministic relationships with the firm demographic variables would imply that business managers might enjoy considerable freedom of choice as far as growth is concerned. However, the systematic relationships give reason for managers to consider that some growth strategies appear to be more compatible with resources, goals, and environmental constraints than are other growth strategies. The results may help owners and managers of businesses question the validity of prescriptive advice about firm growth that may be based on oversimplified, unidimensional views of this phenomenon. A high relative growth rate in sales (the criterion celebrated in *Inc. Magazine*) is just only one aspect of how firm growth may occur, and this type of growth appears to be appropriate, only, for certain kinds of firms in certain situations. Does the focus on this one criterion of firm growth in many popular business publications distract attention from other forms of growth? Prior research has shown that many small business managers are reluctant to expand their firms (Davidsson, 1989b; Wiklund et al., 1997). A more careful look at these different types of growth patterns may reveal growth options that are not in conflict with other important goals of these manager(s) or other important stakeholders.

Limitations of the Study

The data used in this study have some weaknesses. Sales data were only available for half the population of firms. Thus, we were no longer dealing with a census but a subpopulation that is somewhat biased towards larger firms and towards the manufacturing sector. It should also be noted that, by design, this study focused on firms that were in existence at the end of the measurement period. The study, therefore, focused on the growth history of surviving firms, at a particular moment in time, rather than all growth firms that may have been in existence during the measurement period. Given that the primary research issues revolved around the differences in the measurement of organizational growth, and the recognition of a diversity of organizational growth processes, the study of the growth histories of surviving firms was thought appropriate. This study can, therefore, describe ways that established high-growth firms have achieved high growth. The study cannot specify whether certain processes of growth may have led to the failure of some firms along the way.

With respect to the fact that we included only firms that had achieved a size of 20 employees or more at the end of the period, we would argue that in terms of employment growth a firm cannot be a high-growth firm – that is, a member of our target population – for extended periods of time without reaching that size. However, with respect to growth in sales, this censoring of employment-wise smaller firms is a limitation.

There are forms or aspects of growth that our data did not capture. For example, if a firm first grows as an independent unit and then grows further by adding new firms (that is, if a company group is formed), our data set does not count these firms as one unit of analysis. This is a potentially important form of growth that should be considered in the design of future studies (cf. Levie, 1997; Shulman et al., 1998). Likewise, we lack data on an issue that has attracted a lot of attention in research on large corporations but which is largely ignored in research on growth of young and small firms, that is, the extent to which growth is achieved through penetration or diversification. Finally, we have deliberately refrained from offering any causal explanations for why firms end up with different growth patterns. However, this would be an interesting topic for future research.

CONCLUSION

This study shows that identifying a high-growth firm depends on the measurements used. To focus, for example, on relative sales growth percentage as the only criterion for selecting a high-growth firm will likely ignore a substantial number of firms that, by other measures, are, indeed, high-growth firms. The 'high-growth firm' is a heterogeneous phenomenon. Recognizing that 'high growth' is multidimensional in nature, that 'high growth' can be achieved in a variety of ways, and that it is related to the demographic characteristics of the firm are important insights for researchers and for practitioners.

NOTES

1. Previously published as: Delmar, F., P. Davidsson and W. Gartner (2003), 'Arriving at the high-growth firm', *Journal of Business Venturing*, 18(2), 189–216.
2. We have chosen Statistics Sweden's *Centrala Företags-och Arbetsställeregistret* (CFAR, the Central Register of Enterprises and Establishments) as the basis of our data set. This register comprises data on each enterprise's name, address, legal form, industry, number of establishments, number of employees, entering date, active/inactive, and a few other variables. Applicable variables are available also for establishments. In order to enhance the quality and usefulness of the study, data from CFAR were combined with two other Statistics Sweden registers, viz. the *Koncernregistret* (the Register of Company Groups) and the *Registret över utlandsägda företag* (the Register of Foreign-Owned Companies). This gives additional information that is useful for characterizing the firms.
3. More specifically, for us to accept at time 1 (t1) that firm A_{t0} is the same unit as firm B_{t1} the following has to apply: i) at least 50 per cent of the former employment in A is now found in B and ii) this same employment constitutes at least 50 per cent of B's total employment. This criterion is programmable and can establish unique links in the great majority of cases. Because of mergers and splits, the above criteria do not always lead to a unique and satisfactory solution. In these cases, the two foremost business register experts at Statistics Sweden used a manual procedure for deciding, according to their best collective judgment, which of several links should be used or neither. For any individual year, 0.7 per cent was the maximum fraction of cases for which a link was accepted on the basis of manual inspection rather than fulfilling both of the '50 per cent' criteria.
4. Out of the 5541 cases, 711 had one missing value on sales, 541 had two, and 513 had three.
5. For example, a firm may grow from 100 employees in Year 1 to 200 employees in Year 2 (a factor 2.0 change), and in Year 3 retract to 95 employees (a factor 0.48 change). Over the period, the firm would in total have lost five employees, but show an average growth rate of 1.24.
6. With respect to growth rate, Evans (1987) provides convincing evidence that age and size have separate effects.

REFERENCES

Ardishvili, A., S. Cardozo, S. Harmon and S. Vadakath (1998), 'Towards a theory of new venture growth', paper resented at the 1998 Babson Entrepreneurship Research Conference, Ghent, Belgium.

Barkham, R., G. Gudgin, M. Hart and E. Hanvey (1996), *The Determinants of Small Firm Growth*, vol 12, Gateshead: Athenaeum Press.

Barney, J. (1991), 'Firm resources and sustained competitive advantage', *Journal of Management*, **17**, 99–119.

Barron, D.N., E. West and M.T. Hannan (1994), 'A time to grow and a time to die: growth and mortality of credit unions in New York City, 1914–1990', *American Journal of Sociology*, **100**, 381–421.

Blixt, L. (1998), *Tillväxtföretag i Sverige 1993–1996* [Growth Companies in Sweden 1993–1996], Stockholm: NUTEK.

Brush, C.G. and P.A. Vanderwerf (1992), 'A comparison of methods and sources for obtaining estimates of new venture performance', *Journal of Business Venturing*, **7**, 157–70.

Carroll, G.C. and M.T. Hannan (2000), *The Demography of Corporations and Industries*, Princeton, NJ: Princeton University Press.

Chandler, G.N. and D.A. Baucus (1996), 'Gauging performance in emerging businesses: longitudinal evidence and growth pattern analysis', in P.D. Reynolds, S. Birley, J.E. Butler, W.D. Bygrave, P. Davidsson, W.B. Gartner and P.P. McDougall (eds), *Frontiers of Entrepreneurship Research 1996*, Wellesley, MA: Babson College, pp. 491–504.

Chandler, G.N. and S.H. Hanks (1993). 'Measuring the performance of emerging businesses: a validation study', *Journal of Business Venturing*, **8**, 391–408.

Churchill, C. and V.L. Lewis (1983), 'The five stages of small business growth', *Harvard Business Review*, **61**(3), 30–50.

Collings, J.C. and J.I. Porras (1994), *Built to Last: Successful Habits of Visionary Companies*, New York: HarperBusiness.

Cooper, A.C., F.J. Gimeno-Gascon and C.Y. Woo (1994), 'Initial human and financial capital as predictors of new venture performance', *Journal of Business Venturing*, **9**, 371–95.

Davidsson, P. (1989a), 'Entrepreneurship and small firm growth', dissertation prepared for the Stockholm School of Economics/The Economic Research Institute, Stockholm.

Davidsson, P. (1989b), 'Entrepreneurship – and after? A study of growth willingness in small firms', *Journal of Business Venturing*, **4**, 211–26.

Davidsson, P. and F. Delmar (1997), 'High-growth firms: characteristics, job contribution, and method observations', paper presented at the RENT XI Conference, Mannheim, Germany. This is an early version of Chapter 8 in this volume.

Davidsson, P. and J. Wiklund (2000), 'Conceptual and empirical challenges in the study of firm growth', in D. Sexton and H. Landström (eds), *The Blackwell Handbook of Entrepreneurship*, Bath: Blackwell Business, pp. 26–44, Chapter 3 in this volume.

Davis, S.J., J. Haltiwanger and S. Schuh, (1996), 'Small business and job creation: dissecting the myth and reassessing the facts', *Small Business Economics*, **8**, 297–315.

Delmar, F. (1997), 'Measuring growth: methodological considerations and empirical results', in R. Donckels and A. Miettinen (eds.), *Entrepreneurship and SME Research: On its Way to the Next Millennium*, Aldershot: Ashgate pp. 199–216. Chapter 4 in this volume.

Donckels, R. and J. Lambrecht (1995), 'Networks and small business growth: an explanatory model', *Small Business Venturing*, **7**, 273–89.

Dunne, P. and A. Hughes (1992), 'Age, size, growth and survival revisited', Small Business Research Centre, working paper no. 23, University of Cambridge, England.

Dunne, P. and A. Hughes (1996), 'Age, size, growth and survival: UK companies in the 1980s', *Journal of Independent Economics*, **XLII**(2), 115–40.

Evans, D.S. (1987), 'Test of alternative theories of firm growth', *Journal of Political Economics*, **95**, 657–74.

Flamholtz, E.G. (1986), *Managing the Transition from an Entrepreneurship to a Professionally Managed Firm*, San Francisco, CA: Jossey-Bass.

Gibrat, R. (1931), *Les Inégalités Économiques*, Paris: Sirey.

Greiner, L.E. (1972), 'Evolutions and revolutions as organizations grow', *Harvard Business Review*, **50**(4), 37–46.

Gundry, L.K. and H.P. Welsch (2001), 'The ambitious entrepreneur: high growth strategies of women-owned enterprises', *Journal of Business Venturing*, **16**, 453–70.

Hair, J.F.J., R.E. Anderson, R.L., Tatham and W.C. Black (1995), *Multivariate Data Analysis: With Readings*, 4th edn, Englewood Cliffs, NJ: Prentice-Hall.

Hoy, F., P.P. McDougall and D.E. Dsouza (1992), 'Strategies and environments of high growth firms', in D.L. Sexton and J.D. Kasarda (eds), *The State of the Art of Entrepreneurship*, Boston, MA: PWS-Kent Publishing, pp. 341–57.

Kirchhoff, B.A. (1994), *Entrepreneurship and Dynamic Capitalism: The Economics of Business Firm Formation and Growth*, Westport, CT: Praeger Publishing.

Kogut, B. and U. Zander (1992), 'Knowledge of the firm, combinative capabilities, and the replication of technology', *Organizational Science*, **3**(3), 383–97.

Kumar, M.S. (1984), 'Growth, acquisition, and investment', Department of Applied Economics, occasional paper no. 56, Cambridge, UK.

Law, K.S., C-S. Wong and W.H. Mobley (1998), 'Toward a taxonomy of multidimensional constructs', *Academy of Management Review*, **23**(4), 741–5.

Levie, J. (1997), 'Patterns of growth and performance: an empirical study of young growing ventures in France, Ireland and Scotland', in P.D. Reynolds, W.D. Bygrave, N.M. Carter, P. Davidsson, W.B. Gartner, C.M. Mason and P.P. McDougall (eds), *Frontiers of Entrepreneurship Research*, Wellesley, MA: Babson College, pp. 419–30.

Mata, J. (1994), 'Firm growth during infancy', *Small Business Economics*, **6**, 27–39.

McCann, L.E. (1991), 'Patterns of growth, competitive technology, and financial strategies in young ventures', *Journal of Business Venturing*, **6**, 189–208.

Merz, G.R. and M.H. Sauber (1995), 'Profiles of managerial activities in small firms', *Strategic Management Journal*, **16**, 551–64.

Miller, D. (1987), 'Strategy making and structure: analysis and implications for performance', *Academy of Management Journal*, **30**(1), 7–32.

Milligan, G.W. (1996), 'Clustering validation: results and implications for applied analyses', in R. Arabie, L.J. Hubert and G. De Soetes (eds), *Clustering and Classification*, River Edge, NJ: World Scientific Publishing, pp. 341–75.

Morris, M.H. and J.D. Trotter (1990), 'Institutionalizing entrepreneurship in a large firm: a case study at AT&T', *Independent Marketing Management*, **19**, 131–9.

Murphy, G.B., J.W. Trailer and R.C. Hill (1996), 'Measuring performance in entrepreneurship', *Journal of Business Research*, **36**, 15–23.

Ostgaard, T.A. and S. Birley (1995), 'New venture competitive strategies and their relation to growth', *Entrepreneurship Research Development*, **7**, 119–41.

Penrose, E. (1959), *The Theory of the Growth of the Firm*. Oxford: Oxford University Press.

Peters, M.P. and C.G. Brush (1996), 'Market information scanning activities and growth in new ventures: a comparison of service and manufacturing businesses', *Journal of Business Research*, **36**, 81–9.

Punj, G. and D.W. Stewart (1983), 'Cluster analysis in marketing research: review and suggestions for application', *Journal of Market Research*, **20**, 134–48.

Schreyer, P. (1999), 'High growth firms and employment', DSTI/INT/PME (99) 6, OECD working party on SMEs, Paris.

Shulman, J.M., U.S. Rangan and F.S. Streeter (1998), 'Getting bigger by growing smaller: the use and formation of strategic entrepreneurial units', paper presented at the Babson College/Kauffman Foundation Entrepreneurship Research Conference, Ghent, Belgium.

Siegel, R., E. Siegel and I.C. MacMillan (1993), 'Characteristics distinguishing high-growth ventures', *Journal of Business Venturing*, **8**, 169–80.

Stinchcombe, A.L. (1965), 'Social structure and organization', in J.G. March (ed), *Handbook of Organizations*, Chicago: Rand McNally, pp. 142–93.

Storey, D.J. (1995), 'Symposium on Harrison's "lean and mean": a job generation perspective', *Small Business Economics*, **7**(5), 5–8.

Storey, D.J. (1998), *The Ten Percenters. Fast Growing Firms in Great Britain*, 3rd report, London: Deloitte & Touche International.

Sutton, L. (1997), 'Gibrat's legacy', *Journal of Economic Literature*, **35**, 40–59.

Vaessen, P. and D. Keeble (1995), 'Growth-oriented SMEs in unfavourable regional environments', *Regional Studies*, **29**(6), 489–505.

Wagner, J. (1992), 'Firm size, firm growth and persistence of chance. Testing GIBRAT's law with establishment data from Lower Saxony, 1978-1989', *Small Business Economics*, **4**, 125–31.

Weinzimmer, L.G., P.C. Nystron and S.J. Freeman (1998), 'Measuring organizational growth: issues, consequences and guidelines', *Journal of Management*, **24**(2), 235–62.

Welbourne, T.M. (1997), 'Valuing employees: a success strategy for fast growth firms and fast paced individuals', in P.D. Reynolds, W.D. Bygrave, P. Davidsson, W.B. Gartner, C.M. Mason and P.P. McDougall (eds), *Frontiers of Entrepreneurship Research*, Babson Park, MA: Center for Entrepreneurship Research, pp. 17–31.

Wiklund, J. (1998), 'Small firm growth and performance. Entrepreneurship and beyond', dissertation prepared for Jönköping International Business School, Jönköping, Sweden.

Wiklund, J. and P. Davidsson (1999), 'A resource-based view on organic and acquired growth', paper presented at the Academy of Management Conference, Chicago.

Wiklund, J., P. Davidsson, F. Delmar and M. Aronsson (1997), 'Expected consequences of growth and their effect on growth willingness in different samples of small firms', in P.D. Reynolds, W.D. Bygrave, N.M. Carter, P. Davidsson, W.B. Gartner, C.M. Mason and P.P. McDougall (eds), *Frontiers of Entrepreneurship Research*, Wellesley, MA: Babson College, pp. 1–16. This is an early version of Chapter 6 in this volume.

Zahra, S.A. (1993), 'Environment, corporate entrepreneurship, and financial perform-ance: a taxonomic approach', *Journal of Business Venturing*, **8**, 319–40

Index